Grow

Your Own

Chinese

Vegetables

GROW YOUR OWN
CHINESE
VEGETABLES

BY

GERI HARRINGTON

A GARDEN WAY PUBLISHING BOOK

STOREY COMMUNICATIONS, INC.
POWNAL, VERMONT 05261

Cover illustration by Susan Eder.

The name Garden Way Publishing is licensed to Storey Communications, Inc.,
by Garden Way Inc.

Printed in the United States by Alpine Press

Library of Congress Catalog Card Number: 78-5045
International Standard Book Number: 0-88266-369-0 paperback

Second Printing, September, 1987

LIBRARY OF CONGRESS CATALOGING IN PUBLICATION DATE

Harrington, Geri.
  Grow Your Own Chinese Vegetables

  Includes Index.
  1. Vegetables, Chinese.   2. Vegetable gardening.   I. Title.
SB321.H27   635   78-5045
ISBN 0-88266-369-0

To JEFF

CONTENTS

PART TWO

*Container Gardening
with
Chinese
Vegetables*

ACKNOWLEDGMENTS

In a field such as this where there are, to my knowledge, no books in English that cover the subject comprehensively, and comparatively little home gardening experience, I have had to rely to a large extent on the help of many individuals widely scattered throughout the United States. It would be impossible to list them all, although each piece of information—no matter how small—was a valuable contribution to the overall knowledge I was gradually able to accumulate and draw on in writing this book. The Department of Agriculture, through its research service, was especially helpful, as were the staffs of the Brooklyn Botanic Garden and the New York Botanical Garden. I am indebted also to the Library of the Gray Herbarium of Harvard University.

Among the individuals I would like to single out for special thanks are the following: Shui-Min Block; Dr. Parker Hang, Yale University Press; Mrs. Parker Hang, East Asian Reading Room, Yale University; W. Bradford Johnson, Vegetable Crops Specialist, CES, Cook College, Rutgers University at New Brunswick; Donald M. Mohr, Monmouth County Senior Agent, CES, Rutgers University; Walter Pagels, San Diego, California; Jack Parsons, Extension Agent, CES, Oregon State University; William J. Sanok, Agricultural Program Leader, CES, Cornell University; Perry Slocum, President, Slocum Water Gardens; Pete Slocum, Slocum Water Gardens; Kent B. Tyler, Vegetable Specialist, CES, University of California at Parlier; Bill Uber, Van Ness Water Gardens; Professor Mas Yamaguchi, CES, University of California at Davis.

In addition, I would like to thank all the seedsmen who were so generous with their time and advice that I was able to grow successfully even those vegetables with which I had no previous experience and to enjoy their new flavors and textures in my kitchen. I especially want to thank the people at the Kitazawa Seed Company for hunting up for me seeds which were not available in their catalog.

And—as always—my thanks to my husband, Don, who shared my interest in every new flower and fruit.

INTRODUCTION

Americans used to be considered somewhat insular by the rest of the world—and, in a way, we were. Most of us traveled very little outside of the United States, Canada, or Mexico, and when we did, we preferred hamburger or steak to the local cuisine. American housewives prided themselves on their excellent cooking, but they had little interest in most "foreign" food; a superb roast beef or a flaky pie crust was the ultimate test of the cook.

All that has changed sharply in what seems a very short time. Today, cooking classes in French, Indian, Chinese, Japanese, Persian, and other cuisines are given under the conservative aegis of adult education, and the courses are regularly oversubscribed by both men and women. What is even more interesting, many of the people who take these courses do so in order to learn how to cook food they have already eaten and liked on their travels abroad. There is another interesting point: in most cases, the teacher is both a local resident and *a native of the land whose cookery she is teaching.* In the small town of Wilton, Conn., for instance, in just the past three years, courses have been offered by Wiltonians who are natives or long-term residents of China, Japan, Iran, and India.

Inevitably, as we become interested in the food of other countries, we want to be able to cook and eat truly *authentic* dishes. If the cook substitutes celery for water chestnuts in a Chinese stir-fry dish, both she and her guests know they are eating what is only approximately Chinese food. The more conscientious cook will buy canned water chestnuts and canned bamboo shoots.

But canned vegetables—whether Chinese or American—do not taste the same as fresh, especially vegetables just picked from your own garden. The more I ate and cooked Oriental food, the more I realized that I would have to grow my own Chinese vegetables if I wanted to taste the real thing. Even going to Chinese restaurants became unsatisfactory; most of them limit themselves to a very few authentic Chinese vegetables—snow peas, bok choy, bamboo shoots—and often even these are canned. If you live near a great city, you may be fortunate enough to have access to fresh Chinese vegetables in season, but you aren't going to use them very often when buying them means a special trip some distance away from your usual shopping areas.

When I first considered growing Chinese vegetables in my own garden, I found there was no literature on the subject—no books even to tell me what the vegetables were or how to obtain seeds, let alone how to grow them. But I started hunting up seed sources, and soon had my own Oriental vegetable garden. Since then, I have found the situation somewhat improved; more and more regular seedsmen carry Oriental vegetables and identify them as such, and some are now offering the home gardener seeds imported from the East.

I predict that Chinese vegetables will slowly become an everyday part of our diet. They are not in any way limited to Chinese cooking; Chinese vegetables fit in comfortably with familiar American recipes, and their use is practically unlimited. When you reflect that many of the "American" foods we all take for granted—carrots, beets, apples, and many more—are not native to this country, you realize that a foreign vegetable is just one we have not yet incorporated into our daily menu.

Growing Chinese vegetables is no stranger than trying a new hybrid tomato or corn. One significant difference I have noticed is that in most cases Chinese vegetables seem to be somehow prettier—snow peas are more attractive to grow than English peas; snow-white eggplants are more glamorous (or perhaps just less familiar) than large, purple ones; Chinese pumpkins are far more handsome and more interesting than jack o' lanterns. Another difference, an important one to the home gardener and especially to the container gardener, is that Oriental vegetables generally seem to be more prolific than most of the ones to which I am accustomed. Here again, snow peas are a perfect example.

It is important for the American home gardener to realize that Chinese vegetables are not novelties developed to win blue ribbons at a country fair; they are the mainstay of densely populated countries whose people consume much larger amounts of vegetables, and much less meat, than we do.

Growing Chinese vegetables is good nutrition as well as great fun.

A fringe benefit of growing Chinese vegetables is the pleasant relationship that develops with the various seedsmen. I send them more questions than orders and am constantly amazed at their patience in answering me. Sometimes, if my inquiry concerns a vegetable they cannot quite identify, they send me complimentary packets of seeds, with the suggestion that I grow a few plants and see if they produce what I am looking for. As I write, the product of one of these packets is growing in my garden. It is a beautiful vine with dinner-plate-sized heart-shaped leaves. A profusion of lacy white flowers rises above the leaves on long slender stalks. The vine has competed successfully with my vegetable spaghetti (I didn't think anything could), has grown over the fence and across the meadow, and is now well on its way up a 50-foot cedar standing conveniently nearby. It is, presumably, some kind of cucumber or squash, and so far has one enormous, light-green, slightly furry fruit—about 36 inches long and 4 inches in diameter. There are numerous smaller fruit coming along, so I think I will let this one grow to maturity and see what it is. Meanwhile, as soon as I have a minute, I will drop a line—to Kitazawa, as it happens—and ask if he knows the Latin name of what he sent me.

A word about nomenclature

Not the least of the problems I encountered in writing this book was determining the correct Chinese or Japanese name for each vegetable, and the correct English equivalent. I had not realized how different Cantonese is from Mandarin, and how much they in turn differ from other Chinese languages. Two Chinese friends would invariably give me two different names for the same vegetable; others could pronounce the name but would leave it to me to work out the spelling phonetically. As a result, I have had to arrive at the Oriental names by consulting a number of different sources, and I suspect that I may not always have been consistent—sometimes I may give the Cantonese name, sometimes the Mandarin. There is also very little consistency in the English spelling among Chinese reference books, since transliterating the Chinese word to an English phonetic equivalent has often been an arbitrary decision on the part of a Chinese writer. I found that most of the various spellings could be resolved by pronouncing them aloud. For instance, "gai choy" and "kai choi," if spoken aloud, are quickly recognized as the same thing. This system works best with Cantonese; if a word seems almost unpronounceable, chances are—in my experience—it is Mandarin.

To complicate matters further, I discovered that there has also arisen a "language" known as California Chinese, a variation of Cantonese. Many of these vegetables are grown commercially in California, and I sometimes thought I had come upon a new vegetable when I had merely found the California Chinese name for one I already knew.

After some study and considerable research—often having to go to the garden to compare a plant with my notes from a telephone conversation—I finally arrived at what I think is the Chinese name most commonly used in America for the various vegetables. In cases where the most commonly used name was Japanese, I used that instead, since my intent was to provide the most useful name, not to be consistent for the sake of mere scholarship. There is a complete chart in the appendix which gives the English equivalent, if there is one, and several if there is more than one, the Chinese or Japanese name, and the Latin name. Latin names are universal, regardless of the country in which the vegetable is best known, and should always be your final arbiter in identifying any plant. All the names appear in the index for easy cross-reference.

I hope you will have as much pleasure growing and eating these fascinating vegetables as I have had in introducing them to you. If you have any interesting experiences, I would very much like to hear about them.

In closing I would like to tell you an old Chinese proverb: "To be happy for a week, get married; to be happy for a month, kill a pig; and to be happy for a lifetime, plant a garden."

GERI HARRINGTON

Wilton, Connecticut

PART ONE

The
Chinese
Vegetable
Garden

1 *Where It All Begins—The Soil*

In the gardener's world, soil, sun, and water are essential elements: soil to provide nutrients; sun to aid the plants in utilizing the nutrients in the soil and converting them into food for the plants; water to make the nutrients available. Nature manages to maintain a delicate balance in a seemingly casual, almost offhand way; man cannot be quite so casual when he interferes with nature in order to grow a vegetable garden.

In the wild only the strongest, most rugged plants survive; in the vegetable garden, the most precious crop is sometimes a comparatively delicate plant which must be specially tended. The vegetable gardener can, however, take a tip from nature; even in the vegetable garden, the healthiest plants are the ones which will produce the most fruit, and the tastiest crops, and be the ones most resistant to disease and the vagaries of the weather. But what can the gardener do to produce this ideal crop?

As with all difficult questions, there is no easy answer. Some seasons you do everything right and are still defeated by a sudden hailstorm, a drought, or a spell of unseasonable temperature. All gardeners must be philosophers and take the bad with the good. Fortunately, even in the worst season, the home gardener will always have some unexpected successes. Unlike the commercial farmer who has put all his money on a single crop, the home gardener grows such a variety of things that poor conditions for one vegetable turn out to be ideal for another. Sweet potatoes, for instance, will revel in a dry summer that is hard on cucumbers and melons. Also, since the home gardener has a comparatively small area to watch over, he can give each of his crops individual attention.

One of the most important things to learn is that lack of success with a vegetable doesn't mean the gardener is a failure. Seedsmen, who grow vegetables for a living, often have to leave a seed order unfilled due to "crop failure." If even these experts can have a bad year, certainly allowances can be made for you. Nature has the last word, and there is very little mere mortals can do about it.

I do not mean to say, however, that the gardener is totally at the mercy of the elements. There are many ways he can improve the natural situation in which his garden exists; if there were not, we would still be eating the tough, comparatively tasteless root of Queen Anne's lace, instead of the sweet, delicately flavored carrot.

The first item on the gardener's list of things to improve is soil.

Soil and what to do about it

At first glance, it might seem that nothing is simpler than soil. It is there under our feet—perhaps under concrete, blacktop, and shopping center—but still there. Soil, it would seem, is no problem; it has always been there and it always will.

Unfortunately, this is not true. Most gardeners first learn something about the limitations of soil when they try to grow a lawn. If there is one thing that will not grow by itself, it is a lawn. Everything conspires against what is basically an unnatural, man-made product. Lawns are probably one of the most intensive forms of gardening man has ever attempted. In order to achieve a beautiful lawn, grass must be made to grow—and thrive—under unnatural, severely overcrowded conditions. The how and why of a good lawn is not the subject of this book, but it deserves a passing mention because it is often the gardener's first encounter with soil that won't grow *anything*—subsoil. If subsoil is on the surface, instead of under the topsoil where it belongs, it is usually because the builder has stripped off the topsoil and left you with the second layer, or subsoil. If so, you have your work cut out for you. If you have had this problem and conquered it, the experience is not wasted; vegetable gardeners must deal with many similar problems.

Soil comes in two grades: topsoil, which is the first thing, we hope, that you encounter when you dig into the ground; and subsoil, which is the next layer of soil and is in the process of gradually turning into topsoil. This process can require over two hundred years; obviously you should cherish your topsoil. To determine how much topsoil you have, dig a hole with straight sides with a good spade. Examine the cross-section you have exposed and you will see that one layer—the thinner—is dark, crumbly, and somehow rich-looking. The much thicker layer beneath it is lighter in color and very different in texture. The first is topsoil, the second subsoil. In digging over your garden, never bury the topsoil. If you want to incorporate humus and fertilizer into the subsoil, put the topsoil aside on a tarpaulin or sheet of plastic, dig over the subsoil, and replace it in the bottom of the trench. Then put the topsoil back *on top*. It is surprising how many conscientious gardeners make things much harder for themselves by digging the topsoil under. This comes partly from following old gardening books, which simply told you to turn over the soil; in those happy days the topsoil was 12 inches thick in most places and you weren't likely to dig down much deeper than that. Today topsoil is only a few inches deep at best and if you aren't careful you can easily bury it all.

Topsoil

Not all soil on top of the ground is good topsoil, and even if it is, there often isn't enough of it for your purpose. Good topsoil, when dampened, smells like a forest after a rain. You may have good soil but it may be too clayey (small particles) or too sandy (large particles). If it is good soil, chances are it will have numerous earthworms, but that is not an infallible guide; a pile of fresh manure will soon become loaded with earthworms, but it is not topsoil.

If you want to see what good topsoil looks like, buy a bag of the potting soil sold in small, expensive bags in garden centers. It is sterilized, so it doesn't contain soil bacteria, but it will show you what you're aiming at.

Today topsoil is an endangered resource. On the average, an American farm loses about 5 tons of topsoil per acre per year. Recent droughts in the United States have accelerated this process. It is estimated that under drought conditions, a brisk breeze can remove an inch of topsoil just by passing over the land.

During the recent long droughts, we have obviously lost a great deal of this almost irreplaceable resource—and more droughts are predicted for the future. This is why some agriculturists are predicting another dust bowl. It is not something to leave for our grandchildren to cope with; it is very much a current problem.

The gardener's contribution to soil depletion is comparatively simple to explain. Growing cultivated flowers and vegetables depletes the nutrients in the soil. If these are not replaced, the soil becomes poorer and poorer, and less and less able to support vegetation. As man has developed farm machinery, and large one-crop farms, he has depleted the soil at an alarming rate. True, he replaces the nutrients—otherwise, he wouldn't be able to continue to produce crops commercially—but he has done it with chemical, rather than organic, fertilizers. Until recently, this was the most economical and easiest way to fertilize; unfortunately, it is not good for the soil.

Chemical fertilizers do not enrich the soil, nor return nutrients to it. They use the soil purely as a carrying medium; that is, the soil merely holds the fertilizer in place until the plant roots take it up. Meanwhile the soil itself is left poorer than before, and without the soil bacteria or earthworms which are essential to the production of new topsoil (these helpful, natural soil factories cannot co-exist with chemical fertilizers). Chemical fertilizers do not enrich or help to create topsoil; on the contrary, they hasten its destruction.

There is, in addition, a hidden price the consumer pays for this widespread use of chemical fertilizers. Recent studies in Japan show that the nutrients in the soil directly affect the nutrients in what is grown in that soil. A *New York Times* story from Tokyo reported a Japanese owner of thoroughbred horses as claiming that the legs of his race horses were getting weaker because the grass they ate was grown on chemical fertilizer. The article further reported that Japanese industrialists and farmers were turning to earthworms—breeding and utilizing them for agricultural use—and that one farmer who had mixed worm castings into the soil of his rice paddy as an experiment had discovered that the plants became stronger and more resistant to mold.

Our own Department of Agriculture, in spite of a disposition to chemical fertilizers and insecticides, reports: "Soils that have a high content of organic matter usually have many desirable physical properties. For example, they are easy to till, absorb rain readily, and tend to be drought-resistant. Because soils high in organic matter have these desirable properties, some people have speculated that they might also produce plants of superior nutritional quality and that the use of organic composts or manures would result in plants of superior quality to those produced with inorganic fertilizers." Subsequent studies have shown this actually to be the case; vegetables grown on organically fertilized soil are richer in essential vitamins and minerals. Here is where the home gardener has complete freedom of choice; he can easily use wholly organic fertilizers and reap the benefits in improved nutrition, better flavor, healthier plants, and richer soil.

The simplest way to do this is to recycle your own "garbage." Potato peelings, eggshells, coffee grounds—everything organic except meat (but fish is good, and fish bones)—should go into the soil, instead of into the garbage pail. Many city container gardeners put their vegetable leavings in the blender with a little water and add the resulting "soup" to the soil in their containers. This is some of the best potential fertilizer you can use and it is absolutely free.

Another source of free fertilizer is the seashore. Seaweed is an excellent all-around fertilizer. It can be applied directly on the soil as mulch, or dug in a little below the surface. Digging it in will be more beneficial, but even as a mulch it will improve the soil.

If you live near a stable or in a town like mine where there are a number of horses, chickens, and pet rabbits, you have another source of free fertilizer. This is a little messier, because stable manure must be well rotted before it can be used on plants. It can, however, be dug into an in-the-ground garden in the fall; it will then be ready for spring planting. Chicken and rabbit manure can be dug in right around the plants—and it is amazing how much excellent fertilizer is produced by even one pet rabbit.

If, of course, you have room for a compost heap, you need never buy fertilizer again. If not, your own organic matter can be supplemented with commercial organic fertilizers; they come in both dry and liquid forms for every use and purpose.

Since, however, you cannot tell the fertility of the soil by looking at it, how do you determine what nutrients it requires? The answer is by a soil test.

Soil tests

A soil test is simply a chemical analysis of the soil. You can do it yourself with a soil-test kit, or you can have it done by your local Extension Service. This used to be a free service but now, I believe, they charge $1—which is still a bargain. Send in the sample in late fall or early spring so that you will have time to correct the soil balance before sowing your seeds. The Extension Service will also advise you whether liming is needed. Lime makes the soil more alkaline, necessary in areas where the soil tends to be acid. In other sections of the country, you may need to correct an excessively alkaline condition by adding peat moss. Your Extension Service soil test will tell you if this is the case. The soil's alkaline or acid condition is expressed in terms of the pH scale.

Just a few years ago, pH was a term unfamiliar to most people unless they were scientists or experienced gardeners. Today it is a magic symbol used to sell shampoos, moisturizing lotions, and other cosmetic items. Even so, the average consumer doesn't know what pH means, so an explanation is in order.

In gardening, another term for pH is soil reaction, indicating whether the soil, when tested, reacts as acid or alkaline. If you want to know this about a liquid, you can buy a piece of litmus paper at any drugstore and determine the acidity/alkalinity of a liquid by seeing whether the moistened paper turns pink or blue. You will get a similar reaction with moist soil, but you won't know just how it stands on the pH scale—that is, *to what extent* it is acid or alkaline. What you need that will tell you this is a soil-testing kit, which operates on the same basic principle as the litmus paper. A kit runs about $14 and provides enough chemicals for several pH tests. I prefer to send in my dollar to the local County Extension Service. In addition to telling me the pH of whatever soil samples I send, the Extension Service also tells me how the soil samples rate as to calcium, magnesium, phosphorus, and potassium. It recommends several fertilizer formulas—the last time, for instance, it was "25 pounds of 5-10-10, 20 pounds of 6-12-12, 15 pounds of 8-16-16, or 10–25 pounds of 10-20-20." It suggested using this amount for 1,000 square feet of space, so I could easily work it out in terms of my own garden area. If you have any questions after you receive your soil analysis, you are welcome to call your County Agent and talk with him about your problems. There is an Extension Service in every county in the United States. See the list in the Appendix for the address of the one in your state; it can tell you the phone number of your local branch. And if you are not on the Extension Service's mailing list, drop it a postcard asking to have your name included; the Extension Service offers a great deal of useful material, some free, some costing a few cents.

The pH reaction of the soil is measured on a scale that runs from 1 to 14. A measurement of 7 means the soil is neutral—neither acid nor alkaline. Above 7 is alkaline, all numbers from 7.5 to 14; below 7 is acid, all numbers from 1 to 6.5. Soils in various parts of the country have a natural tendency toward one or the other; in Connecticut, for instance, most soil was originally acid. The Connecticut gardener cannot, however, count on this, because generations of farmers have worked to correct this acidity, and there is always the possibility that they have overcorrected and the soil in a given area is now alkaline.

Most vegetables are content with a pH between 6.0 and 7.0, or slightly acid. Potatoes require higher acidity, not because that is the nature of the potato plant, but because that is the easiest way to discourage some of the most prevalent potato pests and diseases. Lettuces, beets, and watercress—to name only a few—prefer an alkaline soil. The degree of acidity or alkalinity that plants find best is usually slight—the difference may be, for instance, no more than an increase from 7.0 to 7.5. Excess of either acidity or alkalinity is destructive to plant growth. In correcting the pH, always do so gradually, with several small applications rather than a single large one.

Once you have determined the acidity or alkalinity of your soil, the next step is to bring it to the desired pH. This is quite easily done. If your soil is too acid, add ground limestone. Limestone also acts as a soil conditioner and contains magnesium and calcium. Sea shells and eggshells are a good source of lime, but need to be ground up because they decompose slowly. Wood ashes are another excellent source.

If your soil is too alkaline, the simplest way to bring it into balance is to add organic material. In fact, organic material will correct either an acid or an alkaline condition; in some magical way, it brings the soil into balance regardless of which way it has gone. In addition, it encourages the growth of soil bacteria and earthworms and decomposes into humus, which improves the texture of the soil and fertilizes it as well.

Unlike limestone, *it is impossible to add too much organic matter to the soil;* it is never harmful. This is why organic gardeners prize their compost heaps so highly; they are a cureall for so many garden problems. An easily available organic matter is peat moss; pine-bark chips are another. The only precaution necessary in the use of organic material—whether to correct the soil's pH or to serve as mulch or fertilizers—is that the bacterial action that breaks down the organic material requires nitrogen. Since the nitrogen in the soil is its most fragile ingredient, this could result in a serious deficiency unless you take steps to add supplemental nitrogen. See the section on nitrogen for sources of this important fertilizer.

Note: Your County Extension Service soil test will not include a recommendation on nitrogen. This is because the Department of Agriculture has found that the amount of nitrogen in the soil can vary from day to day, let alone from month to month, and you could not use any one sample's measurement as a guide. Nitrogen is easily leached out by rain and watering, and is used up in various natural soil processes.

Fertilizer

There are three kinds of fertilizers that are easy to obtain: nitrogen, phosphorus, and potassium. The numbers on bags of fertilizer or manure—10-5-10, 5-10-10, and so on—stand for these three fertilizers, listed in alphabetical order. The numbers indicate the percentage of each that the mixture contains. Since they do not add up to 100 percent you are obviously paying for a good deal of material that is of no use to you. This is apparently unavoidable, but it makes price comparison of various commercial fertilizers a little difficult. Since nitrogen is your most expensive fertilizer, use the percentage of nitrogen as a rough check on price. A 5-10-5 formula, for example, should be less expensive than a 10-10-5. If you buy chemical fertilizers, this rule may no longer apply, since most chemical fertilizers are made from petroleum and the inflated price of petroleum is being reflected in the increasingly high price of all chemical fertilizers.

Organic fertilizer mixes will have a formula on the bag which you can use as a general guide but which does not tell the whole story. Because they are made from natural substances, organic fertilizers will also contain trace elements, while chemical fertilizers generally will not. This is a valuable bonus; it is only in very recent years that we have come to realize the importance of trace elements.

They are called trace elements because they are present in the soil in such minute quantities that there is often merely a "trace" of them. Now that we have equipment which can detect a millionth part of an element in a substance, we have begun to realize that a millionth part of some substances can be just as helpful or deleterious as a much larger quantity of others. Until we know a great deal more about body chemistry, our diet should be as varied as possible so that we increase our chances of including some of these important substances of which we may not yet know the value. Since it has been shown that plants reflect the deficiencies of the soil in which they are grown, it behooves us to make our vegetable garden soil as rich, proportionately, in the trace elements as in the "big three." This can only be done through the use of organic materials and fertilizers; chemical fertilizers deplete the soil of these essential trace elements and the plants grown with them are, in turn, also deficient.

Let us see, specifically, how we can obtain these necessary elements through organic fertilizers.

Nitrogen

Nitrogen is the first element in a fertilizer formula (10-10-5, for example). Each element has its particular function in plant growth, just as certain nutrients contribute to the health of certain parts of the human body (for instance, the calcium in milk builds bones, the iron in spinach contributes to the red blood cells). The chief function of nitrogen is healthy, leafy growth. Any part of the plant that grows above the ground owes its health to a large extent to the amount of nitrogen in the soil. In addition to iron, nitrogen is responsible for the dark-green color of foliage, and a lack of nitrogen may be indicated by pale-green or yellow leaves. (A lack of iron may have the same effect; as with the human body, the same symptom may result from more than one disease.)

Nitrogen is not a difficult fertilizer to obtain. You can buy large sacks of cottonseed meal, which is probably the least expensive of the high-nitrogen fertilizers, or small, expensive sacks of dried blood. Rabbit and chicken manure are also high in nitrogen—so much so that some gardeners keep a pet rabbit just for the fertilizer it produces.

One of the best ways to add nitrogen is to occasionally plant that part of your garden in legumes—peas and beans—which improve the nitrogen content of the soil. If for some reason you are leaving a garden area unplanted for a season, sow it with alfalfa and plow it under in the fall. Even clover adds to the nitrogen in the soil.

Castor plants are very high in nitrogen. Dried seaweed contains more than fresh and shellfish more than other fish. If you should find any feathers on your lawn, bury them in the garden—they too are high in nitrogen.

As long as you use organic sources of nitrogen it is unlikely that you will apply too much; the soil bacteria must work on organic material to convert it into a form the plant can utilize, and they usually maintain a good balance. If, on the other hand, you use chemical fertilizers, it is all too easy to apply an excess of nitrogen, and the effect on your vegetable plants can be quite serious—and irreversible.

See the fertilizer table in the Appendix for an at-a-glance listing of organic sources. After applying nitrogen, do not use lime or wood ash for three or four weeks. They cancel out the nitrogen.

Phosphorus

The second number in a fertilizer formula always stands for phosphorus.

Phosphorus is like the electrolyte balance in the body—it makes everything else work. In addition, it promotes strong stems and aids in setting fruit. It is essential to root crops since it directly affects both feeder and base root development. If you get skinny roots instead of fat radishes, you probably have a deficiency of phosphorus.

Phosphorus is easy to apply and should always be included in side-dressing for root vegetables. It is most easily available in the form of rock phosphate, and comparatively inexpensive. A more expensive but also excellent source is bone meal. Additional sources are fish and shellfish (if you have a fisherman in the family, encourage him to bring home the "trash fish" together with the edible fish he catches).

Potassium or Potash

The last of the big three fertilizers is potassium or potash.

In addition to its own useful contribution to healthy plants it has one very important function: it can increase the plant's resistance to an excess of nitrogen. Its chief function, however, is to make plants winter-hardy; it acts like the antifreeze in your car's motor and is, obviously, particularly important to vegetables like Jerusalem artichokes which are harvested late in the season, or throughout the winter.

A sufficient supply of potassium will grow healthy, sturdy plants, more resistant to fungi and other diseases and less affected by extremes in temperature. It gives main roots the strength to push deeply into the soil, and is the most important of the three fertilizers in the production of satisfactory root crops.

Potassium is easily obtained if you have a source for wood ashes (which also add lime); they can be incorporated in the soil and used as a mulch. Greensand and granite dust are other organic sources that are comparatively inexpensive and pleasant to use.

A nitrogen deficiency will sometimes show up among the lower leaves of the plant; they will turn brown and die. It will also cause weak stems and stunted base roots.

Trace elements

There is a lot we still don't know about trace elements. The best way to ensure that your vegetable garden has enough of them is to use compost or organic materials to fertilize and condition the soil. All organic materials contain one or more trace elements. Rock phosphate, for instance, also contains molybdenum; granite dust contains boron, a particularly important trace mineral in which soils are often deficient. Since a deficiency in trace minerals in the soil leads to a deficiency in the plants, you are not getting your full value in nutrition if you eat plants from inadequately supplied soils. The effects of a deficiency of trace minerals can be serious. A recent news item reported growing support for a theory that epilepsy is caused by a magnesium deficiency.

How to fertilize

In the discussion of individual vegetables, I have given fertilizer recommendations. I hope, however, that you will not take these recommendations as exact prescriptions. The organic gardener is dealing with natural materials which differ in their composition from one source to the next as well as from one season to the next. As much as some manufacturers would like you to think so, fertilizing is not really a science under our control. Variables of weather, soils, temperatures, seeds, and many, many other factors affect how much fertilizer to apply and when. You can follow some general rules, but you must be quick to notice the condition of your garden and of the individual plants in it. You will soon learn to distinguish between a healthy plant and one that is under stress. In the table on fertilizers in the Appendix, I have given some of the symptoms which will occur as the result of a deficiency of the various elements.

Pests and diseases

Sometimes the problem will not be with the fertilizer but with insects or disease. The healthier your plants, the more resistant they will be, but aphids, whitefly, flea beetles, and the like will still make some inroads even on healthy plants. Many times these insects can be deterred sufficiently with just a strong spray from the garden hose. Other times, companion planting may prevent their making their home in their usual haunts. As a last resort, the organic gardener can use pyrethrum or rotenone.

Last year I gardened without the use of any spray or dust other than wood ashes. The only problem I had was with squash borer. I cut the borers out, covered the stems with moist earth, and had no further difficulty. I did have an early attack on my eggplants from voracious flea beetles, but I became quite adept at catching them between thumb and forefinger and soon disposed of them.

Leaf miner appears in my spinach and Swiss chard every year. I keep it under control by removing the leaves as soon as I notice any. This seems to spur new growth and I always get a good crop.

A few insects here and there won't do much damage, so don't get nervous just because you see something walking around on a vegetable leaf. I long ago discovered that the parasitic wasp that attacks tomato hornworms takes care of every single one my tomato plants attract. Since I leave the hornworms alone, I apparently have bred a good supply of the wasps and they do their job efficiently every summer. Unless you are on your way to losing your whole crop, give nature a chance to work for you.

Remember that a vegetable garden is part of nature and you cannot run it like a machine. Your attitude should be more like that of the old farmer who philosophically planted three cherry trees for every one he hoped to harvest. "One for the bugs, one for the birds, and one for me."

2 The Chinese Greens

Generally speaking, "greens" means the leaves of vegetables that are eaten cooked, as opposed to "leafy greens," like the lettuces, which are primarily eaten raw. The dividing line is a purely arbitrary one, and not at all consistent. For example, spinach was once considered edible only when cooked, until some brave soul nibbled on a raw leaf and found it good. Now even restaurants, naturally conservative, feature spinach salad when it is available. On the other hand, Belgian endive—normally a raw salad vegetable in the United States—is excellent braised, and escarole, when cooked in the Italian fashion with a little olive oil, is almost better hot than raw.

Traditionally in the United States the term "greens" has been mostly applied to kale, collards, Swiss chard, dandelions, and mustard greens. Since greens by their nature contain a good deal of water, they are best cooked briefly in just the rinse water that remains on their leaves. In this way they retain most of their nutrients. The Southern custom is to boil them for a long time with a piece of salt pork. Most of the nutrients are thus lost to the cooking liquid, but this does not do any harm nutritionally, since the "pot liquor" is also consumed.

In the old days, greens were available in the spring after a winter that was barren of fresh vegetables; they could be sown and harvested before almost any other crop. Their taste was usually slightly bitter, and this bitterness had a tonic effect on winter-weary appetites. It was thought to benefit the body and purify the blood. Whether or not this is medically sound, everyone looked forward with great anticipation to that first mess of spring greens, and always felt better for having eaten them.

15

Nowadays we have so many fresh vegetables available to us all year round that we have lost some sense of the rhythm of the seasons, and often can no longer tell what our bodies crave. In spite of this, it is interesting that our appetite for early spring greens persists, and spinach and dandelions are grown and gathered today with a good deal of the same enthusiasm as in colonial days.

Now, in addition to old favorites, you can grow and enjoy the greens of the Orient: amaranth, Chinese mustard, mizuna or potherb mustard, and garland chrysanthemum. They are easy to grow and take up very little space. They thrive in both vegetable and flower gardens, are worth their weight in nutrition, are low in calories, and are deliciously different from any of the more familiar greens. For an unexpected treat, try them in your garden this season.

AMARANTH   HINN CHOY

[*Amaranthus gangeticus*]

Amaranth, or Chinese spinach, is an ancient vegetable widely known in many parts of the world. In the Caribbean it is sometimes known as *callaloo;* the Japanese name is *hiyu;* and in India it is called *bhaji.* For some reason, however, it is virtually unknown in the United States except as an ornamental. It is certainly showy enough for the flower bed, with brilliantly colored leaves and bright clusters of small flowers which bloom steadily for many months. Perhaps you have been growing amaranth for years and never knew it was edible.

Most American catalogs list amaranth, but the majority of them place it in the flower section. If you want to order seeds and can't find it in the vegetable section, check the flower index. Always specify that you want an *edible* variety; not all varieties are suitable.

Amaranth is often called Chinese spinach because of its great popularity in that country. It is not botanically related to spinach but it can be cooked the same way, and is even more nutritious. One of our so-called "summer spinaches," tampala, is a variety of amaranth.

In addition to its use as a green vegetable, certain varieties of amaranth are valuable grain crops. In the Americas, before the Europeans came, this was a favorite food of the Aztecs, who cultivated the prolific plant as their main grain crop. History records that 200,000 bushels were paid annually as tribute to Montezuma, and use of this grain can be traced back in this hemisphere for 20,000 years. The Spanish conquistadors, disturbed by its use in Aztec religious ceremonies, forbade the Indians to grow it, but its cultivation continued surreptitiously.

For some reason, amaranth has been used in religious ceremonies wherever it has been grown. The ancient Greeks considered it a symbol of immortality (hence its name, which means "unwilting"), and pronounced it sacred to Artemis. It was supposed to possess exceptional qualities of healing, and was frequently depicted in the decorations on tombs and temples. India, China, Japan, and Guatemala also have many legends about amaranth, and have, at one time or another, used it in their own sacred rituals. The Eastern Star Chapter of North American Masons—the largest Masonic woman's organization in the United States—has the Order of the Amaranth. The initiation ceremony of this order is based on a similar ceremony in Sweden's Amaranter Order of Knighthood, established in 1653 by Queen Christina, who obviously chose the name because of the legendary reputation of the amaranth plant.

Culinary and other uses

The flavor of amaranth is variously described as meaty, spinach with a pinch of horseradish, rather hot (or rather bland, depending on the variety), aromatic, slightly sweet but tangy. Some of these apparent contradictions are due to the many varieties of edible amaranth; they vary in taste as well as in appearance. All amaranths have a unique flavor, unlike that of any other vegetable.

Although occasionally used as a salad, amaranth is mostly eaten as a potherb. It cooks in a few minutes, and can be steamed like spinach just in the water left on it after it is washed. A crushed clove of garlic added to the pot, and a dressing of sesame oil tossed with the cooked, coarsely chopped leaves, makes a delectable vegetable.

If allowed to cook more than five minutes, amaranth becomes quickly mushy. Take advantage of this fact and simmer it longer in chicken broth. When it becomes thoroughly limp, purée the leaves in some of the broth (easy in the blender), add heavy cream or yogurt, a bit of curry, an extra pinch of turmeric, and perhaps a little salt. Reheat in the pot of broth, without boiling. Stir to blend thoroughly and serve as an unusual hot or chilled soup. A garnish of crisp, thinly sliced water chestnuts is a good finishing touch.

In China and Japan, amaranth is widely used in soups and stir-fry dishes, and steamed as a side dish. It combines well with garlic, ginger, grated radish, scallions, pork, soy sauce, lemon, and saki to make a delicious Oriental main dish. Wherever your Chinese cookbook calls for spinach, use amaranth.

It is a popular ingredient in buffets throughout the East Indies and the traveler in the West Indies will encounter it cooked with rice, tomatoes, and ham and simmered until the rice is tender.

Its use as a potherb is, however, only a small part of the potential of this amazing plant; worldwide, by far its greatest use is as a grain. It is very prolific—much more so than wheat, for instance—and a mere square yard of garden can yield up to 2 pounds of grain. The seed is easily gathered (unlike wheat) by the home gardener, and then ground into flour. Amaranth flour can be added to breads, cakes, sauces, soups, stews, and many other dishes; its 20 percent protein content makes it a welcome addition to diets throughout the world, and it could well be used in American diets to cut down on our high consumption of cholesterol-rich beef. It is, of course, a boon to vegetarians, although most of the ones I have met have never heard of it. Since the grain is so easy to grow and the flour so easy to make, it is a home product everyone can enjoy.

Appearance

The appearance of amaranth varies greatly in the color of the foliage, the shape of the leaves, and the height of the plant.

Sometimes known as Joseph's Coat because of the brilliance of its red coloring, it ranges from a rosy crimson to a highly colored variegated leaf that is both red and green. The cloverlike flowers are small and would be insignificant in themselves, but they occur in such large numbers that the overall effect is outstanding. If you are growing amaranth for the leaves, you won't want to encourage the flowers or let the plants go to seed, but amaranth has such a long growing and harvesting season that you are bound to reach a point where you will welcome a few weeks without this leafy vegetable on the table; the plants left at that time can be allowed to flower and go to seed. If you grow it for its grain, you will naturally have a long season of beautiful flowers.

The shape of the leaves can vary so much that you will not always recognize them as belonging to an amaranth plant. To get the most delicious varieties, be sure when you order to specify edible amaranth, so that even if you don't get *A. gangeticus,* you get one of the other excellent edible varieties. Flower seedsmen will discourage you from considering their amaranth edible; don't argue with them when there are so many vegetable seedsmen who carry it. Thompson & Morgan, for instance, is most enthusiastic about theirs, which they promote as a grain. Other growers—Tsang & Ma, for one—call theirs Chinese Spinach to make the most of the "greens" use. Redwood City has two kinds: one for greens, the other for both grain and greens. This is a fascinating vegetable. Try different kinds in different years until you find the variety you like best. Since amaranth is so ornamental, you might even try several different kinds in one season, planting them in flower beds and letting the neighbors think you are simply into foliage plants.

Most of the plants grow from 2 to 3 feet in height, although some reach considerably higher. Some of the lower-growing varieties tend to be somewhat straggling in habit; others are very compact and bushy. They require good air circulation, so if you do put them in the flower bed, do not crowd them with petunias, zinnias, marigolds, or the like. If the plants get too tall, you may need to stake them with thin bamboo poles, as you do delphiniums. The grain varieties are usually erect and need no support.

When to plant

Because of the number of varieties, it is difficult to say when to plant the particular seeds you may have. Most of the low-growing amaranths should be planted when the ground warms up, but some of the grain varieties can go in with the leaf lettuce and peas. You won't lose anything by trying for an early crop.

How to plant

Here again, you will have to be guided by the directions that come with the seeds. Generally speaking, seeds should be shallowly sown, no more than ¼ inch deep, ½ inch apart, in rows 18 inches apart. You will eventually thin the plants so that they finally stand from 10 to 18 inches apart; you will get a good crop just from these thinnings. Always take every other plant so you will never have crowding and won't thin excessively either.

Although amaranth will tolerate—in fact, it almost seems to thrive under—dry conditions, keep the seeds moist until the first set of true leaves appears.

Transplanting

There is considerable disagreement as to whether you can transplant amaranth. Some gardeners have good luck; others find it impossible. Transplanting is very time-consuming and I, frankly, see no need for it. The crop grows quickly from seed in the open garden. If you just can't wait to enjoy some fresh greens, sow regular spinach, which doesn't need warmed-up soil; you can eat the amaranth all summer when spinach has bolted and been pulled up.

If you still want an early crop of amaranth, try a small sowing. Plant the seeds in Fertl Cubes and keep moist. This should be done four to five weeks before you usually plant your green beans. As soon as the first true leaves have fully opened, put the cubes in 2½-inch peat pots of Cornell Mix. Keep them moist and keep an eye on the growth. The seedlings will start to branch when they are very young. Put the peat pot, sides and bottom slashed, into a larger peat pot and continue to transplant if necessary. Since amaranth is undoubtedly fussy about transplanting, be even more careful than usual about disturbing the roots. If you thoroughly slash and soak the peat pots and keep putting them into larger ones, you will minimize root disturbance and the plant won't even realize you have moved it.

As soon as the soil has warmed up, place them where they are to stay in your garden, shading them if a hot spell coincides with this move. Keep the soil around them moist so that the roots will move into it with the least possible difficulty.

Culture

Amaranth grows freely in many climates, in the North as well as in the South. It requires full sun but isn't fussy about anything else, including soil, mulching, and so on. Fertilize lightly; if you over-fertilize, the leaves will get very large and may become too tough.

When seedlings are 2 inches high, thin plants to 2 inches apart. This is your first crop. Pull up the entire plant you are thinning. Cut off the roots and wash the leaves in lukewarm water to remove sand. Then steam or stir-fry for two minutes for a delectable treat available only to the home gardener.

Continue to thin until the plants are standing from 10 to 18 inches apart.

Harvest

For greens, start to harvest the plants when they are 6 to 8 inches tall, taking only some of the leaves from each plant. Your plants will continue to put out new leaves, and to flower for some time. In Connecticut, for instance, they will flower from July through September, slowing down when the weather turns cool.

The plants will mature in about 40 days for greens, 90 days for grain.

To harvest the grain, wait until the seeds are fully mature and almost dry. Pull up the entire plant and hang upside down in a warm dry place in a paper bag. If you label the bags, you will be able to keep the varieties separate; this is important both for taste tests and for next year's crop (you will want to know which variety of seed you are planting). When completely dry, shake the plants in the bags. Most of the seeds will fall to the bottom and can be easily collected. Check the plants for any seeds that remain and hand-pick.

When the seeds are completely dry, store in airtight containers in a cool dry place. Grind into flour as needed, making sure to reserve some of the seeds for planting the following spring. The flour contains gluten and combines well with other flours in biscuits, breads, and other baked goods.

Amaranth and nutrition

Amaranth is not only versatile and delicious, it is also one of the most nutritious vegetables and grains you can eat. On a scale of 100 for a complete "protein," amaranth rates 75, higher than milk, soybeans, or whole wheat. The leaves are rich in vitamins and minerals—even more than beet greens—and are easily digested.

CHINESE MUSTARD   GAI CHOY

[Brassica juncea]

If the only mustard greens you have ever eaten are the common garden variety, you may be inclined (unless you are from the South) to turn away from this vegetable without another thought. It is true that American mustard greens are too pungent for many tastes. Chinese mustard is not; in fact, it is one of the most delicious greens in nature's repertoire.

A native of Asia, where it has been under cultivation for thousands of years, Chinese mustard is grown commercially in this country only in California and New Jersey, mostly for the Oriental trade. It is so well regarded by those familiar with it that a delicious California honey is made by bees that have been allowed to feed solely on the nectar of mustard flowers. I would very much like to try it but I have never found it in any market in my area.

As a member of the genus *Brassica*, it is a close relative of the common mustards, but its taste is quite different—as one member of a family may be peppery in temperament while another is only mildly so. Chinese mustard is not usually to be found in the produce section of supermarkets, unless you live near a Chinese one, and must, therefore, be grown in your garden if you are to have it at all.

Culinary and other uses

Medicinally and nutritionally, Chinese mustard has all the valuable properties of common mustards. It is considered useful as a spring tonic and for purifying the blood. It is also rich in vitamins and minerals, especially when eaten raw.

Chinese mustard can be used in salads like lettuce or spinach. I prefer it in combination with other greens, but a small salad of just this attractive green makes a zesty side dish. Garnish it with minced hard-cooked egg and use a vinaigrette dressing with a dash of lemon juice (but no mustard) in it.

In cooking, treat it just like spinach. Steam briefly in a very small quantity of boiling water (longer cooking makes it less flavorful) and toss with sesame oil and soy sauce. Use it instead of spinach in your favorite quiche recipe and combine with a cream sauce for delicious crêpes. It also makes an interesting green sauce for pasta, whirled in a blender with melted butter and a couple of garlic cloves and briefly heated.

Chinese mustard adds character to clear soup and makes an excellent vegetable to stir-fry with ginger, bok choy, bean sprouts, snow peas, and mushrooms. For a heartier version, add a bit of shredded chicken or pork.

The root of this versatile plant is also edible. It is a specialty of northern China, where it is boiled whole, then peeled, sliced, and served with soy sauce and sesame oil. It can also be very simply prepared, Western-style, like celeriac. Just boil, slice, and serve with a little butter and salt. If you like cream soups, this makes an excellent one, garnished with curly parsley.

Appearance

Chinese mustard comes in many forms, just as do the leaf lettuces. The leaves may be broad and flat, richly curled, deeply savoyed, or feathery. It can grow from 6 to 12 inches in height. Since the flavor of one will vary slightly from another, the only way to determine which you prefer is to try them all—which you can easily do in a single season, since this is a fast-growing crop and lends itself to successive sowings.

The seeds are small, round, and dark red, sometimes almost black. In India and Asia they are pressed for their oil, which has medicinal as well as culinary uses.

When to plant

Almost all varieties can be sown in early spring as soon as the ground can be worked, and again from early August until the first frost. Most varieties will not do well in midsummer. If you want to have this vegetable at that time, hunt up a variety that resists all but the most determined heat wave; with any luck and a little planning, you can enjoy it all summer long.

How to plant

The seed is small and should be shallowly planted, about ¼ inch deep. Set the seeds ¾ inch apart, in rows 12 inches apart.

When the seedlings are 2–3 inches tall, thin to stand 4 inches apart. Crop when 6 to 8 inches in height. Taller than that, the leaves become very pungent, more like common mustard, and are best left to go to seed.

If you get seeds of the *rugosa* variety, they should be planted farther apart—about 2 inches—and thinned to stand 10 inches apart, as the clump takes up somewhat more room than the *foliosa* variety. Seeds can be sown up to ½ inch deep.

If you are not sure which variety you have, you will be able to tell by the time you are ready to thin; *rugosa* leaves will be brownish rather than green.

It is sometimes hard, when ordering Oriental vegetables, to determine exactly what variety you have received. Since some Chinese mustards may turn out to be the kind that requires a full 10 inches between plants, use common sense in dealing with them. If they seem to be getting too crowded, thin them out more.

Culture

Chinese mustard does best when it is kept growing briskly. For the finest crop, fertilize weekly with a 10-10-5 fertilizer, plus a little manure every two weeks. Keep well watered. Needless to say, weeds should be kept down and the plants mulched to conserve moisture.

Harvest

Maturity dates range from 35 to 50 days, depending on the variety. Do not wait this long, though. Harvest from the time the plants are 3 inches tall. Any remaining plants which grow above 8 inches should either be pulled up or allowed to go to seed. (On the other hand, don't take my word for it—you may like the more mature leaves. Try them cooked Southern-style, with a bit of lemon, a dash of vinegar, and some bacon bits.)

Varieties

Basically, Chinese mustard, *Brassica juncea*, comes in two varieties, *rugosa* and *foliosa*. In appearance they differ primarily in the color of the foliage. As we mentioned above, the *rugosa* has brownish-red leaves, the *foliosa* has dark-green leaves. From a culinary standpoint, the difference is a little more marked. The *rugosa* has broader, thicker stems—more like chard—which can be used separately from the leaves and cooked like asparagus. In the Orient, the stems, prepared separately, are very popular and are used in stir-fry dishes as well as frequently pickled. If you wish to try pickling *rugosa* stems, save the liquid from your next batch of pickles (your own or commercial ones), heat to the boiling point, cool to lukewarm, and pour over the cut-up stems. Refrigerate for three or four days and your pickles will be ready to serve. Just be sure the liquid isn't too warm when you pour it over the stems or you will sacrifice the crunchiness that is essential to a good pickle.

Tsang and Ma lists the *rugosa* variety as Dai Gai Choy, the *foliosa* variety as Gai Choy. Johnny's offers Taisai, described as "attractive Japanese mustards . . . rounded leaves on thick white stalks which form a bulbous, celery-like base." Kitazawa, among its mustards, lists Aka Takana, a *rugosa* variety which doesn't take up any more room than the *foliosa*.

POTHERB MUSTARD   MIZUNA

[Brassica japonica]

This is an Oriental green that seems to have no common English name; potherb mustard is as close as I can come, and that is a name which is also sometimes used for other greens. If you live in California, you may occasionally encounter it under the name "California peppergrass," but even this is a misnomer since it is not related to peppergrass, and is not at all peppery. Nor, although

Chinese potherb mustard   mizuna

technically a member of the mustard family, docs it have the pungency of either the common or Chinese mustards.

Mizuna is so widely grown in Japan that in China it is called Japanese greens. If you order it from the sources I have given, mizuna will do very well.

Culinary and other uses

Mizuna can be eaten raw but it won't do much for you; the taste is so mild as to be almost without character. It's pretty, though, and in a leafy tossed salad of mixed greens, its feathery foliage is very attractive. If you use it this way, do not combine it with Chinese cabbage, escarole, or other strongly flavored salad greens; it would be better with salad bowl and similar mild varieties. A bit of dry mustard in the vinaigrette dressing would be welcome.

Mizuna is rich in vitamins and minerals, and is available from the garden long after most of the other greens have been harvested. When the weather is cool, and hot food more welcome, combine it (at the last minute) with a steaming dish of turnips and carrots; stir-fry in sesame oil with ginger and soy sauce for flavoring; use in clear soups or as a last-minute addition to minestrone. It makes an unusually fine cream soup, garnished with a sprinkling of Chinese chives.

Appearance

Like so many Oriental vegetables, mizuna is worthy of being grown purely as a decorative plant. When not in flower, its feathery, light-green leaves form an ornamental clump up to 12 inches in diameter— compact and upright. Use it as a graceful bedding plant, a delicate foliage accent, or a beautiful background for low-growing ageratum or alyssum.

It is particularly useful in filling up that awkward period in the flower garden, when the spring crocuses and daffodils, tied and awaiting maturity, must still be accommodated in the flower bed, even though they are no longer an asset. Mizuna grows quickly and high enough to hide bent-over daffodil foliage. When you are ready to remove the bulb foliage and plant your annuals, mizuna can be harvested for the kitchen, leaving the flower bed free and clear for new plantings.

When to plant

As an early spring green, mizuna is ideal; it is both cold- and wet-resistant. In Connecticut, where springs are so often chilly and wet, it compensates for failures due to the too early, overenthusiastic sowing of other seeds that cannot possibly germinate under these adverse conditions. If your green beans are rotting in the ground, it is comforting to see a fine row of mizuna seedlings well on their way.

Grow mizuna successively from early spring on, until stopped by a hard frost. Do not hesitate to continue sowing even after midsummer (although seedsmen will discourage this); take the chance that the weather will not freeze hard until late in the fall. Sometimes mizuna will even survive the first snowfall and give you greens to gather well after the rest of the garden has given up for the season. This is an example of how appearances can be deceptive; it looks so fragile you would expect it to blacken on the first cold night. I have actually had mizuna green and fresh after a frost that destroyed my zinnias.

On the other hand, in spite of being comfortable with cold weather, mizuna—unlike lettuce—will not go to seed in a spell of hot weather. Some summers, of course, may be too much for it, but it is surprisingly heat-tolerant and I have grown it through a week of 90°F. temperatures without any ill effect except a slight wilting of the leaves—and that corrected itself when the temperatures cooled off in the evening.

How to plant

The seeds can be sown 2 inches apart, about ½ inch deep. Rows should stand about 18 inches apart. Once the plants begin to crowd one another, thin to stand about 12 inches apart. For use as a bedding plant, thin to 10 inches apart. The thinnings are delicately delicious.

Culture

Frequent watering and applications of 10-10-5 fertilizer three weeks after germination are all the attention this vegetable needs. It seems remarkably free from pests and diseases.

For successive sowings, prepare the soil before seeding by digging in a little wood ash, dried manure, and 10-10-5 fertilizer to replenish that used up by the previous crop. Do not overdo the fertilizer, however; growth should be brisk but not headlong.

Harvest

Take a few leaves from each plant anytime from three weeks after germination. The major harvest should be completed in 35 days. This can mean removing the whole plant or just most of the leaves. You can take advantage of the biennial character of mizuna by leaving enough foliage for it to grow on; in the flower bed, this may be the most satisfactory way to have your mizuna and eat it, too.

I generally prefer to harvest the entire plant, and replant with seedlings that have been started elsewhere. This is because I am constantly changing my garden plan and often want to put a plant in quite a different spot. It is very easy to have a flat of mizuna seedlings ready for transplanting. If you aren't so fond of it as a vegetable that you want a continuous harvest, drop in a seed whenever you harvest a whole plant and you will have a rest between harvests. What with lettuces, chards, mustards, cabbages, and other leafy vegetables, I must admit that sometimes some of them get away from me, but I have discovered this happens to all enthusiastic gardeners—*all* of us always plant too much zucchini, for instance.

Just as an experiment, I tried cutting back some mizuna plants to within an inch of their bases. The part that remained grew new leaves overnight; a week later the plants were 3 inches high. This is even easier than reseeding or transplanting seedlings, a tremendous time-saver. Try it for your second crop, but fertilize as if you were reseeding.

Varieties

There is only one kind offered, and no varieties specified.

Kitazawa lists it under "Mustard," and adds the other name by which it is sometimes known, Kyona. Japonica lists it under "Greens"; Johnny's under "Assorted Greens"; Hudson under "Japanese Greens." Redwood City also carries it.

If you want to inquire of your regular seedsman, use both the Latin and the Oriental name to avoid confusion; but you will find that not many of the larger American growers carry it.

GARLAND CHRYSANTHEMUM   SHUNGIKU

[*Chrysanthemum coronarium*]

If you grow many of the wonderful Chinese vegetables in this book, your neighbors are going to be very confused; they won't be able to tell your vegetable garden from your flower garden.

Shungiku is a case in point; it is a true chrysanthemum, with recognizable chrysanthemum flowers. Only *you* will know that it is also a superb vegetable.

Garland chrysanthemum shungiku

Don't, however, rush out to nibble at your flower-bed chrysanthemums; you will find them much too bitter to be edible. Actually, I should qualify this statement by saying that our usual garden chrysanthemums aren't *generally* enjoyed as food. They are distinctly unpleasant to the palate and a taste for them can be cultivated only through great determination. There is on record the experience of a Japanese gentleman of limited means who worked to develop a taste for this flower. After experimenting with it in his diet over a period of years, he finally grew to like it. To his delight, he reports, he then realized that he no longer suffered from a disease he had had, a rare type of diabetes which had not, up to then, responded to medication or diet. He still feels strongly that this "cure" was a direct result of his eating chrysanthemums, but there is no scientific corroboration of his conclusions.

To grow edible chrysanthemums, be sure to order the so-called "cooking chrysanthemums."

Shungiku is a native of the lands around the Mediterranean, but the Oriental countries have taken it as their own, along with all other chrysanthemums. In China, the chrysanthemum is a symbol of a life of ease and joviality; it is also a flower appreciated by the over-thirty adults as the symbol of late-blooming beauty. In Japan it is the national flower, and it is used in a variety of stylized designs as a decorative element in almost every aspect of Japanese art and architecture.

The high regard in which it is held in Japan is also shown by the fact that it is an ingredient in one of the very special dishes served as part of the tea ceremony.

The chrysanthemum is also used as a medicinal herb in Japan. In the sixteenth-century herbal *Honso Komoku*, it was the chief ingredient in a formula for promoting longevity and for turning gray hair black again. This formula called for gathering the various parts of the plant (the young shoots, flowers, stems, and roots) at their peak—which meant at various times during the entire growing season—then drying them so completely that they could be reduced to a fine powder. This powder was taken three times a day for one hundred days. Within a year, according to this book, hair would return to its natural color; within two years, new teeth would replace those which had been lost; within five years, "an old man of 80 would become like a boy again."

In the West, the chrysanthemum is known to believers in astrology as the flower sign of the solar wheel, governing the house of Sagittarius, where it symbolizes the good life.

Culinary and other uses

Shungiku is a potherb, which means it is used for cooking rather than eating raw, as in salads. It should always be cooked *very briefly*, in a small amount of water, somewhat like spinach. The unusual feature of this green is its aromatic flavor; it tastes exactly the way chrysanthemums smell. When you first try it, combine it with other greens or vegetables, until you see how much you like it. Coarsely chopped and added to chicken broth, with a thin slice of fresh ginger, it produces a soup that is like an instant trip to China. Nothing could be simpler than its use, yet it adds flavor and distinction to whatever it accompanies.

Stir-fry dishes make good use of this "fragrant green," as it is sometimes called. Combine it with bamboo shoots, snow peas, and bean sprouts for a rich variety of texture and taste that is typically Oriental. A little sesame oil, soy sauce, and a dash of sherry make it a memorable side dish with pork or chicken. Or be completely Chinese and shred the pork or chicken directly into the same skillet or wok.

Shungiku can be cooked with spinach, beet greens, or the leaves of chard to create a vegetable melange, but do not confuse the palate by combining it with any of the mustards.

Among friends, you might like to try the Japanese custom of dipping the flowers in saki at the beginning of a meal. This is said to confer good health and long life on the diner. (I think you will find it more to your taste if you dipped the flowers in boiling, salted water before serving them.) The saki should be slightly warmed when served. If saki is not handy, a medium-dry sherry will do almost as well.

Dried flower petals are used in soups, stir-fry dishes, and tempura. They should be soaked in tepid water before adding to the pot.

A very fragrant Japanese pickle, *kikumi*, is made with fresh chrysanthemum petals. Gather them, remove the green base, and separate the petals. Dip in boiling, salted water and drain. Pat dry with paper towels. Marinate for an hour in saki and soy sauce. To be completely authentic, the marinade should also include chopped, pickled peaches or pickled apricots. Serve with the marinade as a condiment—it will keep in the refrigerator for several days.

Appearance

Shungiku is a true chrysanthemum, so it is not surprising that it looks like our common garden chrysanthemum. Usually, however, it has been eaten up as a green long before it has had a chance to flower. Always let a few plants flower, partly because they are pretty, and partly because it is fun to eat flowers. The flowers vary in color from white to yellow to orange; the plant grows from 2 to 4 feet high.

Like all chrysanthemums, shungiku is long-flowering and will bloom in your garden from August until killed by the frost; since it is very hardy, this may be as late as December.

The foliage is dark-green, pleasantly scented, and very attractive.

When to plant

Shungiku can be planted as early in the spring as the ground can be worked, and sowed successively until early summer, and again in late summer for a fall crop. If grown during hot weather, it is liable to become slightly bitter.

How to plant

The seeds are small and should be sowed thinly, if possible, ¼ to ½ inch deep, about 2 inches apart in rows 18 inches apart. Thinning is part of the harvesting procedure, since young leaves, which are gathered while the plant is still immature, make the best eating.

Culture

Like most vegetables, shungiku likes a rich, humusy soil, with manure and compost dug into it 10 inches deep.

Keep the plants well weeded and watered—a mulch is a big time-saver—and they will thrive without any other particular care. If you have fertilized properly upon sowing, they won't need further feeding.

Shungiku will tolerate partial shade, so save your sunniest spots for more demanding vegetables.

Harvest

The leaves should be gathered when the plants are no more than 4 to 6 inches tall.

Spring-sown plants can be gathered, plant by plant, as wanted. Plants sown in late summer should be harvested in such a way as to thin out the row, leaving room for mature plants which will eventually reach the flowering stage (in about 60 days from seed). The chief reason for this is that the flowers look so pretty in a vegetable garden which, by then, is practically flowerless. The full-grown plant will stand from 2 to 4 feet high and make quite a show. Plant between rows of ruby chard and you will find yourself out in the vegetable garden with a camera full of color film.

How to dry chrysanthemum flowers

To dry chrysanthemum flowers for culinary use, gather them when they have fully opened. Remove the green base and separate the petals, one from the other. Dip the petals in boiling, salted water, and dry on a paper towel. Spread the petals in a single layer on a flat surface and sun—or oven-dry (150° F.)—before storing.

In Japan only yellow flowers are used, but this seems to be an aesthetic consideration rather than a culinary one, since there is no discernible difference in flavor when other color flowers are used.

Varieties

Many seedsmen carry shungiku but some call it Chop Suey Green, and Redwood City lists it under "Japanese Greens." The latter, incidentally, offers two varieties: one small, with medium-lobed leaves, and one, with deeply serrated leaves, that grows somewhat taller. Both mature in about 65 days, so you might order both and see which one you prefer to continue growing.

Japonica, Johnny's, Kitazawa, and Hudson also carry seeds.

Another variety, *Chrysanthemum morifolium* (*shokoyu-qiku* in Japanese) is frequently used in Japan for making dried flower petals. There are also many other kinds commonly grown in China and Japan. So far, none of these is available in this country, but they are worth watching out for since new varieties are being brought in each year.

3 The Chinese Cucurbits

BITTER MELON • WINTER MELON • FUZZY GOURD •
SWEET MELONS • CHINESE PUMPKINS • PICKLING MELONS •
CHINESE OKRA • CHINESE CUCUMBERS

The Cucurbitaceae are a large family which includes all melons and all the gourds, pumpkins, cucumbers, and squashes. They tend to be plants which take up a great deal of room in the home garden, and the majority of them are vines. They are all subject to the same pests and diseases, and there is considered to be a danger of cross-pollination if they are grown next to one another; cantaloupe, for instance, will reputedly taste like cucumber if planted next to that vegetable. I have never had this experience but I do know many gardeners who claim that they have. Since cucurbits tend to take up a lot of room, it is almost impossible in a small garden to keep them separate enough to prevent cross-pollination; you can either take your chances, as I do, or grow one or the other each season.

If you have had a problem with poor pollination of other bee-pollinated vegetables, a few cucurbit plants will attract more than enough bees to your garden; they feed so heavily on the mostly orange or yellow blossoms that harvesting the fruit is sometimes hazardous—although I ignore the bees and usually find they are too busy with the flowers to pay any attention to me.

Do not hesitate to try growing these fascinating plants even if you are told, for instance, that "melons don't do well" in your area. I was always warned off cantaloupes in Connecticut, and when I finally got up my courage and planted some anyhow, I had a huge crop of cantaloupes that spoiled me forever for store-bought ones. Conditions in garden sites vary so much that you may have luck with a vegetable your neighbor can't grow at all; the only way to tell is to try it for a couple of seasons.

You will find, in this chapter, many very unusual things to grow. They are great fun and good eating; I hope you will be tempted into giving them a try. Even the Chinese cucumbers are very different from our own—especially the extraordinary shapes. As I write this I have, sitting on my desk, a serpent cucumber—curled around in a circle with its "head" raised as if to see what I am up to.

BITTER MELON   FOO GWA

[*Momordica charantia*]

Like so many Oriental melons, this is not, as you might suppose, a fruit, but a vegetable. It is more closely related to gourds than to our familiar cantaloupes, honeydews, and other melons.

Virtually unknown in the United States as a vegetable, bitter melon is grown in both North and South America as an ornamental vine, and its edible qualities may come as a surprise to many a gardener who has looked at but not eaten its attractive foliage and strange fruit.

Culinary and other uses

Bitter melon is one of those vegetables for which there is no equivalent in the roster of our Western foods. As you may gather from its name, its flavor is definitely bitter; at first it startles the taste buds, then it becomes a delight. A taste for bitter melon is quickly acquired by both children and adults. The bitterness is due to the presence of quinine, and because of this ingredient, the dried melon is used in Oriental medicines. If you took to the Bitter Lemon soft drink and mixer which was introduced to this country from England (and which also contains quinine), you will surely like this vegetable. Even if you didn't, make room for it in your kitchen; you will find it a welcome change from the flavors to which you are accustomed.

In classic Chinese cuisine, there is a bitter melon dish prepared with soybean sauce. You can easily make this dish yourself if you can obtain one special ingredient, fermented black soybeans. Any market that carries Chinese foods will have them; they are called dow sei. Soak the beans in water for ten minutes before using, as they are heavily salted. To make the sauce, combine dow sei with minced garlic and set aside. Then take the unpeeled melon and cut it in half or slice it.

Combine raw minced pork, raw minced shrimp, finely chopped

water chestnuts, soy sauce, cornstarch, and sugar; blend together with the bean-and-garlic mixture. Remove the seeds from the melon and stuff the cavity with these combined ingredients. Heap the stuffing high, because it will shrink in cooking. If cut in half, the stuffed melon can be baked or braised. If sliced (and stuffed), it can be dipped in cornstarch, lightly browned on both sides in a little sesame oil, and steamed. Either way, cook until the melon is tender. Steaming, for instance, will take about forty minutes.

By the way, if you have not used up all the black beans, stir-fry them with minced garlic in sesame oil for one minute and store them in the refrigerator. They are called for in many stir-fry, baked, and steamed dishes.

A quick and easy-to-prepare Chinese dish is stir-fried melon and chicken. If very bitter, the melon should be parboiled for three minutes. Then cut both chicken and melon into small chunks. Stir-fry melon one minute, add chicken, and fry a few minutes more. Add soy sauce, minced garlic, ginger, and a bit of chicken broth, and reheat, stirring to blend. If you prefer less garlic flavor, add the garlic when you first cook the melon.

For an American dish, try parboiling bitter melon for five minutes, then adding it to a skillet of braised veal and carrots for the last thirty minutes of cooking. Quickly made Chinese soup is chicken broth to which small chunks of bitter melon are added and simmered until tender. Parboiled bitter melon can be marinated in rice or cider vinegar that has been mixed with an equal amount of water, a little sugar, and less salt. Two hours is sufficient for the marinade. Drain the melon, slice thinly, and serve as a tangy relish. This is especially good served with a flaky white-fleshed fish.

The young leaves of bitter melon can be steamed and used as a potherb, but *do not attempt to eat the seeds;* they are a strong purgative and definitely not to be experimented with.

Appearance

Since bitter melon is often grown as an ornamental, you know it must be an attractive plant. It is a very handsome vine with attractively lobed bright-green leaves and numerous small, gay, yellow flowers. The fruits, or melons, are really odd-looking. They grow up to 12 inches long, about 2 inches in diameter, and are oval, tapering to a point at each end. When immature, the fruit is yellowish-green or dark green. As it matures it turns the same bright yellow of the flowers, then bright orange. It is very showy when fully fruited. If the fruit is allowed to ripen, the melon will split open; the inside it reveals is even more striking than the flowers and fruit. This is a fascinating plant to grow, and to eat.

When to plant

Bitter melon, like almost all melons, is a warm-weather crop. Seeds should be sown in place when all danger of frost is past and the ground is thoroughly warm.

How to plant

Sow seeds next to a fence or trellis 1 inch deep, 6 to 8 inches apart. A well-fertilized soil, high in nitrogen, will suit it best. The seeds are slow to germinate (up to 14 days), so be patient. Keep seed bed moist until seedlings appear. Since copious watering is required throughout the growing season, you might want to dig a ditch next to the planted row. Scoop out about 4 inches of soil from the ditch, and fill with sand. If you water the ditch as well as the soil around each vine, you will get the moisture down to the roots and not have to water the surface soil nearly so long. Even a light rain will penetrate this sand ditch more deeply than if it merely fell on the surface soil.

Culture

Bitter melon requires a good deal of fertilizer. It should be side-dressed every couple of weeks, always with a high nitrogen formula. Dust the vines with wood ashes and use a wood-ash mulch. Water every four days if the season is dry; deep watering is the only kind that will do any good.

When the vines are about 10 inches long, tie them to their support. From then on, you can weave new growth in and out of the support. If you are growing it ornamentally as well as for the fruit, tie it in such a way as to train the foliage where you want it to go.

Harvest

Depending on what you want, harvest the young leaves or wait for the immature fruit. For best eating and least bitterness, fruit should be picked when no more than 6 inches long. If you find you like the taste very much, try more and more mature fruit, until you reach the degree of bitterness you draw the line at. The younger the fruit, the longer it must be cooked before it will get tender; older fruit cooks up more quickly. Once the fruit has turned from its green color, you won't want to eat it, but you can let it go to seed, both for the looks and for next year's seed crop.

Varieties

There are no varieties offered. Seeds can be obtained from Grace, Kitazawa, and Tsang & Ma. Keep an eye on other catalogs; more Oriental vegetable seeds are coming in every year.

WINTER MELON   DOAN GWA

[Benincasa hispida]

There is a very good chance that you have never seen, let alone eaten, a Chinese winter melon, even if you often eat in Chinese restaurants. In China and Japan, however, it is a staple, widely grown and used in almost every kind of dish—from steaming to stir-fry.

Unlike some Chinese vegetables, this is one with many names. It is commonly called white or wax gourd, because of its appearance, and is also known as ash melon for the same reason. Because it makes a delicious pickle, it is sometimes called Chinese preserving melon, and the Japanese call it *togwa*. Occasionally, you may find it in Spanish-American markets under the name *calabaza China*.

Even if you are not familiar with its culinary properties, grow a few vines just for fun. It will be very decorative in your garden and sensational in the kitchen. Its use in everyday dishes ranges widely from soup to relish tray to main vegetable, and will be limited only by your own imaginative approach to cooking. Most amazing is its keeping quality; properly stored, it will stay fresh for a whole year.

Culinary and other uses

There are many easy ways to use winter melon, but probably the most famous dish of all is a rather elaborate one. Both the preparation and presentation of this dish make it suitable only for a banquet or a very special occasion. When you are having a particularly important buffet party, you could stake your entire culinary reputation on this one dish.

First of all, the melon must be completely ripe; you can tell this because a mature melon will be covered with a heavy, waxy, white coating. Scrub off the waxy coating with a stiff brush and you will reveal the beautiful celadon-green color of the skin. Carve the skin, like a cameo, into a bas-relief dragon or some other suitable design (in China these are sometimes amazingly detailed and elaborate). The result can look for all the world like a rare Chinese bowl. If your own artistic skills are not up to this, and you don't have an artist in the family, even simple geometric designs are attractive. The green outside and the cream underskin make it easy to create a work of art.

Once carved, cut off the top with a saw-toothed edge, like a jack o'lantern, and reserve. Remove seeds and fibers.

Now—and this is the hard part—you need to find a pot that will hold the whole melon. Since a mature winter melon may be 12 inches long and 8 inches thick, you will have to use your very largest pan. A pail might do the trick, or a small washtub. If you have a pot that is wide enough but not quite deep enough, another pot laid upside down over it might work, but you would have to seal them together with foil to keep in the steam.

Since the melon is so large, and since it will become a little soft when cooked, it is a good idea to make a sling out of a piece of old sheeting or several thicknesses of cheesecloth. This should go under the melon and hang out of the pot on both sides so that you can get hold of the ends to help lift the melon out of the pot when it is done.

Carving a winter melon (doan gwa) **for a special feast**

The melon will be very heavy because it will be filled with broth and vegetables, so make your sling sturdy and easy to manage.

The melon is meant to be steamed, not boiled, so a rack must be rigged or some other method of keeping the melon above the boiling water. If you use a colander with feet, you might make handles of wire, instead of the sling described above.

Once you have the melon in the pot, fill the melon with Chinese vegetables cut into ¼-inch chunks. These might include lotus root, bamboo shoots, mushrooms (whole button, or sliced larger ones), water chestnuts, and so on. In addition, raw chicken and pork and baked ham, also cut in small pieces, are usually added. Pour hot chicken broth over the vegetables until the melon is three-quarters full. Dried tangerine peel which has been soaked in water for thirty minutes is usually added at this time, and removed just before serving. If you don't have this, stir in grated orange rind just before taking the melon out of the pot.

Cover the filled melon with its top, then cover the pot. Steam for three or four hours, or until the inside of the melon is tender.

To serve, bring the whole melon to the table on a flat platter, and serve from it at the table, stirring to mix the ingredients each time. This dish is a bit of fuss, but it is worth it both for flavor and appearance. It isn't something to make every Sunday, however.

A simpler version of the same soup can be made by scrubbing, peeling, and seeding the melon, and cutting it up in small chunks. Put the chunks into chicken broth with the other vegetables and simmer until the melon is tender. It is just as good and much quicker—even though not nearly so spectacular—as cooking the melon whole.

All parts of the winter melon vine can be eaten—young leaves and flower buds, as well as immature and mature fruit. The seeds are somewhat bitter and an acquired taste, but as long as you will have them anyway, toast a batch and see how you like them.

Winter melon is good stir-fried with pork, scallions, and mizuna; the immature fruits are delicious in seafood curries. If you want an interesting pickle, prepare the rind like watermelon pickle.

Appearance

Winter melon grows on a *single*, somewhat hairy vine, rather than a branched vine like other melons. Because of this it is easy to train on a fence or other support where it takes up much less room than on the ground.

The melon itself is very large. It may grow 12 inches long and 8 inches wide at maturity, and weigh as much as 25 pounds. It is oblong in shape and a pretty green which gradually becomes coated with a white waxy substance as it matures.

The flesh is white and looks something like a honeydew, although it tastes more like a slightly sweet zucchini—if we must have a comparison.

When to plant

Winter melon is a warm-weather crop and, like most melons, requires a long growing season. Tsang & Ma estimates 150 days. If, on figuring back from your first frost date, you decide you won't have enough warm weather out of doors, start the seeds in peat pots indoors. Set out as soon as the ground has warmed up and all danger of frost is past. If you grow watermelon, set out winter melon at about the same time, or a little earlier.

How to plant

If you start the seeds indoors, sow two seeds to a peat pot and thin to one as soon as seedlings appear well started. If sown outdoors, plant seed 1 inch deep, 8 to 10 inches apart. The best way to assure a good crop is to dig a trench 8 to 10 inches deep and fill it 4 inches deep with a high-nitrogen fertilizer plus manure. Mix the remaining soil with the same formula and fill in the trench. Then sow the seeds. Water thoroughly and keep watered until seedlings appear; the ground should be kept moist at all times.

Culture

Moisture and fertilizer must both be supplied heavily. If you have pre-fertilized as suggested above, side dressing will not be so necessary, but it is still a good idea. Side-dress when the flowers begin to fruit and every two weeks thereafter.

Water weekly—even oftener in excessively dry weather. If you don't have too many vines, a coffee can with holes punched down the sides all around and the bottom removed can be sunk in the ground between each vine. Fill this can with water several times when you do your regular surface watering; the results will amaze you.

Because of frequent watering the soil will be moist a good deal of the time. This is bad for fruits that rest on the ground, and hay or straw or some other dry mulch material should be furnished for the fruits to rest on.

If you want to try growing the vine up a support, be sure the support is sturdy enough to hold the large fruit. The legs of old panty hose or strips of sheeting make good slings when the fruits get too heavy for the vine and need to be hung from the trellis.

Harvest

Young leaves and flower buds can be harvested whenever they appear. Immature melons can be picked with clippers as you want them. Mature melons are unmistakable; they will be covered with a heavy white waxy coating when they are fully ripe. Pick with clippers, leaving some stem attached to the fruit.

Storing

Not the least of the virtues of this extraordinary melon is its ability to keep for long periods. It may be stored for six months to a year if you have the right place for it.

First of all, keep the melon in the position in which it was growing; this is the way it should be put on the shelf. The storage area should be cool (but not less than 50° F.) and dry. So long as the rind is not broken, the flesh will stay sweet and fresh for many, many months. If you cut into a melon, store the rest in the refrigerator; it will keep for about a week.

For short-term storage, a warm place—even an out-of-the-way spot in your pantry—will work as long as it is dry.

Varieties

There is only one variety of winter melon available in the United States; seeds can be had from Tsang & Ma and from Grace's.

FUZZY GOURD   MAO GWA   [*Benincasa hispida*]

This is the little cousin of the winter melon, and is sometimes called the little winter melon. If the size of winter melons intimidates you, the fuzzy gourd will be just right. Its culture and habit of growth are similar to the winter melon; you would probably choose to grow one or the other rather than both—unless you are especially fond of these Chinese melons, in which case this will give you an earlier crop than the winter melon.

Culinary and other uses

Like winter melon, fuzzy gourd is a vegetable rather than a fruit. It can be used in all the ways yellow summer squash and zucchini are—for soup, bread, casseroles, stir-frying, and so on.

The outside has a distinctly fuzzy coat, like an especially fuzzy peach, which must be removed. Rub the gourd with paper toweling to take off the fuzz, then peel off the green skin. This should always be done (in that order) no matter how you are going to prepare the melon. Do not cut it open until you have done this.

Fuzzy gourd is a good size and a nice shape for stuffing—just big enough so that each half makes a single portion. You can stuff it as the Chinese do, with shrimp, pork, bamboo shoots, bok choy, and scallions all cut up and mixed with soy sauce, sesame oil, ginger, and minced garlic. Or you can use your favorite zucchini recipe, which might include tomatoes, chopped beef, oregano, basil, garlic, olive oil, and minced onion (the beef lightly browned in the garlic and oil). The seeds and core can be chopped up and added to this just as with zucchini.

Appearance

Fuzzy gourds are vaguely pear-shaped, but without a waist. They taper top and bottom and are either plumply oval or round. The vines are single-stemmed and should be tied, one to a pole, or in a straight line up a fence. The fruit is an attractive green with sweet white flesh.

When to plant

Fuzzy gourd is a warm-weather vegetable; plant when the ground is warm and all danger of frost is past, in well-fertilized soil. Keep the soil moist until seedlings have their second set of true leaves.

How to plant

Set seeds 1 inch deep, 2 inches apart next to a fence, trellis or pole. Be patient; it will be 10 to 14 days before the seeds germinate. When the seedlings are 3 inches tall, thin to stand about 5 inches apart.

Culture

Fuzzy gourd, like winter melon, is a heavy feeder. When the seedlings are 3 inches tall, fertilize lightly—fish emulsion plus cotton-

seed meal is good (one is liquid and will help water in the other) once
a week. When the fruit begins to form, fertilize every two weeks but
more heavily. Provide plenty of moisture all through the growing
season. Many vines may either be staked or allowed to sprawl; fuzzy
gourd *must* be staked and the fruit allowed to hang free from the vine.
You needn't provide slings or other supports for the fruits because
they won't be that heavy.

Harvest

Like all members of this family, fuzzy gourd should be harvested
when young. Pick them when 4 to 6 inches long, unless you want to
let some mature to provide next year's seed.

Varieties

The difference in varieties is mostly in the shape rather than the
taste, so it needn't concern you. You don't have much choice
anyhow, since only Tsang & Ma and Grace's offer the seeds.

SWEET MELONS   CHUNG GWA   [*Cucumis melo*]

The Oriental sweet melons are the kind of melon with
which we are familiar—similar to our honeydews and cantaloupes.
They are very superior melons and you will find some of them much
easier to grow than our common varieties. If you like to grow melons,
don't miss these. Even if you have had difficulty with regular melons,
give them a try. A detailed discussion of varieties at the end of this
section describes the ones for which seeds are available.

Culinary and other uses

The uses of melons in desserts, fruit cups, and so forth are too well
known for me to detail here. Use these melons any way you would
use regular honeydews and cantaloupes; if anything, they are even
sweeter and more fragrant than the finest melons you have ever
tasted.

Appearance

Oriental sweet melons look much the same as our melons, with
somewhat the same variations in size and color of rind and flesh.
Most of the varieties run from 1 to 3 pounds in size, which makes

them very convenient for a limited home garden—although they still take up more space than most crops.

When to plant

Like our melons, Oriental sweet melons require unvarying warm weather, and in the North—Connecticut, for example—are usually started indoors in 3-inch pots about a month before the ground warms up; June is the recommended month. I must confess I seed melons *in place* in June, and have had unusually good luck with them, but you can try both methods and see what works for you.

How to plant

Pre-fertilizing works well with melon. Dig out about 12 inches of soil. Fill the bottom 6 inches with a 5-10-10 fertilizer plus a generous amount of manure. Fill the hole with plain soil. Plant seeds 1 inch deep. Prepare the soil the same way for transplants.

If you plant in hills, plant four seeds to a hill, about 4 feet apart each way. Thin to two or three plants per hill when seedlings are about 4 inches high.

I don't plant in hills at all, though it is what is recommended. I plant my melons in a row, about 18 inches apart, and train them up a fence. As the fruit grows heavy, I support it with individual slings. This keeps the fruit off the ground and away from all sorts of pests and insects, including slugs, that are attracted to the sweet fruit. The melons grow beautifully shaped and clean, and I can keep the soil well watered without spoiling the melons. I don't know of anyone else who does this, but most people in Connecticut have trouble with melons and maybe they wouldn't if they tried this method. It is a tremendous space-saver, too.

In addition, I sink coffee cans, top and bottom taken off and holes punched all up and down the sides, between vines. I always fill them with water three or four times when I do my regular watering (as well as watering the soil around the vine), and my melons come out juicy and sweet. One year I didn't plant any melons and we bought them in the market; we were amazed at the difference in flavor and texture and decided to grow our own again the next season.

If striped cucumber beetles are pesky in your area, then do consider starting your melons indoors. This gives the plants time to gain strength before they are attacked, and makes it much easier for you to keep ahead of the beetles by hand-picking them whenever they appear. Young seedlings could be eaten up before you even realized the bugs were around. I hesitate to jinx myself by saying so, but I have never had this particular problem.

Harvest

Recognizing a ripe melon is a knack, and no one can really teach it to you; it takes experience. Aroma is one good test—a melon that smells fragrant and ready to eat usually is. With the cantaloupe type, the melon will slip easily from the vine when it is ready. Just give a little tug; if it is meant to be picked, it will come off in your hands. Maturity dates are also a guide but only to a limited extent. The moment of perfect ripeness is something you develop a sixth sense for, and some people are just better at it than others.

Varieties

It's always nice to have a choice, and here you really do.

Nichols offers Cantaloup Honey Gold No. 9, which they describe as "a real gem. A small Japanese cantaloup producing fruit that only weighs 10 ounces each. Egg-shaped fruits with smooth, shiny golden-yellow skin. White crisp flesh is sweet and very aromatic. Good keepers."

Thompson & Morgan and Japonica offer Honey Drip, which the former describes as "intolerably sweet." I already find honeydews too sweet, so that variety wouldn't necessarily appeal to me, but they mean it as a good thing and are most enthusiastic about it. "Actually contains over 14% of sugar," says T & M, "considerably easier to grow than the honeydew which it replaces."

In addition, Japonica offers five other melons, both cantaloupes and honeydews, from creamy white to golden rinds, smooth and netted, with flesh ranging from pale green to salmon. Johnny's offers three varieties of "small-fruited Japanese melons," Sakata's Sweet, Takii's Honey, and Honey Gold. They are all mouth-watering and freeze well for out-of-season enjoyment.

CHINESE PUMPKINS   NUNG GWA

[Cucurbita pepo]

The only problem you will encounter in growing Oriental pumpkins is one of nomenclature. "Pumpkin" and "squash" are terms that are used interchangeably to describe these vegetables. In the United States, "pumpkin" is almost never used to describe winter squashes, but "squash" is often used to describe pumpkins. Since the difference lies not in the vegetables themselves, but in the fact that "squash" comes from an Algonquin word and "pumpkin" from the Greek, it is understandable that there should be no real distinction between the two.

The English, who have become very fond of our native American squashes, call all of them "pumpkins."

You can see therefore that it might be a little difficult to be sure what you are ordering when you look at Oriental seed catalogs. To make it even more difficult, Oriental pumpkins do not look like our pumpkins; they come all shapes and various colors, and they are usually much smaller and flatter than our big orange giants. See the section below on varieties for a more detailed discussion.

Chinese pumpkins are native to Asia and highly esteemed in China, where the pumpkin is known as the "emperor of the garden." It is a Chinese fertility symbol (which anyone who has ever grown this prolific vine can easily understand), and a symbol of good health. Pumpkin seeds are a rich source of the B vitamins and of phosphorus and iron; in folk medicine they are used in the treatment of urinary-tract disorders.

Chinese pumpkins   nung gwa

Culinary and other uses

Oriental pumpkins can be used in all the ways you use winter squash or regular pumpkins—in soups, as pies, puréed, baked, or fried.

Pumpkin makes an unusual soup, beautiful in color with a delicate flavor. Peel, seed, and slice the pumpkin and boil it in a little salted water until tender. Drain, and purée in blender. Meanwhile brown chopped onion, and add to pumpkin, with pepper, salt, and a little curry powder. Stir in a cup of yogurt, and reheat without boiling. Garnish with thinly sliced raw chestnuts when serving.

Puréed pumpkin has many uses; it can be mixed with eggs and made into a vegetable custard—just follow a standard recipe for corn or other vegetable custard. This is not a dessert, but it could be if you added sugar and nutmeg with a pinch of cloves. Put it in a pastry-tart shell, and garnish with whipped cream laced with sherry.

For a very easy Japanese pumpkin dish, cut peeled pumpkin into chunks. Add the chunks to chicken broth, as well as a little *dashi* (which can be bought like soy sauce, already bottled), and simmer for thirty minutes. Then add sugar, soy sauce, and salt if necessary. Simmer until the pumpkin is tender. During the last three minutes of cooking, add Japanese noodles.

Irish lamb stew, with pumpkin chunks, potatoes, onions, and carrots, is another tasty but easy dish to prepare.

To stir-fry pumpkin in peanut oil, peel, seed, and cut it into small chunks. Blanch for ten minutes, drain, and cook with bamboo shoots, scallions, and snow peas, and at the last minute add mizuna. Stir in soy sauce just before serving. This is especially good with toasted sesame seeds sprinkled over each portion.

Appearance

As I have said, compared to ours, most Oriental pumpkins are small and flat. The rind may be dark green, brown, or almost gray, with or without stripes, and often deeply ridged. The flesh varies in color from orange to yellow, and is usually very sweet. Some varieties are quite "warty"; all are very decorative and would be a most interesting addition to your garden.

Most Oriental pumpkins have short vines—rather than the large sprawling vines of our native pumpkins—and are more suitable for the small home garden. They will climb on anything, and can be sown among corn or up a fence or trellis.

When to plant

Oriental pumpkins can be started indoors about four weeks before the ground warms up. Or, if you have a long enough growing season, just seed them in place as soon as the ground is warm.

How to plant

Pumpkins are traditionally planted in hills, but planting them along a fence or other support is a space-saver for small gardens. If planted in this fashion, the seeds should be sown 1 inch deep, three to four to every foot. Thin to 18 to 36 inches apart as soon as the seedlings are about 3 inches long.

You will save yourself a lot of work if you dig in fertilizer at the bottom of the row, about 7 to 10 inches deep, before sowing the seeds. A 10-10-10 fertilizer mixed with manure will give good results. Do not feed too heavily from then on or you will create vines that are overlong and easily broken. Regular *light* feeding is advisable.

Culture

Like all cucurbits, Oriental pumpkins require constant moisture. As the vines grow they will shade the earth beneath them and make it easier to keep it moist; in dry weather, however, you may have to water every day.

To cut down on pests and diseases, dust the leaves with wood ashes and mulch with wood ashes. This will have to be done again after every rain, but wood ash is inexpensive, and quicker to use than commercial pesticides, which have to be handled so carefully that they are quite time-consuming to apply. In addition, pesticides do nothing for the soil, while wood ashes add nutrients as they wash down into it.

If any of the pumpkins rest on the ground, put black plastic or hay under them to keep them dry.

Harvest

You don't have to guess when a pumpkin is ripe; it tells you. The stem by which the fruit is attached to the vine turns brown and dry. When this happens, just cut off the pumpkin. You will get a lot of pumpkins on one vine, so don't overplant.

Storing pumpkins

Oriental pumpkins store very well and, under the right conditions, will last through the winter. Cure them in the sun for several days (taking them in, out of the dew, at night) and then store them in a cool, dry place; a temperature of 45° to 60° F. will hold them well as long as they are kept dry. Check them over every so often in case it has been more humid than you realized, and wipe them off if any moisture has formed on the skin. A pumpkin will keep for months as long as the skin is not punctured.

Varieties

Nichols, Kitazawa, Redwood City, Japonica, and Johnny's all carry Oriental pumpkins, but in some cases you will have to look under "Squash" to find them. Green-and-orange Hokkaido is a reliable variety, with fruit that weighs about 5 pounds. Kikuza, a pretty silvery green, is slightly smaller, and Red Kuri twice as big.

Regardless of the variety, they all take about 100 to 130 days to mature.

PICKLING MELONS   CHUNG CHOY

[*Cucumis conomon*]

It's a puzzle to me why Oriental restaurants don't serve more pickles. Americans are very fond of pickles, and many an otherwise undistinguished restaurant has made its reputation with little more than loaves of home-made bread and an assortment of unusual relishes. Americans aren't even aware that there are such things as Oriental pickles, yet the variety and number of them would turn Mr. Heinz green with envy.

Almost every vegetable—cabbages, radishes, and turnips, as well as melons—finds its way into the Oriental pickle barrel, and here, to prove the point, is a melon grown just for pickling (as West Indian gherkins are grown just for their famous sweet pickle).

The Oriental pickling melon is native to China and Japan; it is easy to grow in this country and lends itself to a wide variety of delicious pickles. If you like pickles, you'll love the Oriental pickling melon.

Culinary and other uses

Pickling melons can be used in any standard pickling recipe. Don't limit yourself to sweet pickles; they make an unusual and delicious sour pickle. And while you are trying these pickles, make some the way the Japanese do, pickled in white bean paste *(shiro-miso)* which you can buy at any Oriental grocery store. They take only a week in your refrigerator to reach the fully pickled stage. Or you can pickle the melon like pearl onions, in salt, vinegar, sugar, and chilis. These pickles take three months. If you can't wait that long, some Oriental pickles are ready to eat in just twenty-four hours. I am sure you will also find many easy American recipes, if you want a quick preview of the pleasure these pickles can add to a simple meal.

In the Orient pickles are eaten not only because they are delicious; they are considered healthful as well. Since nutritionists have discovered only recently that vinegar is good for you, who can tell what they may eventually find out about pickles? In any case, we all enjoy them, and it is getting increasingly difficult to find good commercial pickles. To make your own, start with the shorter, simpler recipes, then work up to more elaborate ones. No pickle recipe is really complicated; some are a little lengthy, but most of that time is spent waiting for the pickles to mature. The hardest part of the pickle maker's job is having the patience to wait until the pickles are ready to eat.

While this melon is grown primarily for pickling, it also can be cooked and eaten as a vegetable. Pickling melon has a particular affinity for seafood, and makes a delicious fish soup. Simmer fish stock, together with melon chunks, soy sauce, sugar, and a little rice vinegar, until the melon is tender. Serve with a garnish of thinly sliced scallions as a starter to either an American or a Japanese meal. For a more filling soup, add chunks of cod.

Appearance

The foliage of pickling melons is very dense and forms an excellent windbreak. Do not use it on all sides or you will cut down on the air circulation within the garden. It can be allowed to grow on the ground, but since it is liable to spread 10 or more feet, you would have to have a large garden to want to give it this much space. A better method is to train it up a fence or trellis; it will be easier to find the fruits and, since they should be allowed to ripen on the vine for some uses, the fruit will be better protected from pests and diseases.

The melons themselves vary from dark to light green to silvery gray to white. They are oval in shape, about 12 inches high and 4 inches in diameter. The flesh is white and dense. Their close relationship to the common cucumber is evident, both in their looks and in their flesh; cut in half they look almost exactly like a short, stubby cucumber but with somewhat denser flesh and smaller seeds.

When to plant

Like all members of this family, pickling melons are a warm-weather crop. Sow the seeds in place when all danger of frost is past.

Their growing season, 65 days, is short enough to come to maturity in just about any part of the United States, and the young seedlings can be protected by hot caps or some similar covering if a cool spell strikes early in the planting. In Connecticut, June planting is usually reliable, but even here we occasionally have a cool June.

How to plant

Seeds should be set ½ inch deep, about 4 inches apart in a row that has been pre-fertilized by digging in manure and 10-10-10 fertilizer 6 inches down from the soil surface. The last 2 inches from the surface should be plain soil.

Culture

Side-dress when blossoms begin to turn to fruit, and every two weeks from then on. The vines are aggressive and need to be turned constantly in the direction in which you want them to grow. Let them go over the top of the fence and down the other side, if necessary; pinch off the tips when they get as long as you have room for. Water copiously; they must never be allowed to dry out.

Harvest

The time to harvest depends—as with cucumbers—on the kind of pickle you want to make. Some Oriental cooks prefer the young immature fruit; others say the melons must be mature. Do not allow the fruit to more than just start to whiten even for mature fruit; it will soon pass the point of goodness and get too dry.

Fruits will ripen steadily over a period of four to six weeks, so you will have ample time to try out a number of different ways of preparing this interesting vegetable.

Varieties

Nichols carries Japanese Pickling Melon, which leaves the variety pretty much up in the air; Johnny's is very specific with Nuname Early and a complete description including "the earliest maturing Japanese selection." Kitazawa has two varieties, one light and one dark green. That's a wide choice for such a rare melon, and you may want to try them all out to find the one that suits you best—one variety a season could keep you in melon pickles for the next four years.

CHINESE OKRA   CEE GWA

[Luffa acutangula; L. cylindrica]

If you want to garden intensively, no single vegetable I can think of produces as much useful "material" as the Chinese okra. "Material" may sound like an odd way to describe a vegetable, but Chinese okra is much more than a vegetable, as you will see when we come to its uses. All parts of the plant, except the root, are good for either culinary or household use. In addition, Chinese okra grows rampantly with little care; a single vine will produce over twenty-five large gourds.

It may be that you, like many American gardeners, already grow Chinese okra as luffa—an ornamental gourd—without realizing that it is also a fine vegetable. If so, you are in for a pleasant surprise when you taste it.

Luffa originated in India, but was brought to China long before records were kept. Today it is grown throughout the world, especially in tropical and semitropical countries. Although considered a warm-weather crop, it can be grown as far north as Connecticut, and starting the seedlings indoors a little earlier makes its culture possible in even colder regions.

Culinary and other uses

"Chinese okra" is a misnomer, since the name refers to its appearance, not its taste. The fruit is much larger than okra but has the same sort of pronounced ridges.

Chinese okra   cee gwa

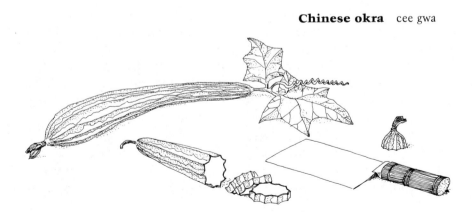

Both the leaves and flower buds are edible when very young. Use them as a potherb; simmer in boiling salted water until just tender, then serve with butter which has been heated with a pinch of curry powder.

The fruit, which is edible only when immature, can be prepared exactly like zucchini—although it doesn't taste like zucchini—which gives you a wide range of raw, cooked, and pickle recipes to choose from. It is delicious sliced, or diced and tossed in a salad, like cucumber. The flavor is delicately sweet, and everyone seems to like it the minute he tastes it. Try it stuffed, mixed with browned chopped meat and vegetables, and baked in a 350° F. oven for an hour. Or simply simmer until tender, and serve with butter and a teaspoon of lemon juice; it will taste something like early English peas. The Chinese stir-fry it in sesame oil, with bamboo shoots, snow peas, scallions, water chestnuts, soy sauce, and grated fresh ginger. For a heartier dish, add shredded chicken, pork, or beef. Or dice and stir-fry with shrimp, scallions, and a finely chopped green chili. Chinese okra is also good simmered briefly in a clear soup, or deep-fried as tempura.

Always pare off the ridges with a potato peeler to prepare the gourds for eating; the skin can be left on.

The seeds of the mature gourd can be oven-roasted, lightly salted (and oiled, if you like), and served as a nutritious snack.

The Chinese consider the dried gourd a special culinary treat. To make this, slice the young fruit, and sun- or oven-dry. Store in tightly covered jars (checking occasionally to make sure there is no mold). They are especially prized when cooked in broth, but can be combined with other vegetables and meats where you would ordinarily use squash.

Once you have harvested all the young fruit you want to eat, let the remaining gourds mature to full growth, then remove and put in hot water. You don't have to keep the water hot, but change it daily. When the outside skin begins to rot away, remove it and you will find the inside is a spongy fibrous mass. Dry the individual gourds in the sun, and eureka!—you will have a vegetable "sponge." This is the famous loofah of Egypt. It is sold in all our better drug stores as a shower aid—it's great as a back-scrubber and when used all over gives the skin a gentle glow, without ever being abrasive. I have always kept one handy in the shower, but it was years before I knew what it was or that I could grow it. It is quite expensive to buy, very inexpensive to grow enough for yourself and for Christmas gifts for family and friends. Even used daily in a humid bathroom, a luffa sponge keeps almost indefinitely, without getting the least bit unpleasant or musty. It has practically replaced real sponges, which are almost out of reach from a price standpoint, and hard to find besides.

The luffa is also known as dishcloth, dishrag, or towel gourd, which tells you some of its other uses. Because it is a good scrubber, both cooks and gardeners find endless uses for it. It doesn't get offensive or retain odors, like plastic sponges, and is much more effective for cleaning dishes, pots and pans, flower pots, and plastic seed trays. It won't scratch no matter how hard you press.

It has innumerable other uses. Our own army and navy buy quantities of luffa sponges to clean automobile windshields, use as superior oil filters, and for the manufacture of equipment which requires a spongy material. In the Far East it is used to make bedroom slippers, bathroom, door, and table mats, sun helmets, and as stuffing for pillows and mattresses (particularly good in humid climates where other materials tend to mold). If you are into crafts, you will think of dozens of uses for this amazing gourd.

Appearance

Like many cucurbits, Chinese okra is a vine. It grows almost rampantly and is best trained on a trellis, where it will take up much less space than sprawled in the vegetable garden proper. Depending on which variety you grow, it will reach as much as 15 feet in length, with numerous pretty, bright-yellow flowers. The gourds or fruit are deeply ridged, like oversized okra, sometimes slightly curved, sometimes straight. You will get straighter gourds if you grow the vine on a trellis or fence so that they hang free. The gourds will vary in length; the longer variety can grow over 24 inches long and weigh up to 5 pounds; the smaller variety usually grows a maximum of 12 inches.

When to plant

Chinese okra is a warm-weather plant and cannot be set out in Connecticut until about the middle of June. As you go south you can plant earlier. Whatever your location, allow about 115 days to maturity. If you cannot be sure of uniformly warm weather for that long in your area, start the seedlings indoors. Chinese okra is not, however, as delicate as it sounds, and Johnny's grows it successfully in Maine, so do not hesitate to try it.

How to plant

If your warm growing season is shorter than 115 days, start it indoors. Outdoors, the seeds should be planted about 1 inch deep, 3 inches apart. Some gardeners like to plant them in hills but I prefer to plant everything possible in rows along a fence—even spaghetti squash, cucumbers, and watermelons; there just doesn't seem to be any advantage to hills. So, unless you have an enormous garden, grow Chinese okra up a support, along a fence or trellis. In this case, sow the seeds about 6 inches apart, and tie the vines to their support as soon as they can reach it.

It may take as long as two weeks for the seeds to germinate; the soil must be kept moist during that time. If you have a very dry spell or the nights turn cool, cover the row with burlap or black plastic, or any kind of mulch, until the seeds germinate. Keep a sharp eye out for the first seedlings and remove the covering immediately. Do not keep it on for the whole twenty-four hours in any case, only during the heat of the day (if hot and dry), or overnight (if cool). It needs light to germinate properly.

Culture

When seedlings have reached about 4 inches in height, and you are sure they have germinated and are healthy, thin to about 24 inches apart. If necessary, seedlings can be transplanted so that none are wasted.

If you have more than you have room for, maybe a neighbor would like some.

Remove all of the first flowers; this should be done when they are still in bud and make good eating. If any gourds develop but don't look healthy, remove those also. By doing this, you will increase fruit production and ensure a uniformly usable crop.

Chinese okra is a heavy feeder and will repay a generous application of manure and 10-10-10 fertilizer in the bottom of a trench (about 6 inches down) before the seed is planted. Once the seedlings are up, side-dress every three weeks with manure and a high-nitrogen fertilizer. If you plant Chinese okra where you have had peas, alfalfa, or other nitrogen-fixing crops the previous season, you will have superior results with less work. The pH should be slightly alkaline, so a little lime may be in order. In the event of a rainy summer, add additional lime (in small quantities) about the middle of the season.

This is a thirsty as well as a hungry plant and should be kept well watered. In most areas, rainfall will not be sufficient.

Harvest

There are two harvest periods—early for the immature vegetable, late for the mature "sponge." For use as a vegetable, pick the gourds when they are 4 to 6 inches long. You can either crop all your vines or choose some to eat when young, and some to mature to the sponge stage. It is more efficient to do the latter, since you can pull up the vines you have chosen to use only for a vegetable once that harvest is completed and put that space to fall-sown crops, or use the area as an above-ground storage for root vegetables. Since you can figure on about twenty-five gourds per vine, you won't need many mature vines unless you are planning a cash crop. Actually luffa is an excellent crop for the small gardener who would like some extra income from his garden; local drugstores will be glad to buy your sponges once you have acquired the knack of drying them properly, and you might even expand into manufacturing other items. Your raw material is so cheap that almost any price you charge for your products will be profit. Since the sponges are very light and easy to ship, this might well be a profitable mail-order item.

Species and varieties

There are numerous kinds of Chinese okra, but most seedsmen will carry one of two: *Luffa acutangula* or *L. cylindrica*. Both are edible and grown as food throughout the world; both form good sponges. Of the two, *L. cylindrica* is thought to be tastier, and since it is also much larger, is more useful in the household. This is the one that grows up to 5 pounds in weight. You cannot always tell which one the seedsman is offering you until after you have grown it and measured the fruit, but both are acceptable.

Again, you will have to be a bit of detective to find whether your seedsman has it in his catalog. Since it is commonly grown in this country as an ornamental gourd, it is frequently listed under "Flowers." Thompson & Morgan, for example, lists it under "Hardy & Half-Hardy Annuals" as Luffa Vegetable Sponge. If you don't know which variety you want, order from them; they sell it as a mixture of varieties so one packet will give you several different kinds. Next year you can concentrate on the variety you have found most satisfactory.

Tsang & Ma carries it, as does Hudson, which calls it Dish Cloth

Gourd (under "Gourds"). Redwood City carries *L. cylindrica* as Luffa Sponge; Japonica also carries *L. cylindrica* under "Gourds," with the Japanese name *hechima*. Park lists it under "Flowers" as Dishrag Gourd, and Johnny's has it under "Gourds" as Luffa. Nichols has *L. cylindrica* but calls it Japanese Bottle Luffa, and Gurney simply says Luffa Sponge, although mentioning that it can be baked and eaten like squash.

CHINESE CUCUMBERS   KEE CHI
[*Cucumis sativus*]

If you have ever grown cucumbers you already know they are one of the easiest and most satisfying crops. Although radishes are always the vegetable of choice for children's gardens, I think cucumbers should also be considered because they grow with such abandon and produce in such tremendous quantities. Gardeners sometimes think space is a problem, but if you grow cucumbers up a fence or trellis, the room they take up is air space, rather than ground space, and even a small garden like mine can accommodate a large cucumber crop, with a number of different kinds to add interest.

Most American gardeners who grow cucumbers seem to stick to the standard types—the ones that look like supermarket cucumbers, though they are not waxed and have immeasurably more flavor. The Burpee Hybrid, Gemini, and all the other familiar ones are certainly delicious, and I still include at least one of them in my cucumber row, but now that I have discovered Oriental cucumbers I wonder why I took so long to try them.

Perhaps you have noticed that in recent years many seedsmen feature "burpless" cucumbers, a type of cucumber with smaller-than-average seeds that is more digestible than the large-seeded types. If, as I did, you have avoided ordering them because you thought they were the result of tampering with a good natural product, and if you suspected that this variety had been developed at the expense of crisp cucumber taste and texture, blame it on the seed-catalog descriptions. There is nothing "new" about the "burpless" cucumber; it is simply an Oriental cucumber now available in the United States. I don't know why seedsmen are so coy about identifying some of their varieties as Oriental, but that is the way it is and you have to be a keen gardener to recognize some of these vegetables behind the descriptive smokescreen of some catalogs.

The origin of the cucumber is so ancient as to be unknown; it is

Chinese cucumbers kee chi

thought that probably it first grew in India. It was introduced to China at a date well before written history, and it has been found in Egyptian tombs dating from the twelfth dynasty. The Romans were inordinately fond of it. Charlemagne gave it a favored place in his fabulous garden, and it is one of the vegetables mentioned in the Bible.

Culinary and other uses

Surprisingly enough, most people do not know how to use cucumbers. I can see your eyebrows going up as you wonder what could be so complicated about the use of a simple garden salad vegetable. That is just the point; most cucumbers in the United States are eaten raw in salads, or as a finger food along with radishes and celery. Recently, Americans have taken to serving them with sour cream (as in Russia) or in yogurt (as in the Near East), but even that barely scratches the surface. It is curious that in both Japan and Germany cucumbers are served thinly sliced and marinated in a slightly sweetened vinegar— for instance, 1 cup of water, ½ cup of vinegar, 2 teaspoons of sugar, a pinch of salt—for about an hour, then drained and set out as a relish at almost any main meal. In Japan the vinegar will be rice, the salt may be in the form of soy sauce, but the basic recipe is similar. I prefer cider vinegar for its snap; you may prefer white vinegar. This is a refreshing and easy pickle, good for unexpected guests because it is so quick.

Stuffed cucumbers make a good summer salad, a great dish for a buffet. Take a slice off each end, and the seeds can be easily scooped out with an iced-tea spoon. The cavity can be filled with a wide variety of mixtures: anchovies, celery, and hard-cooked eggs in curry mayonnaise; shrimp, bean sprouts, and chives in dill yogurt; red caviar, minced onion, and sour cream—these are just a few suggestions. After stuffing, wrap the cucumbers in plastic and chill thoroughly in the refrigerator. To serve, slice ½ inch thick and arrange on Bibb lettuce or rounds of a firm bread; melba rounds will work, too.

It is in cooking that cucumbers offer the most surprises. Peeled, seeded, diced, and sautéed for three minutes in sesame oil, sprinkled with chopped chives, and simmered in a half-cup of chicken broth, cucumbers turn translucent—they look more like pickled watermelon rind than anything else I can think of—and the beautiful pale green contrasts with the dark green of the chives to make an Oriental picture. Cucumbers cooked in this fashion stay crisp and are very digestible; even people who think they can't eat or don't like cucumbers will enjoy them this way (in fact, many of your guests won't even recognize what vegetable they are eating).

Another quick company dish combines shredded cooked pork, seeded, peeled, and sliced cucumbers, thinly sliced scallions, and julienne strips of boiled ham. Sauté the vegetables for three minutes in safflower oil. Add a bit of freshly grated ginger, a little turmeric, and a hint of ground cloves. Add all other ingredients, heating briefly. Turn heat down low and stir in a cup of yogurt. Reheat (but do not boil), and serve immediately. This should be a very meaty dish, and is good with rice and greens. It's a great recipe for leftovers—chicken, fish, or beef can be substituted for the pork, and other vegetables can be used.

In some countries, the young cucumber stems and leaves are eaten as a potherb; I mean to try them every year, and always forget until it is too late.

Appearance

At first, Chinese cucumbers look exactly the same as standard cucumbers. The vines, flowers, and leaves look so much alike that even growing them side by side you would need markers to tell them apart. The fruit, however, is noticeably different almost as soon as it begins to form.

Characteristically, most Oriental cucumbers are very slim; Kyoto, for instance, which grows up to 15 inches long, never exceeds 2 inches in diameter. If you have seen the long slim "burpless" cucumbers that are turning up—at a price—in some fancy markets, they have the typical Oriental cucumber shape.

The serpent cucumber may really startle you the first time you see it nestled under the leaves (even when you grow the vine up a fence, some will form on the ground). Some will grow curled around with the "head" raised inquiringly; others will seem to be uncurling, ready to slither away. Even hanging free on the vine, they will persist in curling into snakelike shapes. They are sweet, crisp, and delicious, as well as fascinating to look at. Children love them.

Another variety is a very pale green—almost greenish-white—and oddly ribbed. It grows up to 2 inches thick and 8 to 12 inches long. The flesh is much denser than that of most of the other Chinese

A baby serpent cucumber

cucumbers and cooks up more like a squash. It can, of course, be eaten raw as well.

Grown on a trellis or a fence, cucumber vines form an excellent windbreak and the fruit is much easier to harvest. This latter point is important, since cucumbers must be harvested frequently and never be left to completely mature; a vine on a trellis is easier to scan for fruit ready for picking.

Some of the Oriental cucumbers will grow straight on a fence, curved on the ground. Some will grow curved even on a fence, but the curve will be less pronounced.

If you have a problem attracting bees to your garden, plant at least one or two cucumber vines; the bees will come from miles around to sup at the bright-yellow blossoms, and once they have made the journey they will attend to your other vegetable flowers as well.

When to plant

Like so many garden "rules" the rules for planting cucumbers can be stretched quite a bit. So long as you do not set out seeds or seedlings until the ground is completely warm, you may start them quite late and still get a good crop over a long period. I never have the patience to start cucumbers indoors. I sow them in the open garden as soon after June 1 as I can manage, and I have noticed that my cucumbers seem to ripen just as fast as those of my friends who have set month-old seedlings at the very same time.

How to plant

Here again, traditional garden practice says to plant cucumbers in hills. As there are more and more small gardens, we are all turning to fences and trellises, and this means planting in a row, rather than a hill. Sow seeds about 3 inches apart ½ to ¾ inches deep. When the seedlings are 4 inches high, thin to about 12 inches apart; you can transplant if the best seedlings are not naturally spaced this way.

Before sowing the seeds, dig down 24 inches and put in manure mixed with wood ash, and a 5-10-10 fertilizer down to the deeper roots, which are otherwise hard to fertilize.

Culture

If your cucumbers are bitter, you've let them get too dry; it's as simple as that. Always water copiously. Cucumbers sometimes worry new gardeners when the leaves wilt dramatically in hot weather. This reaction hardly seems fair, since the plant requires and thrives in hot weather. It can be quite unnerving to go out and see whole cucumber vines apparently dying from lack of water. Unfortunately, maybe they are; you can't tell just by looking at them. A cucumber that is protecting itself from the heat wilts during the day but looks fresh and fully recovered early the next morning; if it doesn't, get out the hose quickly. A better system is to water regularly in hot weather—every three days is not too often if rain is scarce. It is essential that you give the ground enough water to reach well below the surface. As with so many vegetable crops, the moisture content of the soil deep down around the cucumber roots is more important than the surface moisture content. Even with eggplant, which has surface feeder roots that like shallow watering, the deeper roots must still be able to find moisture. Cucumber vines will shade their roots to some extent—even when grown on a fence—but you must keep the water coming on a regular schedule.

If you have run into a period of drought and your cucumbers are bitter, all is not lost. Pick off all the ones maturing at that time, then water well and regularly—and your new batch of cucumbers will be sweet and back to normal.

A midsummer side dressing of manure and 10-10-10 will keep your vines producing generously; a mulch of wood ashes may discourage some pests. I have never had the slightest problem with disease or insects on cucumbers, but if you do have trouble with cucumber beetles, hand-picking is the best recourse. Other diseases are best avoided by growing disease-resistant varieties, but don't worry about this unless you or your neighbors have had a problem.

Harvest

Cucumbers can be picked at any stage in their growth before maturity. As the fruit reaches maturity, it is no longer a choice; you *must* pick the cucumbers before they mature or the vines will relax, work done, and stop producing. If you miss a cucumber and it turns yellow, that vine may stop forming new cukes. Let any remaining cucumbers go to seed, and for a unique treat, try your hand at pressing cucumber oil from the dried seeds.

It is not easy to spot all the cucumbers; daily harvesting is the only safe procedure (especially with Oriental cucumbers, which are so slim they may be easily overlooked). Any small cucumber can be pickled, so pick them young if the harvest is beginning to swamp you with more cucumbers than you can manage.

Varieties

Unlike some Chinese vegetables, cucumbers offer a wide choice and are carried by many seedsmen. Not all catalogs will identify them as Oriental, but you will get to understand the catalog jargon and know that any burpless cucumber is basically Oriental, and that any long, slim type probably is, too.

Johnny's, Harris, Seedway, Hudson, Japonica, Redwood City, Burpee, Stokes, Nichols, and Thompson & Morgan all carry Oriental cucumbers. The commonest, and one of the best, is Sooyow Long (spelled various ways, but say it phonetically and you'll recognize it).

Armenian Yard Long has interesting curved fruits, even on a trellis. "Armenian" cucumbers are sometimes called "Syrian" or "Turkish," but don't let that bother you; they are all Oriental. Green Knight, Tokyo Slicer, and Yamato Extra Long all make easy-slicing cucumbers. Only Redwood City has Heiwa Green Prolific, and only Johnny's has Early Ochai.

To really learn about the different varieties quickly, grow several— just two vines each—next season. I grew five different kinds this year and had a wonderful time. You will find some are early, some a little later, but all will be prolific and delicious. Have fun!

4 Snow Peas

HO LON DOW [*Pisum sativum, var. macrocarpon*]

If you love fresh garden (English) peas but don't have the room for more than a short row, you know how frustrating it is to look forward to a feast and end up with a mouthful. When I raised garden peas, I seldom had enough for even one meal because I grew them along the side of the garage and members of my family snacked off the vines every time they passed by, picking a few pods and eating the peas raw. I never fussed because even if they hadn't there wouldn't have been enough for dinner.

Since I discovered snow peas, all that has changed. I don't think I will ever again bother growing garden peas.

Snow peas are very expensive to buy in the produce sections of supermarkets—over $3 a pound. Apparently people like them so much they are willing to pay the price. I don't quite understand why they should be such a luxury vegetable when they are so easy to grow that even a small patch can feed a family of four.

You will find snow peas a worthwhile addition to your vegetable garden in every way; they are not only good eating but are beautiful, actually showy, when in flower.

In Chappaqua, N.Y., where I grew up, my mother's sweet peas were famous. When I moved to Connecticut and had my own garden, I was very disappointed to learn that sweet peas don't do well here. Once I started growing snow peas, it was as if I had rediscovered the sweet peas of my mother's garden. In fact, people unfamiliar with the appearance of snow peas sometimes think I am growing sweet peas and stop to ask me how I do it in this area. The flowers do not come in various colors, like sweet peas, and they do not really grow in anything like the same profusion, but they have the lovely, pastel violet-lavender found in the coloring of a true sweet pea and the same general appearance. They are pretty enough to use as a cut flower and attractive enough to grow—as I do—in the front of the house. I understand that not *all* snow-pea flowers are violet-lavender; some varieties are snow-white. I have never grown any white-flowered varieties but I imagine they are pretty too. The catalogs describe my

Snow peas   ho lon dow

violet-lavender flowers as "red" or "reddish," which hardly does them justice. If you have a choice, pick the variety so described; it's a feast for the eyes as well as the palate.

The chief reason I prefer snow peas to garden peas is the yield. Once you have shelled a bowl of garden peas, you have a great pile of useless pods (except for the compost heap) and a small handful of peas for dinner. A bowlful of snow peas, on the other hand, gives you a bowlful for dinner. No tedious shelling, no waste—you eat pods and all and they are sweet, crisp, and meaty.

I would almost be willing to guarantee that if you grow snow peas for one season, you will feel as I do that garden peas are not worth good garden space in spite of their delicious taste.

Culinary and other uses

Snow peas combine the best features of snap beans (tender and crisp) and garden peas (sweet and meaty). They can be used in any way you would use either of the other vegetables. They are, of course, essential to Oriental cookery and are used in soups, beef, and other meat dishes, stir-fry dishes, and sukiyaki. If you have vegetarian friends who won't eat shrimp tempura, give them snow peas tempura as a special treat.

Snow peas go with fish and combine well with other vegetables. They are especially useful for busy cooks because they require little preparation—just remove the ends and any strings, wash, drain, and cook quickly. You can steam them for about ten minutes in a little boiling water, toss with butter, and serve. Or stir-fry for two or three minutes in sesame oil and toss with a bit of soy sauce.

Ideally they should be cooked as soon as they are picked, and that is a treat reserved for the home gardener alone. Garden books are contradictory on this point because they say to pick the pods in the early morning, not in the heat of the day, and then they also say to cook them as soon as you pick them. Much as I like snow peas, I really don't eat them for breakfast; I compromise and pick them just before dinner when I am ready to use them. It is usually cooler that time of day even if not quite so fresh as early morning.

It is not necessary to be that much of a purist, however. If it is more convenient, pick them early in the morning, rinse in cold water, drain, and refrigerate in the vegetable compartment. They will be all ready to stem and cook for dinner, and the flavor will still be first-rate. I must confess I have kept them as long as a week in the refrigerator. If you have to keep them longer than that, blanch them, drain thoroughly, and freeze for out-of-season use.

Snow peas are high in Vitamin C, thiamin, niacin, and iron. They also contain Vitamin A, riboflavin, and considerable protein; their caloric content is about half that of garden peas.

Appearance

Snow peas look like garden peas except for the color and size of the flower; the shape of the leaves and flowers is much the same. Some snow peas, however, are dwarf and have a bushy rather than a vining habit. I have grown only the vining kind, but I understand the bush varieties are good space-savers for small gardens and, of course, they don't have to be supported. Since it is convenient for me to grow mine up the side of a fence, I don't think the bush type would save me space; in fact, it would probably use up more space. Vines are less work than bush types; they grow by themselves with only an occasional assist if the winds are from the wrong direction at a crucial time. I also prefer vines because I grow them in back of tomatoes and eggplants. The peas are finished long before they would interfere with air circulation around other crops, and the vines pull up easily without disturbing the soil to any extent. When harvesting, vines are much easier on the back once the lower branches have been picked.

Incidentally, you can't always count on dwarf peas bushing. I grew Kitazawa's China Pea this year. It's supposed to be a small-podded pea, "dwarf, needing no support." Well, maybe. Mine grew 5-foot-high vines, and the pods were anything but small. They were absolutely delicious and I have no complaints, but I might have been a little upset if I had counted on bushes. I understand this often happens with the so-called bushing types, so prepare to put up a support if your bushes take off and start vining. The same thing happens, in a way, with vines. Most of them are described as growing about 5 feet tall, but in practice many will grow considerably taller.

Generally speaking, the bush varieties are earlier than the vine varieties, but this doesn't always run true to the rule either. The earliest variety, vine or bush, that I have found is Nippon Kinusaya from Redwood City, which matures in an amazing 50 days.

When to plant

Snow peas are planted where they are to grow as early in the spring as the ground can be worked. They do not mind cold, wet ground and can be seeded as much as six weeks before the date of your last killing frost.

They will not usually tolerate the heat of midsummer but can be planted again for a fall crop. In the fall, sow seeds from August to mid-September in the North (count days to maturity backward from your first killing-frost date). In mild climates, they can be sown in October or even later and grown throughout the winter for a spring harvest. In any case, the first frosts of winter won't bother them a bit, and if you have a warm spot—like the side of my garage—and a lot of luck, you can get a crop surprisingly late in the fall.

How to plant

Almost no one ever tells you this, but the best way to plant snow peas (or any peas, for that matter) is in a 6-inch-deep trench. The reason for this is that the plants will grow better if earth is pushed up to cover the first few inches of stems as the plants grow taller. This is much easier to achieve if you are filling in a trench than if you are hilling up earth from the surface of the soil. I have tried hilling and always had trouble with spring rains washing the hilled-up soil away. With a trench this never happens. In addition, sowing in a trench makes watering more efficient and keeps the roots in the moister area below the drought line, as well as in cooler soil during an unseasonable hot spell.

Dig your trench deep and incorporate a high-nitrogen fertilizer in the soil. Many gardeners think this isn't necessary with legumes, which they know are nitrogen-fixing plants, able to utilize the nitrogen in the air. What they don't realize is that the nitrogen-fixing action does not take place immediately and even legumes need help. Once a legume has access to nitrogen, it needs phosphorus and potassium to utilize it; so a 10-10-10 fertilizer, applied generously, is the best formula. Wood ashes, manure (including rabbit or poultry), bone meal, and dried blood are all good for snow peas.

Cover this fertilizer-rich soil with plain soil in which to set your seeds. They should be sown thickly, about 2 inches deep, since germination rates are sometimes low. If vine seedlings are less than 2 inches apart, thin them. This is closer than most gardeners will advise, but I find peas don't mind being crowded if you keep them well watered. Bush varieties will have to be thinned to stand 3 inches apart.

The soil pH should range between 6.0 and 7.0; if yours is more acid, lime at least two weeks before sowing.

Vines will grow from 16 to 60 inches or more, so plan your supports accordingly. Bush varieties will theoretically stop short of needing support but, as we have said, don't count on it.

Culture

When the plants are 8 inches high, fill in the trench to almost soil level; leaving it a little below soil level will make thorough watering easier. Keep the soil on the moist side at all times. The easiest way to do this is by mulching, and this is especially important for peas; it not only keeps the soil moist, it keeps it cool, which is equally important. Do not let the mulch actually touch the vines or it will rot them.

Before mulching lay down an inch of wood ash, if you have it. During the growing season, side-dress frequently and lightly with a 5-10-10 fertilizer. If your soil is deficient in nitrogen, use 10-10-10. There is a commercial bacterial mixture which aids legumes in nitrogen-fixing; a soil seriously deficient in nitrogen will need this if you are to get a satisfactory crop. It is easy to use and accepted by organic gardeners. If you think this is an unnecessary bit of bother, try it on one patch and leave the others to their own devices. When harvest time comes, you can decide how much of a difference it made. This product should be used at sowing time, so look into it when you order your peas; most seedsmen carry it. In days gone by the Department of Agriculture used to send little "cakes" of it on request to home gardeners. As far as I know this practice has been discontinued.

Harvest

The peas will form quickly and in tremendous quantity; I have never known a vegetable with a more prolific yield. It is important to pick the pods while they are still immature, but sometimes it's hard not to overlook some. My husband, Don, worked out a really good system. The peas grow in groups of two, so he learned to pick them two at a time, which makes it really fast to strip a vine. In addition, he taught me to shake the vine gently. This makes the peas swing back and forth, and the movement makes the pods easy to spot. Since I have used his method, I never miss a pod; before, I used to hunt and hunt and still some always got away from me. If you let any pods go to seed, the vine will stop producing.

When I say the yield is great and the pods mature quickly, I mean that at the height of the season you may have to pick your snow peas twice a day. This sounds incredible to anyone who hasn't grown snow peas, but you will find it is no exaggeration. I end up with pounds and pounds in my refrigerator and usually have to take off a morning to freeze a batch. This at a time when snow peas are selling in the market for $2.50 to $3 a pound. I should add that this is from a small garden, with snow peas planted only along three sides.

Snow-pea bonus

The bonus is not for you—at least not right away—but for your garden. Since snow peas are nitrogen-fixing plants, use the dried vines and roots as a nitrogen-rich mulch and rototill them in at the end of the season. I think they are wasted on the compost heap and should be returned to your garden soil at the earliest opportunity. Nitrogen is our most expensive and one of our most essential fertilizers, and this is an easy and organic way to obtain it.

Varieties

With most Oriental vegetables, there are not so many seed sources that you have much of a selection; with snow peas, you can really choose just the ones you want. Here is a rundown of some—but by no means all—of the varieties available.

Mammoth Melting Sugar (72 days) is a tall-growing vine, about 5 feet, with large 4¾-inch pods. Most seedsmen who carry snow peas have this variety.

Dwarf Grey Sugar (65 days) is the "bush" variety almost everyone offers.

Dwarf De Grace is an early, low-growing variety offered only by Thompson & Morgan.

Dwarf White Sugar (60 days) is carried by Gurney in addition to the usual varieties.

Nippon Kinusaya (50 days) is the earliest I have found anywhere. Only Redwood City has this.

Little Sweetie (60 days) is a Stokes offering.

China Pea (55–60 days) is carried by Kitazawa only.

Oregon Dwarf Sugar (63 days) is "a vast improvement over Dwarf Grey Sugar," according to Johnny's, the only house offering it. If you want a low-growing variety, this is worth a try even though it is white-flowered.

Tsang & Ma has snow peas but doesn't give them a name. Check your usual seed source before going further afield; it may have just what you want.

5 The Chinese Beans

ADZUKI BEANS • FAVA BEANS • MUNG BEANS •
SOYBEANS • YARD-LONG BEANS

In less favored parts of the world where the standard of living is not so high and consumption of meat not so great as in the United States, beans are the staff of life. Whenever a new bean has been discovered, it has quickly spread around the world and taken hold in whatever countries and climates could maintain it. Unlike wheat, which is not suited for growing in the home garden, beans take up little room; they are high in protein, vitamins, minerals, and overall food value. Beans keep well; they can be eaten fresh, or preserved through canning, freezing, or drying. They are versatile—useful in many ways, from green vegetable to flour—and they combine well with herbs and spices to suit the cuisines of many lands. They are used in famous French dishes, are the mainstay of India under the name *dahl*, feed man and beast as soy, are an important ingredient in Mexican chilis, and provide the chief ingredient in that famous Early American tradition Boston Baked Beans.

As vegetables become increasingly important in our diets, and as the cost of living forces even affluent Americans to lower their meat consumption, the bean is increasingly coming into its own. What better time for the home gardener to discover the delicious Chinese beans? He may be completely unfamiliar with them, but he can grow them as easily as the ubiquitous green or snap bean.

Some of these beans, such as soybeans, are already grown extensively by commercial American farmers; others, such as adzuki, have not been available as seed until comparatively recently. Today all of these beans can be bought from special seedsmen, and I have listed sources for them in each case.

72

ADZUKI BEANS   ADZUKI   [*Phaseolus angularis*]

Adzuki beans (*azuki* in Japanese) have been cultivated in the Far East for thousands of years. They are somewhat different from other beans in that they have a slightly sweet flavor, and this has led to their being used in Oriental desserts. In this country we would not think these desserts nearly sweet enough, but they are much better for you than, for instance, a chocolate fudge cake; they contain relatively little sugar and are high in protein.

The adzuki bean is almost as complete a food as the soybean and, to my way of thinking, it is much better-tasting. Adzuki beans are 25 percent protein, which is very high, and are rich in minerals and almost all of the amino acids, including lysine. As if all that were not enough, they are unusually easy to digest—which cannot be said of all beans.

Culinary and other uses

Most of the adzuki beans sold in this country are used to make particularly delectable bean sprouts; they have a nutty flavor quite different from mung beans. Directions for sprouting can be found in the chapter on bean sprouts.

Adzuki beans make an excellent fresh vegetable. Pick them young, like snow peas, and eat them pod and all. Just cook briefly in a little boiling water or sauté for three minutes in sesame oil. A dash of soy and maybe a pinch of freshly grated ginger, and you have an unusual company dish that everyone will like. For American use, cook any way you would our common green beans.

A handy ingredient to have in your refrigerator is puréed adzuki beans. Simmer the beans in boiling salted water until tender, drain well, and purée in the blender or food mill. This can then be mixed with minced garlic, a pinch of turmeric or Chinese mustard, and a bit of grated ginger. It can be served hot as a vegetable to accompany meat or fish. Or blend in sour cream or yogurt, increase the quantity of spices, and you have a delicious high-protein dip. Use as a sandwich spread with thinly sliced cucumbers and hard-cooked eggs. Or stuff into mushroom caps and broil; serve with a sprinkling of lemon juice.

Be sure, however, to let some of the pods mature so that you have beans to dry. They will be small and probably red and look something like lentils. See the end of this chapter for directions for drying.

Once dried, keep them in a tightly covered jar and they will last indefinitely. When you want to use the dried beans, it is not necessary to soak them overnight; they cook up more quickly than navy or other similar dried beans. Just soak for an hour, and cook in two changes of boiling water to cover until tender. Add to cooked hot white or brown rice that has been mixed with thinly sliced scallions. If you want to make this a main dish for a vegetarian meal, add more vegetables to the rice (carrots, peppers, and other such vegetables should be briefly scalded until just crisp-tender).

Make a bean dinner by simmering in a casserole with chopped green onions, salt-pork chunks, a dollop of molasses, and minced green peppers. For an Indian flavor, simmer the beans with peeled chunks of raw white potato, a pinch of cumin, cardamom, turmeric, cloves, and ginger plus carrots and a green vegetable (spinach, for instance). A few chilis, chopped fine, would make it even more authentic.

Appearance

The plant forms a 2-foot-high bush, something like green beans. The young pods—shorter than green beans—are borne in profusion. When the pods are mature, shell them to release the shiny, red, round beans. If you prefer, you can dry the beans in the pods, without shelling, and then shell them as wanted; this takes up more storage space, so I find it impractical.

When to plant

Plant the same time as green beans, about two weeks after the last frost date for your area, when the ground has warmed up. You can plant successive crops, just as with green beans, by seeding a new row each week.

How to plant

Seeds should be planted in place in a rich, loamy soil, ½ inch to 1 inch deep. Since the seed beans are so large, there should be no need to thin; plants should stand 2–3 inches apart, rows 18–30 inches apart.

Culture

You will get better results with cool nights, but this is not within your control, so don't worry about it. Do not grow adzuki beans in the same part of the garden as beets, because beets like a slightly basic soil and adzukis like a slightly acid soil. I don't believe in working *too* hard at this—a pH range of 5.5 to 6.5 will accommodate most vegetables (except potatoes)—but if you are a perfectionist and try to garden very scientifically, for the highest possible yield, keep the acidity in mind.

If you're into companion planting, plant summer savory among your beans; it's said to improve their flavor and to deter bean beetles. Theoretically, you shouldn't plant onions near any kind of bush bean.

Fertilize after seedlings are about 4–5 inches high and again when flowers start to form pods. Keep the watering consistent and ample.

Harvest

Adzuki beans mature in about 120 days, but that is for dried beans. To harvest as green beans, pick when the beans are just beginning to be outlined in the pod. To enjoy them as a green vegetable, pick every five or six days; otherwise they will get away from you. If you do miss some and they start to ripen, let them; your next row of beans will be along soon in any case.

Varieties

No varieties are offered and the seeds are not widely available, so once you have grown them successfully you may want to save some of your own seed for next year's crop. Johnny's and Thompson & Morgan list them (the latter as "sprouting beans"); generally check the seed-catalog index under all the various headings—"Beans," "Bean Sprouts," "Adzuki," etc.

FAVA BEANS   DOW FU   [*Vicia faba*]

The fava is not a bean in the same sense that limas, green beans, kidneys, and so forth are beans; it is related to vetch, and its Latin generic name shows this—*Vicia* rather than *Phaseolus* or *Vigna*. In spite of these botanical distinctions, we can think of the fava as a true bean for all practical purposes. From a culinary standpoint, it certainly has all the characteristics we expect of a bean: it looks like a bean, grows like a bean, dries like a bean—and for thousands of years was the only bean known to European kitchens.

Because beans have been important as food wherever they are found, it is no wonder that the fava bean, as Europe's only representative of this type of high-protein vegetable, soon became the subject of folklore and legend. It has been found with Bronze Age artifacts in Switzerland and Italy; it is depicted on Egyptian tombs and mentioned in the Iliad; it was unearthed by archeologists on the site of ancient Troy. The Romans offered fava beans, along with bread and circuses, to the populace, who then used them as ballots for voting—which inevitably led down through the centuries to English proverbs linking beans with bribery.

In England ghosts quickly dispersed when beans were spat at them, and in Scotland the witches rode not on the conventional broomstick but on beanstalks.

By the first century A.D. fava beans had been introduced to China, which has regarded them highly ever since.

Culinary and other uses

Although many seed catalogs will assure you that the pods are not edible, this is not true. The very young pods are deliciously edible, a treat available only to the gardener who grows them. In no time at all, however, the pods pass the point of edibility and become useful only as a container for the beans. If you pride yourself on being a gourmet, don't pass up the chance to grow these beans and to enjoy them in this very special way. Just cook the fava pods as you would snow peas—stir-fry or simmer briefly in boiling salted water—and they make a rare dish.

I would not want, however, to denigrate the other uses of fava beans, even though these are available to all. There is still a quality to a freshly picked and shelled bean that you cannot experience even if you could buy "fresh" beans at your market. To enjoy the fava bean at its next-to-earliest—just past the edible-pod stage—shell them like peas and cook them just as tenderly. Many gardeners say they even taste like peas; I am reluctant to always ascribe the taste of a familiar vegetable to an unfamiliar one. Be content that they taste like their delicious selves and never mind looking for similarities.

If you have waited a little longer to pick and shell them, remove the outer, parchmentlike skin on the bean itself. To do so, blanch the beans, rub with a dish towel, or peel with a sharp knife. Then cook just like the immature beans, until tender.

Well drained and served with heavy cream and a little summer savory, fava beans are a treat. They also make an excellent purée (cook with salt, black pepper, and thinly sliced scallions). A deliciously thick bean soup, redolent of thyme and basil, is a warm welcome to guests on a winter's day.

Since they have a short season in Connecticut, I am particularly grateful that fava beans are also a third vegetable—in addition to the pods and the "peas." They dry beautifully, just as other beans do, and can be kept indefinitely in this state. Once you have them dried, cook like navy beans, in casseroles and other slow-cooking dishes, or simmer until tender and add to rice-and-vegetable medleys. A bit of basil, a few tomatoes, tomato paste, and some chopped onion are all in order with this kind of recipe.

In addition to all their other good qualities, fava beans are very nutritious—even more so than wheat.

Appearance

Fava beans are a bush bean, but the bush is quite tall compared to other beans (not pole beans, of course); under ideal conditions they will grow 4 feet tall. The pods are borne in profusion and are large compared to green beans, 7 to 12 inches. Because of the size of the beans, a pod will usually contain not more than five to seven seeds; they are large and very flat, something like limas but more angular. The flowers, as with most beans, are not very conspicuous and are the usual white. The beans are light green, again like limas.

When to plant

Growing fava beans gives you a chance to get the jump on the bean crop because they are much hardier than, for instance, green beans. You can plant them as soon as the ground can be worked without fear of the seed rotting.

How to plant

Fava beans will do well in your regular vegetable garden; their upright habit and early short season make them particularly suited to succession cropping. Plant fava beans when you plant your snow peas and you will be able to replace them with cabbages, beets, and similar vegetables.

The seeds are large and easy to handle, so sow in place where they are to stand. They should be planted 2½ inches deep, 4–6 inches between plants, in rows 18–25 inches apart. The seeds will germinate within two weeks and mature in about 90 days. Some varieties, like Johnny's Windsor, mature in 75 days; Stokes' Windsor Long Pod matures in 65 days. Since you will be cropping these beans at three different stages (as edible pods, edible "peas," and dried beans), you will be keeping an eye on them anyhow and will know when to harvest for whatever stage you are ready.

Culture

Fava beans will do best in a rich soil with plenty of moisture and not too much heat; unlike green beans, they do not thrive in hot weather. Because of their cultural requirements, they are particularly successful in England. In the United States, however, we can approximate the English climate by planting in very early spring in the Northeast and similar climates, and in the fall for a spring crop in the South.

Give them a 10-10-5 fertilizer with an extra feeding of manure. When the pods begin to form, side-dress with the same mixture. Keep well watered and you will have no problems unless you have an early, hot summer.

Since they prefer cool weather, you can easily replace them with green beans once they have finished a season's crop.

Harvest

Begin picking as soon as the pods have started to show the bare outline of the beans. At this point, you can eat the entire pod, as described above.

Your next crop will be the "peas," or shelled-out beans. Last will be the fully mature beans, which should be dried for out-of-season use.

Since there are so many other vegetables that cannot be stored except by freezing (zucchini, for instance), I think it would be a waste of freezer space to freeze fava beans. Eat them fresh while they are available and then contain yourself until the next crop; meanwhile enjoy all the wonderful things you can do with the dried beans.

Allergy to fava beans

Fava beans are an excellent addition to your diet; they are very high in protein (up to 25 percent), high in Vitamins A, B_1, B_2, and C, low in fat, and only 19 calories an ounce. There is, however, one possible problem: it is thought that people of Mediterranean ancestry carry a genetic allergy to these beans; if you are one of these unlucky people, perhaps you will not be able to eat them. This is not invariably the case, however, as is shown by the fact that fava beans are very popular in Italy, Portugal, and Spain.

Varieties

Because of their immense popularity, fava beans are carried by many seedsmen. Thompson & Morgan has the largest and most intriguing selection, attesting to the wide use of this bean in England. They list eight different kinds, and each one sounds more delicious than the one before it. Burpee lists one, Long Pod, is most enthusiastic about it, and recommends it as a substitute for limas, which don't do well in a short summer season. Johnny's features Windsor, Stokes calls theirs Broad Windsor Long Pod, and Nichols settles for plain "Fava beans." In addition, they are carried by DeGiorgi, Demonchaux, Le Jardin du Gourmet, Redwood City, Suttons, and Gurney.

MUNG BEANS LOU TEOU [*Phaseolus aureus*]

Almost no one grows mung beans in the home garden, but more and more Americans are eating them in the form of bean sprouts. If you buy bean sprouts in the market, they have probably been grown from mung beans, since these are regarded as among the finest-flavored; they are also the easiest to sprout. Unfortunately, mung-bean sprouts are also the most expensive to buy—and even come high if you sprout your own.

You can change all that by growing mung beans right in the vegetable garden; they are very easy to grow and will furnish you with a fine supply of an otherwise impossible-to-obtain vegetable, young mung-bean pods.

Mung beans originated in India, where they are known as green gram or golden gram; they are used in innumerable ways in that country. They have been cultivated and eaten in the Far East and in Africa and Greece for thousands of years. Like all beans, mung beans are high in protein, vitamins, and minerals; a deliciously nutritious addition to the diet.

Culinary and other uses

In China and Japan, mung beans are used in the manufacture of cellophane noodles (although these noodles are also made from other beans and other ingredients). In addition, they are eaten in every stage—from immature pods to dried beans.

If you grow them, gather the young pods and cook like snow peas—in soups, stir-fry dishes, and sukiyaki. As the beans mature, the pods can be gathered and dried. Once shelled, boil until tender and season lightly with soy and ginger. The consistency of the beans is slightly sticky, so they lend themselves especially well to bean cakes or to purée. A well-seasoned purée can be Chinese, with the addition of Chinese seasoning, or Indian with garam marsala and minced chilis—the whole simmered or baked for twenty to thirty minutes. The basic flavor of mung beans is pleasant and a little bland, so they take on the flavors you add to them and add their own interesting texture. The cold purée, appropriately seasoned, makes an excellent high-protein dip for parties. A little sour cream or yogurt swirled into it, with a garnish of grated carrot, Jerusalem artichoke, or radish, makes an attractive addition to a buffet.

For an unusual spaghetti sauce, and to add protein to an otherwise starchy dish, mix it with canned tomatoes, tomato paste, oregano, olive oil, basil, minced garlic, and salt to taste. Simmer until the whole is sufficiently thick (at least one hour), adding more oil if necessary. Toss it with spaghetti for a surprise treat. If you want to cut down on calories, toss it with vegetable spaghetti instead—a practically starch-free spaghetti dish.

Appearance

Mung beans come green or golden. (If you are offered black-seeded mung, that is a different variety but it can be used in most of the same ways.) Johnny's has proved that mung beans will grow well in Maine, so you can be sure that these small, olive-green beans will do well in your garden even if you live in a fairly rigorous climate. Burpee carries a variety called Berken, which ripens more quickly (90 days) than Johnny's (120 days); Redwood City and Park both feature theirs for sprouting, but they can just as easily be grown for regular bean use. None of the Oriental seed companies features mung beans, but many of them—Japonica, for one—will order things that you want directly from the Far East if you make your wishes known.

When to plant

Mung beans should be planted at the same time you plant your snap beans—when the ground has thoroughly warmed up. However, you will not be able to make successive plantings in most areas since they require from 90 to 120 days to maturity.

Sow next to a fence or in a corner of your regular vegetable garden. The plant is somewhat twining in nature and liable to bother other vegetables if grown too close. It would be ideal among corn because it could climb the corn stalks and would mature long after you had harvested the last of your corn crop. Don't plant it next to carrots or other long-growing vegetables.

How to plant

The bean is small and should be planted about ½ inch deep. Since the plant may grow more than 3 feet high and bush out quite a lot, set the seeds at least 6–8 inches apart to allow plenty of room. No thinning will be necessary since the seeds are not so small that they cannot be planted in place at the proper distance. If you should find the germination rate low, you may want to plant two beans at a time and thin out one, but I find germination usually reliable. Since they germinate in about three days, you have time to add seeds if you should find this a problem. Rows should be about 24 inches apart.

Culture

A normally rich vegetable loam will do fine if you also give it plenty of moisture and an extra dressing of 10-10-5 when the small yellow flowers start to form pods. Mung beans are very prolific and grow easily without any special care. Give them the same attention you give your snap beans and you will be well rewarded.

Harvest

As we have said, the immature pods must be gathered very early, before the seeds have more than barely defined themselves. To harvest the mature pods, let the plants turn dry; the pods will curve slightly and the beans will be olive green inside the pods.

Pull up the whole plant and pick off the pods in comfort. You will find they have grown to 3 to 4 inches in length and each pod will contain a dozen or so seeds or beans. Dry them in an airy place before shelling and again after shelling to make sure there is no moisture left before you store them.

To dry, see directions at the end of this chapter.

SOYBEANS   SOY   [*Glycine max*]

If you've ever wished you could find a substitute for sirloin steak, had an allergy to cheese but would love to eat it, always longed for your own cow, or get bored with all the green vegetables you know but can't think of a new one, the soybean is the answer to all your problems. It will lower your budget, improve your health, and provide welcome variety to your diet. You will shine as a gardener, be acclaimed as a versatile cook, and join the millions of people all through the Far—and not so far—East who depend on soybeans for much of the quality and nutrition of their food. The soybean is truly a miracle vegetable. It has almost twice as much calcium as milk and twice as much protein as steak, and is rich in Vitamins A and B and niacin.

Culinary and other uses

Soybeans are probably used in more ways than any other single vegetable. They are eaten both as a green vegetable and as a dried one: and they make soy milk, which is a good substitute for cow's milk, as you already know if anyone in your family is allergic to cow's milk—in fact, the soybean is sometimes called the "cow of the East." Soybeans make an excellent cheese called bean curd or, in Japan, *to-fu*. Soy sauce is made from fermented soybeans; *miso*, a special Japanese paste used for seasoning soups and so on, is also made from fermented beans.

In your kitchen, you may already have used soybeans to make your own bean sprouts. They are worth growing if only for this purpose—providing a fresh vegetable even in midwinter.

Roasted, soybeans can be ground into soy flour, pressed to make soy oil—the "vegetable oil" so often found among the dozens of ingredients listed on American processed-food products. The roasted beans are also used to make a product which actually smells exactly like coffee, even if the taste is hardly pure Colombian. And as if all that were not enough, American manufacturers use soybeans in the making of "thick shakes" and other "nondairy" foods, linoleum, shampoo, paint, and many other items of our everyday life.

You will find, in studying the catalogs, that some varieties are particularly recommended for green-shelling, some for drying, and some for sprouting. Grow some of each and see if you agree with the recommendations—any kind can, of course, serve all uses regardless of what it is specially recommended for.

Cook the green soybeans—sometimes identified as green-shelled—in the pod until tender. Drain, season, and serve. In Japan it is customary to serve the cooked, slightly cooled pods, tossed in soy sauce; each diner squeezes his own pods, popping the beans directly into his mouth. You don't need to add any butter or oil because the beans themselves have such a high oil content.

If you want to shell them for your family, blanch the pods briefly in boiling salted water, about five minutes; cool enough to handle and shell. Reheat the beans in a little broth, soy sauce, and sherry until tender, about fifteen minutes. Or cook like baby limas and combine with corn for a Far East succotash. If you like creamed beans, add a little grated ginger to the cream sauce.

You will find the flavor of soybeans mild but nutty and very agreeable. Roasted and lightly salted, they can be served like peanuts.

A popular Japanese festival dish is made with cooked soybeans. Simmer the cooked beans for ten minutes in equal parts of sugar and water plus a pinch of salt. Remove from the fire and let stand overnight on the counter. In the morning, stir in a spoonful of soy sauce and reheat until bean mixture thickens and all the moisture is absorbed. This can be served at room temperature with broiled chicken breasts, a flaky fish, or—with the addition of grated radish—as a dip for tempura vegetables; it also serves as a dessert, and as a filling for pastries.

Appearance

Soybeans come in a fairly wide range of colors—black, green, gray, yellow, brown, and white, some with eyes of a contrasting color, some solid. Among the best-known and most popular varieties is Kuromame, an Oriental black soybean which can be bought as a direct import from Japan. It is especially liked because it is more easily digested than any other type of soybean. Many catalogs list it, although you may have to read the description carefully to recognize it. Johnny's, for instance, calls it Panther and only then identifies it in the text; Nichols calls it Oriental Black Soy Bean before identifying it as Kuromame.

Regardless of the color of the mature bean, the plants all look very similar; there are some variations in the size of the bush. Maturity dates, on the other hand, vary considerably, so be sure to take them into account in making your selection.

The beans are about the size of limas, though not so flat, and grow three or four to a pod. Thompson & Morgan estimates that one plant of their Fiskeby V variety will produce about fifty beans, and a packet is enough for 150 plants. At this rate you could easily dry your own beans for next year's crop and still have plenty left over for eating.

When to plant

Soybeans are a warm-weather crop and should not be planted in the open garden until the soil has completely warmed up. Early planting will be useless as the seeds will rot in the ground. If the variety you want to grow has a longer growing season than the warm months in your area, start them indoors early enough to give you a mature crop. Figure back from your earliest fall frost date to determine when to start the seedlings; set out in the open garden when the ground is warm and all danger of frost is past.

How to plant

There is nothing simpler. Check the maturity date for the variety you have chosen—this can range from 75 days to 115 days, so you must be sure you know what type you are growing. Most catalog listings will tell you—either in actual days or by the description, such as "early and popular," or "early prolific sort," which tells you they have shorter maturity dates.

Once you have determined, by means of the length of growing time required, whether you can plant outdoors or must start the seedlings indoors, the procedure is as follows:

INDOORS   Between April 30 and May 15—depending on variety and climate—plant the beans ½ inch deep in Cornell Mix in 1½-inch peat pots. Be sure to wet the pots themselves thoroughly and fill with dampened mix. Do not allow the soil to dry out until the seedlings have their first set of true leaves; water normally from then on. After all danger of frost is past and the soil is warm, set out pots (breaking down the rims and covering with soil) 2 to 5 inches apart in rows about 24 to 30 inches apart, unless directions for that variety recommend otherwise. The soil should be prepared before this by liming at least two weeks previously, unless you know your soil pH is about 6.5. After setting out the pots, fertilize lightly with cottonseed meal or some other high-nitrogen fertilizer and keep moist until plants are well established.

IN THE GROUND   The seeds are large enough to place where they are to grow, without sowing them more thickly so that you will need to thin. Set them 1½ to 2 inches deep, 2 to 5 inches apart in rows 24 to 30 inches apart. Soil should have a pH of about 6.5 (no higher). If liming is necessary, it should be done at least two weeks before seed is planted. Light fertilizing with cottonseed meal or other high-nitrogen fertilizer should be done about one week before seeding.

Culture

Soybeans are very trouble-free and need almost no attention except for copious watering. Keep the soil on the moist side throughout the growing season. After the initial fertilizing, no more should be necessary.

If the plants get very tall, you may need to stake them, because they bear profusely and the weight of the pods may affect their upright habit. It is not, however, necessary to stake when planting out (as with tomatoes), since you will not need as heavy stakes, and putting them in later won't cause that much disturbance to the root.

Harvest

Harvest twice—once for green shelling, once for dried beans. The green-shelling stage is reached when the beans are fully grown within the pods but before they turn yellow. Generally this is about 30 days before the maturity date, but weather conditions can speed or delay this stage, so keep an eye on your crop.

The dried stage is easy to recognize: the plants and pods turn completely brown. They look dead and ready for the compost heap but are not. Pull up the plants by their roots and pluck the pods in some convenient place but do *not* throw the bushes on your compost heap. Because of its high nitrogen content, soybean foliage should be worked directly into your garden soil. If it is not convenient to do that right away, lay the foliage in a corner of your garden and scatter it over the soil when you are ready to rototill. If you ever have a season when you aren't growing a garden or when you want the soil to lie fallow, plant soybeans and simply rototill them under when they are mature; they are a valuable source of our most expensive fertilizer, nitrogen, and provide it in a highly usable form.

YARD-LONG BEANS　DOW GAUK

[*Vigna sesquipedalis*]

This bean is also called the asparagus bean and is sometimes listed under that name even in Oriental seed catalogs (Japonica, for one). It is an intriguing bean with a flavor variously described as like asparagus, not at all like asparagus, similar to snap beans, etc.; the one thing everyone agrees is that the flavor, whatever it resembles, is delicious.

The yard-long bean is a pole bean, related to the black-eyed pea so popular in the South; it needs a support of some sort to climb on and does best in very warm weather. Even under ideal conditions, it sometimes won't perform and has a reputation for being an unreliable cropper. When it does bear, it bears heavily. I've had very good luck with it. Try it in your garden; if it works for you, you will have an unusual addition to your table.

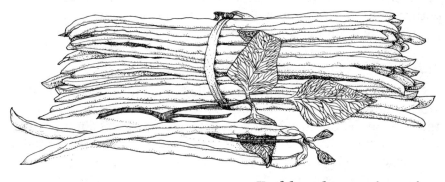

Yard-long beans　dow gauk

Culinary and other uses

Chinese yard-long beans can be used like green beans. In other words, they can be broken into 2-inch lengths, boiled briefly, served with butter, garnished perhaps with a sprinkling of chopped walnuts or sesame seeds. They can be used in stir-fry dishes, such as a combination of shredded pork, sliced mushrooms, burdock, water chestnut, and bok choy leaves and stems, or cut in smaller pieces and simmered in chicken broth along with a tablespoon of grated lemon rind, a teaspoon of grated fresh ginger, and a few chopped mitsuba leaves. For a salad, marinate cooked leftover beans in garlic, lemon juice, soy sauce, and sesame oil.

You will always have to cut them up no matter how you cook them because a vegetable that is almost 2 feet long would be too awkward to deal with otherwise.

Yard-long beans are especially welcome to today's busy cook because they are so quickly done.

Appearance

This bean grows on a vine which is somewhat straggly-looking but very aggressive; it is the only vegetable I have ever grown that can successfully hold its own against vegetable spaghetti. The flowers are large and very pretty, a combination of white and pale lavender. The pods look like elongated, slender green beans and are from 14 to 18 inches long.

When to plant

Yard-long beans are very, very sensitive to cold; on the other hand, it can't get too hot for them. Seeds should be sown in place about two weeks later than bush beans; the ground must be truly warm and all thought of frost a dim memory. In my area this puts planting time to late May or early June. Plant them, however, as soon as you can; they take 60 to 90 days to maturity.

In the South this is a much easier crop to grow, but with a little care it can be successful in New England.

I often take chances and plant bush beans earlier than is recommended; you can't do that with yard-long beans—they will invariably rot in the ground and you will have to plant your row all over again.

How to plant

Place the seeds in the open garden ½ inch to 1 inch deep. The poles should be put in place at that time. If you want to grow this crop most efficiently, put three poles, tepee-fashion, tied together at the top, and let several vines grow up the poles. Poles should be about 8 feet tall. By arranging them tepee-fashion you eliminate the need to dig the poles deeply into the ground, and they make an attractive picture in your garden. Leave 4 or 5 feet between tepees. Of course, you can grow them up any support that is convenient for you—fencing, netting, straight poles, and so forth. In that case, allow about 4 inches between plants.

The seeds are quick to germinate and you will see signs of life in 6 to 12 days.

Culture

Because there is a lot of foliage to feed, a complete fertilizer high in nitrogen should be supplied when seeding and during the growing season; 10-10-5 is recommended. Manure is always desirable, and a side dressing of manure and nitrogen should be added when flowers first appear.

Keep the vines growing briskly with plenty of moisture.

Harvest

Although full maturity is reached in 60–90 days, you should never wait that long to pick them. Chinese yard-long beans, like snow peas, are at their best when immature, with the bean barely outlined against the pod. The idea is to pick them while the whole pod is still tender enough to be edible. They are so prolific (if they fruit at all) that you will be hard pressed to keep up with them, but it is better to pick and freeze the excess than to let them get tough and mature on the vine. Figure on daily picking during the season.

Varieties

There are two kinds, red-seeded and black-seeded. Kitazawa, Hudson, Field, Tsang & Ma, Grace's, Gurney, Burgess, Japonica, and Le Jardin all offer one or the other.

HOW TO DRY BEANS

Drying is a very satisfactory method of preserving food and is the only way to store beans and seeds so that they retain their viability—important for next year's crops and for bean sprouts. The goal is to eliminate all moisture so that the organic material does not rot or the seed begin to germinate unseasonably. It is important, however, not to "cook" the seeds; roasted soy beans are delicious for eating out of hand or grinding into flour but they will not sprout.

The simplest drying method to use is solar—an energy source with which we are becoming increasingly familiar. In this case no expensive equipment is needed. The seeds or beans are simply placed in direct sun until sun-dried (like raisins and some other fruits). This is the least expensive method of drying but it won't work in some climates or during periods of humid weather. Plant material won't wait for a dry spell, so it's best to have an alternative plan available. The only reliable alternatives are your oven or a commercial dryer. Neither is an expensive procedure—in fact, drying is the most inexpensive of all ways of preserving food (except for a root cellar, which wouldn't work for dried foods).

Another advantage to drying is that dried products take up very little space; unlike freezing or preserving, drying does not require bulky containers. Anything that keeps out moisture is a suitable container.

Racks

In drying, the sun or other heat source does all the real work. Your job is providing the proper surface and arranging the material to be dried.

Whatever method is used, the racks are very important. They must allow maximum air circulation, and they should be as large as is commensurate with the method used. In an oven, they will have to conform to oven size; in the sun, they will be limited only by the size you find convenient to handle.

Racks can be ordinary old-fashioned window screens, or you can use the racks from your oven and cover them with wire mesh to keep the beans from falling through. Anything that will support the mesh—trellises, laths, and so forth—is satisfactory. If you have an unused hotbed, stretch mesh across it and use that as a drying surface—it is invariably situated in full sun and usually out of the wind.

Solar drying

Your first requirement is a spell of long, clear, dry, sunny days, and a spot in full sun to place your racks. Since you will be drying at different times during the summer—depending on when your beans mature—everything will depend on the spell of weather at the time you are ready to dry. In Connecticut, July is normally dry, August humid, September dry. Each summer, however, the pattern fails to conform to the norm and sometimes I can dry in the sun for a week in August and then must use another method when September comes around and is humid. Some weeks even the light-bodied stems and lacy foliage of herbs hung up to dry stay limp and moist instead of turning crisp and crumbly. Under such circumstances the thicker,

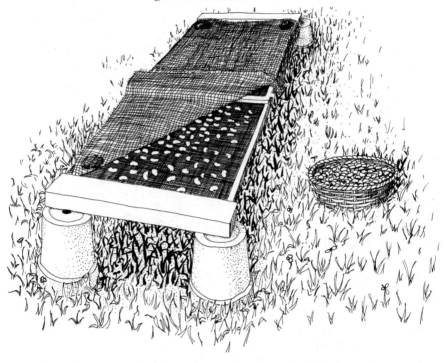

Drying beans in the sun

more solid beans would surely rot. Extension Services in Connecticut don't recommend drying beans here at all—even in the oven—because we have such a humid climate. I find this is an extreme position; while I have my losses, I have dried many vegetables and herbs successfully and brought them for my lecture audiences to sample.

If you have very changeable weather, you might want to get extra oven racks (a good idea anyhow), fit them out with wire mesh, and use those for solar drying. Whenever a shower threatens or a day turns muggy, simply move the racks to the oven and continue drying without interruption. It is very important to dry steadily; intermittent damp and dry conditions will invariably cause your beans to mold or rot.

Note: No matter how dry and clear the weather, be sure to take your racks in at night. The night air is always moister and there is often a heavy dew even during a very dry spell.

Although it may slow drying slightly, it is advisable to cover beans drying outdoors with a single layer of cheesecloth. This will serve the double purpose of keeping them from being blown off the racks by the wind, and keeping them free from insects. It will also deter birds, though it will not be effective against mice. Most of the time, mice won't be a problem during the day anyway.

Needless to say, the cheesecloth must be secured so that it doesn't flap around or get blown off by a breeze. If you plan to do this regularly, run an elastic thread around the edges of the cheesecloth so that it will fit over your rack and stay in place neatly and easily. Or you can thread ordinary string in the same fashion, leaving two loose string ends which can be drawn together and tied in a loose bow. The cheesecloth is easy to wash, dry, and store to reuse year after year.

Attic drying

If you have a nice hot but airy attic, you might be able to use that. I find mine works for herbs but it is not airy enough for beans (aside from the fact that it is too stuffed with accumulated cartons of toys,

Beans on screened racks for oven drying

linens, and books—I can hang plants but not spread them out flat). If you have the attic and the room, it might be worth investing in a good attic fan for this purpose. Be sure your attic is easily accessible or you won't check on your beans often enough and the whole crop may be ruined through neglect.

Oven drying

Use the oven racks prepared as described above, but omit the cheesecloth. Set the oven very low—from about 140° F. to 160° F. (for electric ovens)—or you will roast the beans rather than dry them. It might be a good idea to check your oven thermostat with a portable oven thermometer; a difference of 10° in heat could be critical here, where you might not notice it in roasting a turkey or timing a casserole.

Be sure to preheat your oven before putting in the beans.

About once an hour, rotate the position of your racks. An easy way to do this is simply to move them all down one level—which will put the bottom rack on top, the top rack second down, and so on. That way you don't have to keep track of what you have done last and by the time you've finished, there will have been sufficient variation in placement to assure a uniform product.

In order to assure good ventilation and elimination of moisture, prop the oven door open slightly while drying. You can speed up the whole process by directing a small fan at the oven (through the opening); set it for its lowest speed and be sure it is far enough away not to blow the beans off the rack. (This should obviously be a small fan.) If that is not possible, turn on your ventilator fan over the cooktop; it will cause some circulation of air—more than you would normally have in the kitchen—especially if an open window is nearby.

Oven drying is much quicker than solar drying; it shouldn't take more than six to eight hours altogether.

If possible, the beans should be close but not touching. If this is too tedious to achieve, shake the racks slightly when you rotate them (it will be almost impossible not to) so that the beans shift slightly and different surfaces are exposed.

Storing

After you have removed the beans from the sun or the oven, let them cool *completely* before putting them away. It is important that this be done in a dry place so that they do not reabsorb the moisture you have just driven off.

Once dried and cooled, put in tightly sealed containers (a plastic bag, for instance) and store in a cool, dry place out of sunlight. Cool, incidentally, means a temperature of about 50° F.

Since factors which affect drying are so variable, it is a good idea to check each batch for the first couple of weeks. You may find it is fine, or you may find that some of the beans are developing mold or that moisture is forming on the inside of the container. If this is the case, dry the food for another couple of hours, preferably in the oven, and put into new containers, or containers which have been rinsed out with boiling water and allowed to dry thoroughly.

Commercial dryers

There are a number of good commercial dryers on the market which are designed for home use. You can even build your own with the help of a government booklet.

Most dryers have removable racks and fit on top of your stove. Some of the larger ones provide their own heat source (you can use wood, which is cheaper than gas or electricity). There is one unusual dryer which fits over the entire top of your stove (you don't have to leave it there for the entire drying period) and dries with water—an apparent contradiction but it is faster and cheaper to use than the ordinary method.

6 The Chinese Cabbages

CHINESE CELERY CABBAGE • CHINESE MUSTARD CABBAGE •

FLOWERING CABBAGE • CHINESE BROCCOLI

I have called this chapter "The Chinese Cabbages" to point up the fact that there are so many different kinds. The Chinese cabbages you can now buy in the market don't really have to be identified very accurately, because you either know them on sight (or can ask about them with one in hand), or you don't and are adventurous enough to try them anyhow. When ordering from a seed catalog, however, you need to know exactly what is meant by the different kinds being offered. You may have a specific kind in mind and be very disappointed to receive the wrong one, or you may not know what you want and depend on the seed catalog to help you decide.

Chinese cabbage is one of our most ancient vegetables. Botanists can't determine where it originated because it has been cultivated for thousands of years; it is now found from Newfoundland to southern China. They think that the Celts brought it to the British Isles, but it was grown in the Far East long before that time. Most of the varieties we grow in the United States—where it has been cultivated since 1900—come from Germany or Holland, but in the past few years new varieties have been coming in from Japan and China, so you may, in coming years, see some interesting new cabbages in your local supermarket, and you certainly can obtain the seeds right now to grow these Oriental varieties in your own garden.

The first thing you need to know to grow these cabbages is how to find them in the seed catalogs. This is like looking up a category in the Yellow Pages of your phone book; unless you know exactly what heading to look under, you will never find what you want—and like the Yellow Pages, there is not too much uniformity, so you will have to figure it out all over again for each catalog. In addition, some of the catalogs that specialize in Oriental vegetables don't always describe them in terms that are at all familiar.

As a general rule, look under two headings: "Chinese Cabbage" and "Chinese Mustard." Or sometimes just "Mustard." Occasionally, Chinese cabbages will be lumped together at the end of the common cabbage section (although they are not true cabbages); usually, though, they are singled out in some way in the index. Almost every vegetable catalog offers at least one Chinese cabbage variety, but it's worth sending for catalogs that offer more of a selection than that.

Be sure to read the descriptions carefully; sometimes the "cabbages" and "mustards" are almost impossible to tell apart just from reading the descriptions unless you study and compare them.

Chinese cabbage is usually described as either "heading" or "nonheading or leafy." The heading type is true Chinese cabbage, *Brassica pekinensis;* the leafy type is Chinese mustard, *B. chinensis.* As we have seen, there are many varieties under each group. In addition, there is the flowering cabbage, a colorful vegetable grown for fall harvest, most often used purely as an ornamental. Flowering cabbage looks more like our common cabbage and not at all like the other Chinese cabbages. Another kind, Chinese broccoli, is similar to our more familiar broccoli but different enough to be worth space in your garden.

CHINESE CELERY CABBAGE   PE TSAI

[*Brassica pekinensis*]

This is the type known as a heading cabbage for the obvious reason that it forms a fairly tight, compact head on maturity. It is not, however, round like regular cabbage but tall like romaine lettuce. It is known by many names: celery cabbage, michihli, wong bok, tientsin, napa, shantung, and so forth. The Chinese call it pe tsai, which means "white vegetable"; the Japanese name is *hakusai.*

Culinary and other uses

Chinese cabbage, whether tall or short, can be used all the ways you use ordinary cabbage. It is said to taste more like celery than like cabbage, but I think it tastes like itself. The flavor is more delicate than cabbage, and it makes a truly delicious and unusual coleslaw: shred it finely, toss with ginger, soy sauce, sesame oil, and rice wine

Chinese celery cabbage   pe tsai

vinegar. The Chinese would add a little sugar to this, but that is up to you.

In stir-fried dishes it is added as one of the last ingredients so that the cooking time is especially brief and the natural crispness is retained.

In the Orient it is much favored for pickling, and the result is both similar to and different from our sauerkraut. If you grow Chinese cabbage, you will be delighted with its versatility and want to try all these different ways. It stores well and provides a fresh vegetable when they are otherwise in short supply.

Appearance

The Chinese cabbages most commonly found in supermarkets are tientsin and napa. Tientsin is tall, about 18 inches, and somewhat slender, about 3½ inches thick; napa is shorter, about 13 inches, and chunky-looking, about 8 inches thick. Of the two, the napa is thought to have more flavor and to be tenderer; both are mild-flavored and deliciously crisp. Aside from the difference in height and girth, they look identical, with pale-green to cream-colored leaves, usually rather attractively crinkled in a soft, delicate, fringy way, not in the pronounced, somewhat positive, way of a savoy cabbage. The heads are cylindrical rather than ball-shaped and they look more like a bunch of wide-leaved celery than like our cabbages.

When to plant

There is some disagreement about this since many experts say quite firmly that this vegetable should be planted only as a fall crop. The Chinese do not agree and surely they should know.

It is true that Chinese cabbage is a cool-weather crop that prefers short days, but these conditions prevail in spring as well as fall so it is not true that you cannot plant it in the spring if your season conforms to those conditions. You must, however, plant it in *early* spring or wait until midsummer to plant for a fall crop.

For spring planting, think of it as similar to lettuce and plant it the same time you plant your lettuce. If you are so unlucky as to have a very warm or *very* cold spring, it may go to seed before it has had time to head. In this case you haven't lost much and you have another chance to go for a fall crop. Take the precaution of planting a variety that is described as "early" and "slow-bolting"; varieties that fit that description will tolerate surprisingly warm weather and still head nicely.

How to plant

Here again a lot of books will say you cannot transplant Chinese cabbages and must sow them in place. I didn't believe this because cabbages, in general, can be transplanted; anyhow, I didn't want to believe it because it meant I could never get my spring cabbages planted early enough to suit my plans for early-summer harvesting. I took a chance one spring and found that while it is true that transplanting can set Chinese cabbage back and slow its growth, it doesn't have to. Transplanting isn't a good idea if you can help it, but it certainly isn't impossible. What it depends on is how you handle your transplants; the important thing is not to disturb the roots and to shock the seedling as little as possible. Whatever you can do to fool your seedlings into not knowing they are being transplanted will improve your chances of success.

Start the seeds in Fertl Cubes or some similar medium to get them off to a good start. When they have outgrown the cubes, place each cube in a separate peat pot, the smallest size available, and set firmly in damp Cornell Mix. By the time the seedlings look as if they are ready for a larger container, they will be four to six weeks old with four or five true leaves. At about the third week of growth, start hardening them off and by the fifth week you can safely set them out in the open garden, 14 to 24 inches apart, depending on the variety. The setting-out schedule should be arrived at by figuring back five or six weeks from the last frost date for your area—that will tell you when to start your seeds indoors.

For fall sowing, you can seed directly in the outdoor garden from the middle of August to the early part of September—or three months before the first frost date in your area. Sow the seeds ½ to 1 inch deep, about 1 inch between seeds. When the seedlings have four true leaves and are about 4 inches high, thin the plants to 18 to 30 inches apart (fall cabbages take more room than spring cabbages), in rows 30 to 36 inches apart. Be sure to eat the thinnings; they are a special treat.

Culture

Chinese cabbage grows well just about everywhere in the United States. It likes a lot of moisture, so keep it well watered between rains. It is generally thought to prefer a rich soil, although Johnny's says, "not requiring of a strong fertility, often producing good heads on soil where a normal cabbage is poor." Manure is the favored fertilizer; add it to the soil 6 inches below planting depth before sowing your seed or setting out transplants. Side-dress with more manure plus a complete fertilizer—10-10-5 is recommended—when seedlings are about 4 inches high, and again every five weeks to keep the plants growing rapidly. If your soil is acid, be sure to add lime, since this vegetable will not be happy in an acid soil. Always lime at least two weeks before sowing.

An ordinary loamy vegetable garden soil will do fine, and you need not worry about this vegetable in any special way. It is quite resistant to pests and diseases—much more so than regular cabbage—and you can hedge your bets by getting the resistant hybrid varieties, which should take care of the matter completely. If you need to sprinkle on an occasional saltwater solution, do not hesitate to do so, but in general cabbage maggots and other cabbage pests will pass this by.

Harvest

Although there is some variation among the different types, figure on 70 to 80 days to maturity; harvest when the heads are firm and appear fully developed. Many seed catalogs will give you days to maturity for specific varieties; if so, follow that. For those that don't, figure this as an average.

Chinese cabbage is heat-sensitive but when mature will tolerate quite cold weather. Harvest it before a heavy frost, but don't worry if a light frost should creep up on you; it won't spoil your crop.

Once temperatures drop below 50° F., the plants will stop growing, but they will stand well and you don't have to pick them immediately.

To store

Once harvested, Chinese cabbages store well. They will keep for two to three months in a cool cellar. Keep an eye on them and, if they seem to be getting less fresh-looking, pickle whatever is left. Unlike regular cabbage, it can be frozen.

Varieties

The two varieties available in most catalogs are michihli and wong bok. The michihli is an improved strain of chihli and is much to be preferred to the latter. It is tall like the tientsin; the wong bok is short like the napa. (I should really put it the other way around and say napa is a wong bok type, but it is easier to work from the familiar to the unfamiliar, and many people are familiar with the napa from the produce department of their markets and not at all familiar with the name wong bok.)

The Stokes catalog lists Springtime; Kitazawa lists five varieties, four of them recommended for spring planting; Johnny's features Spring A-1 and Tajii's Spring No. 2 (which is an F1 Hybrid); Thompson & Morgan lists Nagaoka F1 as their early variety; and other catalogs list other varieties. Any catalog or garden book which tells you not to plant Chinese cabbage in the spring must be unaware of these great spring cabbages. Incidentally, all spring cabbages can be sown for a fall harvest equally well—but fall cabbages cannot be sown in the spring. For winter storage, however, fall varieties are better.

In addition, Johnny's lists China Queen and Matsushima as well as the familiar Wong Bok and two others, all suitable for fall crops. Tsang & Ma calls its variety merely Chinese Cabbage and gives Siew Choy as the Chinese name; this is recommended for both spring and fall planting. Redwood City offers five varieties including Paotoulien, which it claims does well in warm weather. Hudson offers all different kinds of Chinese cabbages in one listing and you will have to sort them out for yourself. Grace's has Siew Choy.

Almost every seedsman offers at least one Chinese cabbage in this group, and you will find a larger selection available each year as these vegetables increase in popularity.

CHINESE MUSTARD CABBAGE   BOK CHOY

[Brassica chinensis]

Bok choy (*Brassica chinensis*) is closely related to gai choy (*Brassica juncea*). The former is sometimes called Chinese white mustard cabbage, the latter Chinese green mustard cabbage. You will

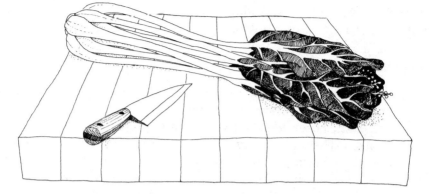

Chinese mustard cabbage   bok choy

find a section on gai choy in Chapter 2, "The Chinese Greens," under the English name Chinese mustard.

Bok choy doesn't look anything like the Chinese cabbage we have been talking about up to this point. You've seen it in your supermarket and you've eaten part of it (the green leaves, not the white ribs) in won ton soup in Chinese restaurants. If you are given to chopsticking the ingredients in Chinese dishes and wondering what each one is, the green leafy vegetable is usually bok choy—and so are the white, crisp, inch-long pieces you find in combination with it.

Bok choy is a mustard and is often found, in properly organized catalogs, under that heading. In Oriental seed catalogs, it is definitely found under that heading and *never* listed under "Cabbages." In spite of this it is sometimes described in American catalogs as a "loose-leaf Chinese cabbage."

Culinary and other uses

Bok choy is two vegetables in one; the leaves are cooked like spinach, the ribs like asparagus. If you are using both in a stir-fry wok dish, put the ribs (cut into 1-inch lengths) in first for a minute or two, then put in the leaves (cut into large pieces) for just a minute. It is also good in chop suey and similar dishes.

The leaves are also used in soup as a last-minute addition, simmered just long enough to get slightly limp. The first outside leaves of really mature plants should either be discarded or reserved for making a vegetable stock.

If you wish to cook the vegetable as a side dish, with roast chicken for example, separate the leaves from the ribs, cut the ribs into 1-inch pieces, and simmer for five minutes in boiling salted water. Then add the leaves, torn into large pieces, and cook three minutes more. Drain well and serve with melted butter with a sprinkling of minced fresh Chinese parsley.

Bok choy is rich in Vitamin C and minerals and is a good addition to a high-fiber diet. It is very popular throughout Europe, especially in France, where it has been cultivated since the 1800s.

Appearance

Bok choy doesn't form a tight head and doesn't look like either a regular cabbage or a Chinese cabbage. If I were to describe it in terms of a more familiar vegetable, I would say it looked like white Swiss chard (as compared to ruby chard), but the ribs are rounder and somehow tenderer-looking.

It is an attractive vegetable. The large leaves are a beautiful, glossy dark green, the ribs are bright white. The blanched hearts are considered a particular delicacy, and Chinese produce stores put a premium price on them. It is often sold with its little bright-yellow flowers nestled in the center, and unlike common broccoli, this is a desirable stage in which to eat bok choy. In your own garden, you can enjoy both the blanched hearts and the flowers without having to pay high prices for them.

When to plant

Bok choy is a cool-weather vegetable. Plant in early spring or the middle of August in the North; as early as March or as late as September in warmer sections. To use as a spring crop, don't crop the outside leaves (letting the rest of the plant continue growing) as recommended to extend fall plantings. Pick the whole plant while it is still small. Then, if a spell of unseasonably warm weather should occur, pick the entire crop right away or you will lose it. The season in spring plantings isn't long enough for leaf-cropping.

How to plant

Sow seed ¼ to ½ inch deep about 6 inches apart in rows 18 inches apart. When the plants are about 4 inches high, thin to stand about 6 inches apart. I don't imagine I have to tell you that the thinnings make good eating.

A little fertilizer mixed in with the soil in the bottom of the row is good if you don't overdo it; bok choy does best with frequent light feedings rather than less-frequent heavy feedings.

Culture

Like all cabbages, bok choy should be encouraged to grow briskly, and the best way to accomplish this is with sufficient moisture. In the spring, nature often takes care of that for you, but fall plantings are liable to coincide with dry weather which you will have to combat with watering.

As I have already said, fertilize lightly every two weeks and give a side dressing of manure when the plants are six weeks old. A rich loamy soil will give you the best crop. Mulch to keep the soil cool and you will come through occasional hot spells without any problems.

Harvest

Bok choy matures fairly quickly—in about eight weeks—but you don't have to wait until maturity to enjoy it, the way you do with a heading vegetable. The outside leaves can be gathered, as with leaf lettuce, from the young pod plant. Just allow the plant enough to grow on and you can crop it throughout the growing season. As I have already said, I don't recommend this procedure in the spring. Always pick the more mature outside leaves; as long as you do not disturb the heart the plant will continue to produce more leaves, completely unconcerned that you have been nibbling at it.

Tsang & Ma suggests an interesting way to preserve the excess bok choy: "Make Choy Gone. Wash and separate each leaf, parboil 5 minutes or until color changes, drain, separate each leaf and dry in sun. Soak Choy Gone about 2 hours before using, boil until tender." This is a very popular Oriental way of using this vegetable; travelers to the East are always bringing back snapshots of lines of bok choy hung out to dry, looking like some strange kind of washing. If you don't have an old-fashioned clothesline, it's worth rigging up one for this purpose. It can be done just as easily on an apartment rooftop as in a backyard.

Varieties

Tsang & Ma offers Pak Choi, as might be expected, but they also have a variety called Choy Sum, which they say is even sweeter. The leaves are smaller and the heart (the "sum" part) is "dominant," so the whole plant is very tender; it is good for a small garden because it can be grown closer together than regular bok choy.

Kitazawa also has Pak Choi, which they identify as Shakushima, and they describe it as bolting easily on exposure to cold temperature, so this might be a good variety for spring planting. Grace's merely lists it; Redwood City lists it in what I find a confusing way, since it describes Pak Choi as *Brassica parachinensis* and says it is like Taisai. It seems to me that their variety Santo, which they label *Brassica pekinensis*, is what is usually meant by bok choy, but I have not grown plants from these seeds and am going entirely by the brief descriptions in their catalog. Since nomenclature in this whole area of Chinese vegetables is still in the process of being sorted out, perhaps they have a sound basis for their listings, but it is not in line with the sources with whom I have worked. They are an excellent seed house and would probably respond to queries if you wished to pursue the matter. If you look at Hudson, which lists similar varieties, it describes Santo as "a popular Japanese variety, originally introduced into Japan from China," and Taisai as "an old Japanese non-heading strain . . . with thick white ribs." It all sounds like good old bok choy in different varieties, and I think you would probably be safe ordering any of them. Nichols also carries it.

FLOWERING CABBAGE   HWA CHOY

[*Brassica oleracea*]

Here again we have a new vegetable unlike any of the ones we have so far discussed in this chapter. It is so beautiful that many gardeners grow it as an ornamental, never knowing it is edible.

Its ornamental feature—aside from perfect shape—is the spectacular range of colors which the foliage turns upon exposure to cold weather; individual plants look like huge cabbage roses and come in striking combinations of red, pink, and green.

If you wonder why you haven't noticed it in your catalog, it may be because you have been looking at vegetables and your seedsman has put it in the flower section. It is only recently that flowering cabbage has come out of hiding among the annuals and perennials and been admitted to the more plebian, but suddenly fashionable, company of edibles.

As you will discover to your surprise when you start to look for it, almost every catalog lists it somewhere.

Culinary and other uses

In spite of its exotic appearance, it is a perfectly familiar cabbage in terms of culinary use. Shred it, boil it, bake it, stuff it—but most of all, use it to make the most decorative salad you have ever seen or eaten. As a buffet dish, it is a show-stopper. The miniature cabbages make beautiful and unusual centerpieces all by themselves and can be interestingly combined with other flowers or with contrasting foliage. For instance, the green-and-white flowering cabbages are beautiful with curly parsley tucked in among the leaves, or the miniature yellow marigolds.

If you want a decorative salad, break up the head and scald the leaves briefly. Then re-form into the original shape (in a bowl) and stuff in between the leaves. The green-and-white cabbages look beautiful with a shrimp-salad stuffing, for example. When you serve, put a single leaf and some of the shrimp salad on each plate.

When to plant

No ifs, buts, or maybes about this one; it is definitely a cool-weather vegetable and you would only plant it for a fall crop. It would be just as edible if planted in the spring, but you wouldn't get the color, which is half the fun. The plants will look like ordinary cabbages until one frosty night; the next morning you will wake up to a row of cabbages that will rival the sugar maples in brilliance and range of colors (though not the *same* colors).

Plant in late July for a fall crop—or 80 days before the first frost date in your area. This vegetable needs really cool weather, but most of the United States experiences that at some time during the year; as long as it gets chilly for long enough to turn the colors, you will want to grow this delightful cabbage.

Where to plant

It just seems a waste to plant flowering cabbage in the vegetable garden, so I usually reserve it for a container or for a bed that is on display, and otherwise full of flowers and herbs. It is an excellent bedding plant because it stays nicely within bounds, and is neat and precise-looking.

If, however, you want to give your vegetable garden a decorative feature, by all means include a row of these cabbages there.

How to plant

Sow seed in any good garden soil ½ inch deep, 8 to 10 inches apart in rows 16 inches apart. If you are using the space for something else and want to start your seeds in flats, cabbages of this sort transplant easily; just disturb them as little as possible when moving into the open garden. If you are planning to put them in a container, start them in Fertl Cubes, then put them into peat pots which can be slashed and put right into the containers once the seedlings are sturdy enough.

Culture

Unlike other Chinese cabbages, the ornamental flowering cabbages grow like common cabbages. Though they are smaller and therefore can be planted more closely together for a breathtaking display, they require plenty of moisture and a rich, loamy soil that is fertilized every four weeks or so with 10-10-5.

Flowering cabbage doesn't seem to appeal as much to pests and diseases as its plainer relatives, and you won't have much trouble with it. The one pest that I have had is the green cabbage worm that comes from the attentions of the white cabbage butterfly. These are always a bother because they seem to spring from nowhere; I can check over a row at dusk and by the next noon, half my leaves are eaten. Even on the purple-stemmed leaves, their camouflage is almost perfect and you have to look carefully to spot them. Get them all each time—even the tiny ones—or you will lose your cabbages. To avoid things getting to this stage, sprinkle your plants with a very mild solution of salt water whenever you see the white butterflies around.

It will develop on thick stalks above the ground, and you should hill up the soil so that the head rests on it; otherwise it may topple over and break. If planted so closely that they support one another at maturity as in containers, this may not be necessary.

Harvest

Pick the cabbages anytime you want after they have formed loose heads; this could be as early as 55 days. The tendency will be to leave them to the point of complete maturity in order to enjoy their color. If you do this, try to use them up as soon as possible after they are picked. Otherwise store them in a cool cellar like common cabbages. Use before other cabbages since they do not have as good keeping qualities.

Varieties

I have never seen any varieties offered. It is usually just listed as Flowering Cabbage and most regular seed catalogs offer it. It is not found in the special Chinese and Japanese seed catalogs.

CHINESE BROCCOLI　GAI LOHN

[*Brassica alboglabra*]

Gai lohn is also, for some reason I cannot fathom, some-times called Chinese kale. I love kale but I don't make it as often as I should because I am always tearing into the kitchen at the last minute to make dinner, and having to strip the leaves from the tough kale stems takes just the extra time I don't have. So we eat a lot more broccoli, which practically prepares itself. All of the Chinese broccoli, like our more common broccoli, is edible, including the stems, and it is prepared like broccoli, not like kale. If you are always in a hurry, you will welcome this delicious, quick-cooking vegetable in your garden and kitchen.

Broccoli is one of the oldest of the brassicas. It was eaten in ancient Greece over two thousand years ago and is a vegetable still enjoyed today both in the simplest cottage and the fanciest restaurant. It is good hot or cold, and the florets can be used as *crudités* with a spicy dip.

Culinary and other uses

Chinese broccoli is very nutritious; one stalk provides one and a half times the daily requirement of Vitamin C, half the daily requirement of Vitamin A. It is also rich in calcium, iron, and other minerals. Since it is quick and easy to prepare and very versatile, you might want to give over a good-sized patch to this valuable vegetable.

Chinese broccoli　gai lohn

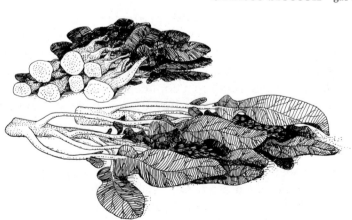

It won't limit your garden potential because it is a two-season crop—spring and fall—and allows plenty of other things to be grown in that same spot during the summer months.

Although regular broccoli is frequently substituted in Chinese dishes by cookbook writers who think if they make a recipe sound too difficult, you won't make it, the cook who really wants an authentic Chinese flavor would never be satisfied with that substitution. It is true that Chinese broccoli resembles regular broccoli, but it is the subtle differences that make life interesting, and the difference between the flavors of Chinese and regular broccoli is substantial enough to be worth being fussy about.

In preparing broccoli, the Chinese usually peel the stems as well as split the thicker ones partway; stems prepared this way will cook faster and can be added to stir-fry dishes with just a minute or two to cook. Here again, I don't have the time to do any unnecessary preparation and I would rather pick my broccoli when it is a little younger and not have to peel it. Splitting the thicker stems is a good idea, however, and not time-consuming.

To use Chinese broccoli in one of its commonest Chinese dishes, you would have to buy oyster sauce in a Chinese grocery. The broccoli, cut into 2-inch pieces, is stir-fried one minute. A little water is added and the broccoli is then cooked covered for two more minutes. Oyster sauce is then stirred into the oil-and-water liquid in the pan, heated, and served spooned over the broccoli. If you want to work with ingredients on hand, don't worry about the oyster sauce; add minced garlic to the first step, and use chicken broth and a little soy sauce instead of the water. Thicken with cornstarch if desired.

For a surprise, serve Chinese broccoli with hollandaise sauce (provided you will take the time to make your own). Your guests will assume they are eating regular broccoli until they taste it. The surprise will be a pleasant one, but I would explain anyhow as soon as they have taken a taste.

Chinese broccoli is good stir-fried with beef, mushrooms, and water chestnuts plus freshly grated ginger root and soy sauce. It holds up well to steaming, although you will find that most of the time the stems will cook up a little more quickly than the leaves.

If you make sukiyaki, this would be an interesting addition to the usual green vegetables. And the florets, dipped in tempura batter and deep-fried, are especially delicious.

Any leftover Chinese broccoli makes a good cold salad with a vinaigrette dressing. Do not mix with the dressing until you are ready to serve or the cooked leaves and florets will get mushy. If you have used just the leaves and florets and saved the cooked stems, these can marinate in a spicy dressing for an hour or so and be served as a kind of pickle. Stems for this use should be just crisp-tender; do not overcook, and do not slice until cooked.

Appearance

Chinese broccoli looks like regular broccoli that didn't quite make it to maturity or was picked too soon by an impatient gardener. It closely resembles regular broccoli, but the stems are long in proportion to the flowers and the heads are much smaller than those we are used to. The flowers are yellow as with regular broccoli, but larger and not so numerous.

When to plant

As a cool-season plant, Chinese broccoli goes into the ground either in early spring or toward the end of summer for a late-spring or late-fall crop. This means you won't get tired of it and can plant other, short-season, warmth-loving vegetables in the same spot between broccoli crops.

Figure on 14 days for germination of the seed.

How to plant

Sow the seed in place ½ inch deep, 1 inch apart, in rows 12 inches apart. Thin seedlings to stand 6 inches apart when they are 3 to 4 inches tall. Cooked very quickly, the thinnings are a gardener's secret vegetable. Only a little butter and salt should be used for this delicate dish.

Do not pre-fertilize; Chinese broccoli is not a heavy feeder.

Culture

Chinese broccoli matures quickly without much attention. Fertilize lightly with a 10-10-5 formula after the first three weeks, more heavily when the buds begin to form. What broccoli needs most is plenty of water.

Harvest

Like regular broccoli, the flavor of Chinese broccoli is best just before the flowers open. Pick the center buds first and the side shoots will be encouraged to send out flowers, giving you a second and third harvest. Always leave a long stub on the stem when you cut the flowering stalk. Once you have picked it, the flowers may open slightly; they won't spoil the flavor.

Varieties

Tsang & Ma lists Chinese Kale under gai lohn, although the catalog promptly admits that it is "broccoli-like rather than kale-like." Redwood City lists it with broccoli but identifies it as Chinese broccoli and calls it Fan-shan rather than gai lohn. This isn't confusing because they also give the Latin, which tells you it is what you are looking for. Grace's simply calls it Chinese Kale or gai lohn. Sometimes you may come across the spelling "kai lan," but if you use our phonetic test, you will recognize it all the same.

1 *A Chinese Vegetable*

Potpourri

ASPARAGUS PEA • BURDOCK • CHINESE RADISHES •

CHINESE EGGPLANT

By dictionary definition, a potpourri is a miscellaneous collection. Since this chapter contains the Chinese vegetables which are too important to be omitted from the book but are not complicated enough to require a chapter of their own and do not fit into any of the other chapters, it qualifies as a truly miscellaneous collection.

Since the types of vegetables will, on the whole, sound familiar to most American gardeners, you will find it all the more interesting to discover what the Chinese varieties are like. You can grow them happily side by side with the old familiar varieties and enjoy the fact that finally, in your own garden, the old adage is confounded—the East and the West finally do meet.

ASPARAGUS PEA   BIN DOW
[*Psophocarpus tetragonolobus*]

The asparagus pea is a legume, as you might expect from its name. It is variously called princess bean and winged bean (from its shape), but the most common name, after asparagus pea, under which it is found in catalogs and garden guides is goa bean. Do not, however, confuse it with the asparagus bean, which is simply another name for the Chinese yard-long bean. Having given you time to read that over, we will now go on.

The asparagus pea originated in India and soon spread throughout the East as far as New Guinea. Today it is an important crop from China to Africa to the West Indies, though somehow it has never caught on in the United States.

Part of the reason for its popularity in these other countries is its high protein content; in lands where meat is scarce or expensive, we find a corresponding dependence on high-protein vegetables. In the

United States, with our high standard of living and sizable per capita consumption of beef, we tend to underutilize high-protein vegetables. Perhaps as food costs continue to rise and the need for nutritious low-cost vegetables increases, we will appreciate the value of some of these delicious foods.

Culinary and other uses

The protein-rich pods, which grow in great profusion, taste just like asparagus, and this is most noticeable when they are gathered—as they should be—well before they are fully mature. Ideally, the pods should be harvested when they are not more than an inch long. At this time they can be eaten without stringing or having to resort to long cooking.

Asparagus-pea pods are delicious stir-fried, alone or in combination with meat or other vegetables. They can be slivered and cooked briefly in a clear broth, and the soup served with a garnish of shredded scallion. They are excellent added to stews (when the cooking is almost complete), or just boiled briefly and served with oil and a very little seasoning. Cold cooked asparagus-pea pods make an interesting addition to a salad if they have been cooked crisp-tender.

In addition to the pods, the whole plant is edible. The tender new shoots, young leaves, and pretty blue flowers are delicately delicious. They make a fine addition to curries and clear soups. The flowers are especially attractive as garnish for a salad, and the leaves can be cooked like spinach.

Since asparagus peas grow so abundantly, you may feel you have enough of a crop to sacrifice some of the plants for the sake of the roots, which are also edible. They should be dug when young and can be cooked in any way you would a sweet potato. Added to an Indian *dahl*, they are superb, and thinly sliced, they make an interesting and authentic addition to stir-fried beef and snow peas. If you try the roots, you may find yourself growing this fascinating vegetable for the roots alone, as they do in Burma.

Since the plant bears so abundantly, it is entirely possible that you will not be able to keep up with it, and the peas will get past the green eating stage. If this should happen, all is not lost. Just let the pods grow to their full 8 inches in length before you pick them. Then shell and roast the peas in the oven. Combine them with hot brown rice for an interesting accompaniment to chop suey or sukiyaki. Or salt them lightly and serve as a snack or with drinks instead of soybeans or peanuts.

This is an easy vegetable to grow and a lot of fun to serve to unsuspecting guests.

Appearance

Although the asparagus pea is sometimes described as a rampant vine, Thompson & Morgan has a variety that grows only 12 inches high. Generally, asparagus peas will take over any area in which you plant them, so it is best in an out-of-the-way corner. The flowers are a pale blue (they whiten as they turn older) and are very showy and attractive; this would be a good vegetable to grow as an ornamental edible in a part of the garden you don't want to have to work over; it will compete successfully with most weeds.

The pods are very oddly shaped; they grow sort of square instead of rounded, and have four sides. Each side has a toothed edge that is very noticeable; this makes it an attractive and unusual vegetable to serve, especially if you slice it across the length. Those you serve it to will immediately notice they are eating something unusual, even before they savor the asparagus flavor.

When to plant

The asparagus pea is not frost-tender and can be sown in the garden a couple of weeks before the last frost date in your area. It does best in cool weather, and since it has a long harvesting season, the earlier you can start it, the better. With vegetables of this sort I usually gamble a bit; if I am unlucky and have a hard frost after I have sown my seed, all I am out is a little seed and a few minutes' work. Most of the time I find my gamble pays off.

How to plant

The seeds should be planted ½ inch deep, about 6 inches apart in rows 18 inches apart. Since they will not need staking, you can do a round bed of just this vegetable. By the time you have finished with it, it will be July, and just the time to put in a fall crop of something else.

It isn't fussy about soil and will do well in any halfway decent vegetable-garden soil. Fertilize it when it flowers by side dressing, and from then on at three-week intervals. A 10-10-10 fertilizer will take care of all parts of the plant; if you wish to concentrate on the roots primarily, then use 5-10-10.

Culture

Like so many of the vegetables in this book, this one is exceptionally carefree. Even Thompson & Morgan says: "It will thrive almost anywhere—it will beat the weeds if you sow it and forget it. . . ." What more could you want?

Harvest

You can begin harvesting the pods about 50 days after sowing. Of course, if you wish to use the leaves, shoots, or flowers, these should be picked earlier.

Sample the roots in about 35 days; then try them again in 50 days. The longer you can let them grow and still find them tasty, the greater the crop you will get. You may even find that you prefer the mature roots, so give those a chance too.

Varieties

No varieties are offered, just "asparagus pea," in the catalogs I looked at. So far as I know, only Park and Thompson & Morgan carry the seeds in this country.

BURDOCK NGAU PONG [*Arctium lappa*]

In the case of this vegetable, you may be more familiar with the Japanese name, *gobo*, than the Chinese name, ngau pong, as the former is the one more often used in the United States. Many people don't even realize that *gobo is* burdock and eat it with relish in Oriental restaurants thinking it is some unobtainable Chinese ingredient. Actually, burdock is so easy to grow in the United States that it is found wild almost everywhere.

On the other hand, if you think of burdock as that bothersome weed with the prickly burrs that the boy behind you in seventh grade used to put in your hair, you may wonder what it is doing in a book on Chinese vegetables. Burdock is not, however, native to America, although—like many other immigrants—it has thrived here. It was introduced by the early settlers and was quickly adopted by the American Indians for their own gardens.

There are two botanical species of burdock, *Arctium lappa* and *A. minus.* The one you find growing wild throughout much of the

United States is *A. minus* and is hardly comparable to the aristocratic, cultivated *A. lappa*.

As *gobo*, it is an important and much enjoyed Japanese vegetable, lending itself to a number of classic dishes. It also has valuable medicinal properties, recognized even by Western medicine.

Culinary and other uses

Gobo is eaten as a vegetable in many countries, but it reaches its culinary peak in Japan and China. While the young leaves and stems are edible—prepared like spinach and asparagus, respectively—the most important part of the plant is the long, slender root.

When very young, the root can be gathered, peeled, and eaten out of hand like a radish, with perhaps a salt shaker handy. The mature root should be peeled, scalded, and then cooked in any way you please. Many recipes don't call for scalding before cooking, so you can try omitting this step and see if the results are satisfactory. Scalding serves a purpose but you may not feel it is worth the trouble.

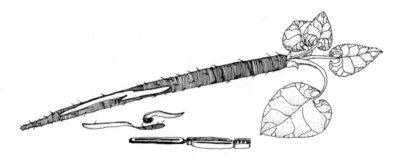

Burdock   ngau pong

The flavor of burdock varies somewhat, depending on the conditions under which it is grown and when the root is eaten. It has been variously described as tasting like Jerusalem artichokes, scorzonera, and parsnips but since most of those vegetables are almost as little used in this country as burdock, I don't think that is going to be of much help to you. To describe the flavor without attempting a comparison, I would say it is sweetly pungent and agreeable; the texture is crisp when raw and retains this quality if used in stir-fry dishes. Unlike wild American burdock, which is very bitter and must be cooked in such a way as to alleviate this bitterness, *gobo* can be cooked along with carrots, turnips, and other root vegetables to make a richly flavored stew. It is an interesting addition to baked beans of all kinds and adds character to a bland broth. It is good scalded, cooled, and shredded, then cooked in butter for about ten minutes. Add 2 tablespoons of vinegar, stir, and cook covered for another ten minutes over low heat. Sprinkle with parsley and serve hot.

In Japan, both the stems and the roots are pickled, and you can buy pickled *gobo* roots in an Oriental grocery store if you want to taste them before making your own. Somehow the pickling seems to make the taste "hotter," so you end up with an agreeably spicy condiment that will do wonders for a platter of cold meats on a hot summer day.

In addition to its value as a vegetable, burdock is used medicinally. Like Jerusalem artichokes, it is very high in inulin—the dry weight of this polysaccharide in a mature root can run as high as 45 percent— and it is used pharmaceutically in this country for that reason. Since inulin is acceptable in diabetic diets, this is a welcome addition to the menu for those who are limited in the carbohydrates they can eat. In the Far East both the root and the seeds (as well as their oil) are used as a diaphoretic, to reduce fever, and for certain skin diseases, boils, and psoriasis. It also is a diuretic and therefore is used in the treatment of kidney diseases. Its somewhat pungent flavor and availability in early spring make it inevitable that it should be esteemed as a "blood purifier," and it is reputed to relieve the symptoms of some kinds of arthritis. Since it is rich in calcium, silicon, and sulfur, some of these medicinal claims are possibly of merit.

Appearance

Gobo looks very much like the wild burdock with which you may already be familiar. It is a tall plant, growing up to 8 feet under ideal conditions. The flowers are purple and numerous, but small and comparatively inconspicuous, quickly turning into burrs if allowed to go to seed. The roots can grow as long as 4 feet but are slender and carrot- or parsnip-shaped. Most of the time they will grow about 24 inches long. They are brown with white flesh.

When to plant

Gobo can be sown equally well in early spring for a fall crop, or in late fall for an early-spring crop.

How to plant

Although the plant itself is very hardy and will winter over almost everywhere, the seeds prefer warmth for germination. In order to encourage them, soak them in fairly warm water overnight (the water will cool, but leave it in as warm a place as possible—short of putting it in a low oven). The next day, drain and sow immediately.

Seeds should be ½ inch deep, set about 6 inches apart in rows about 20 inches apart. A neutral soil is desirable.

The soil—a sandy loam is ideal—must be deeply prepared, down to at least 24 inches to accommodate the long root.

Culture

Since burdock is grown primarily for its root, a 5-10-10 fertilizer is best, with an additional side dressing of rock phosphate one month after planting.

Mulch so that you aren't tempted to overwater, which would give you good top growth but keep the roots smaller than ideal.

Pests and diseases don't trouble this plant much. If your area has nematodes, plant marigolds thickly through your vegetable garden and plow under in the fall when preparing the soil for winter.

Keep the flowers picked off so that the plant doesn't go to seed. You want this vegetable kept under control, not reverting to its wild state.

Harvest

The leaves and young shoots should be gathered in the spring. A special treat may be enjoyed if you gather the young shoots with the tiny roots attached; cook the two together like baby beets and beet greens.

The mature roots are ready about 2½ months after planting, so an early-spring planting will give you a fall crop. If allowed to winter over, burdock—like Jerusalem artichokes—will be one of your earliest root crops. It can also be planted from seed in late fall for spring use.

Like all root crops, just when you gather burdock depends upon what your taste dictates and what use you have for it. It is a good vegetable to plant near Jerusalem artichokes because both are tall, strong-minded plants that outgrow any weeds and produce reliable crops.

To harvest the mature roots, dig deeply with a spade fork until a gentle tug frees the loosened root. If you have succeeded in growing extra-long roots, you may have to dig a trench next to them to get at them. Roots 2 to 3 feet long are the most manageable and therefore the size to aim at.

Varieties

Do not buy any roots that are described by a Latin name other than *Arctium lappa.* In this category, you will find that the most popular and most highly recommended type is Takinogawa Long. Both Johnny's and Japonica have this.

In addition, Japonica offers two other types; Johnny's offers Watanabe for those with clay soil, which does not do well with large rooted vegetables. *Gobo* also can be ordered from Kitazawa, Redwood, Gurney, Nichols, and Hudson—look under "Burdock" as well as "Gobo," except for Gurney which calls it Edible Goberon.

CHINESE RADISHES   LOBOK

[*Raphanus sativus*]

In our cuisine there is nothing simpler than the radish. We think we have exhausted its possibilities when it is served up in a relish dish, alone or with other raw vegetables, to be eaten with the

Chinese radishes lobok

fingers. Occasionally, we go to the fuss of preparing radish roses or, now that salads have become so popular, will slice some into a tossed salad. Compared to these meager uses, the dishes prepared with radishes in China and Japan are incredibly numerous; radishes are grated, steamed, stir-fried, pickled, boiled, sculptured for great banquet dishes, and dried.

Although we do not think of the radish as containing much nourishment, it was part of the diet the pharaohs fed the builders of the great pyramids—along with garlic and onion—to get more work out of them. The Chinese think of radishes as marvelously healthful, and throughout the centuries radishes have always had a reputation for stimulating the appetite. In the Middle Ages, they were considered efficacious in the treatment of insanity, rheumatism, and warts as well as a sure safeguard against poison. Many herbals recommend it as a cure for melancholy—and I can see where the crisp, pleasantly pungent nibble of a chilled radish might have a cheering effect. It was also sometimes used grated, as a poultice.

The cultivation of radishes is very ancient, both in the Orient and in Europe and Africa. The Egyptians have known and used them for over five thousand years, the Chinese perhaps even longer.

Today radishes are relished throughout the world; in Japan, over 25 percent of the entire vegetable crop is devoted to Oriental radishes.

Culinary and other uses

Once you get accustomed to using radishes as an all-around vegetable, you will be amazed at all the years you neglected them. In China and Japan, they are a favorite ingredient in the little dishes of dipping sauce that are served with tempura and other cooked meat-and-vegetable dishes. The radishes are finely grated or shredded, then mixed with soy sauce. Sometimes the grated radish is put on one side along with a little pile of grated ginger, and the diner adds to the soy sauce whichever one he prefers.

You can Americanize this by using grated radish instead of onion on your next hamburger. It is also good on a corned-beef sandwich. Grated radish, instead of sauerkraut, on a hot dog is a whole new ball game.

Another new world of uses opens up the minute you realize that radish is good *cooked.* Stir-fry it with cucumber and chives and a little garlic in sesame oil; add a little chicken broth, cover, and simmer five minutes. All the vegetables should be cut into pieces of the same size so they will cook at the same rate. The Chinese like icicle radish stir-fried with shellfish, and shrimp is a good introduction to this kind of dish. The skin of the radish should be peeled with a vegetable parer and the whole radish shredded. Stir-fry scallions first, then the radish, then the shrimp. The entire cooking time shouldn't be over six or eight minutes. Add a little soy sauce just before serving and perhaps a tiny bit of saki or sherry.

This same stir-fry works very well with pork substituted for the shrimp, and some diced pineapple (canned in its own juice) added.

Grated radishes are added to many Chinese sauces. One of their widest uses is as various pickles. Some of these, like regular pickles, take a long time to cure. But there are some pickles that can be made in a few hours simply by slicing the radishes very thin and marinating in sugar, water, and rice vinegar. An entirely different taste is achieved by marinating in rice wine and soy sauce with a little sugar. Pickled radishes are often used in cooking, where they impart their spicy flavor to the whole dish in a very subtle way.

A simple but surprisingly effective combination is grated radish blended with a little sesame oil. This makes an excellent garnish served as part of a dish of antipasto. Don't worry about mixing your countries; I do it all the time and no one ever knows. The trick is to substitute sesame oil for olive oil for the various ingredients on the dish, and, of course, don't call it "antipasto."

Perhaps you never knew that the foliage of radishes is edible. Young radish tops make an excellent green, briefly steamed and served simply with a little butter. Another treat which no one seems to know about is radish seeds. They are pleasantly peppery and great in a tossed salad. So no matter at what stage your Chinese radish plants are, they are sure to have something interesting to contribute to your kitchen.

Appearance

There is much greater variety among Oriental radishes than among the ones we commonly grow. They come round, long and tapered, short and blunt-ended. They range in color from pure white to rose pink, purple, and black. The most amazing difference between Western and Eastern radishes is the enormous sizes to which some Oriental varieties grow—there are radishes which may weigh up to 65 or more pounds at maturity, as big around as a beach ball. These huge radishes are not freaks but characteristic of the species. They are deliciously edible and an everyday feature—in season—of an Oriental meal.

The foliage of some varieties—daikon, for one—is very decorative.

When to plant

There are spring, summer, and fall Oriental radishes, but the bulk of them are for fall sowing. Many can be stored over the winter as easily as carrots or turnips. Order your variety according to when you want to harvest your crop.

How to plant

No matter what you are going to end up with, all radishes are cultivated the same way and are considered the easiest of all vegetables to grow. They germinate practically overnight and can be eaten in all the various stages of maturity. Since the leaves are also good, they can be eaten even before the roots form or when the roots are barely showing their shape. If you tire of them, you can even let them go to seed and eat that.

The seeds should be sown 1 inch deep, 2 inches apart. How much you thin them depends on what variety you have planted; obviously a radish that will be 2 inches in diameter at maturity can be left closer together than one that will be 10 or 12 inches. You can thin in stages as the seedlings grow, all the while eating the thinnings.

The soil needs to be prepared more deeply for the larger varieties and should be richly provided with a 5-10-10 fertilizer. If root maggots have been a problem, incorporate a generous amount of wood ash into the soil before planting.

Culture

Radishes are of easy culture, and Oriental radishes are no different in this respect from common radishes. They should, like any root vegetable, be given ample and deep watering, and they benefit from a mulch of wood ashes. If roots seem to be forming slowly, side-dress with rock phosphate. In any case, the long-season fall and winter radishes should have an application of 5-10-10 worked lightly into the soil every twenty or thirty days.

Outside of root maggots, radishes are little subject to pests and diseases and can be sown successively throughout the growing season, from early spring to fall. Many varieties will continue to grow until the temperature falls below freezing during the day.

Harvest

Since you can eat the leaves, roots, and seeds, the time of harvest depends entirely on your appetite and patience. Late-season radishes will even hold in the ground for some time after reaching maturity. This is unnecessary, however, since they store well in moist sand in a cool but not freezing environment. A suburban garage, a closet against an outside wall, a sheltered corner, or a city terrace all work well.

They will keep a couple of weeks in the refrigerator, and indefinitely if pickled or dried. If pickling, however, know your recipe; some radish pickles are best eaten the same day they are made and some keep like ordinary pickles.

Varieties

Choosing among radish varieties is as difficult as confronting a tray of French pastries; they all look good. Fortunately you can have your cake and eat it too because most radishes take up so little room and are so quickly harvested that in a single season you can try out many different kinds.

I do not know of any seedsman listing radishes who doesn't carry Oriental radishes. They are not always identified as such but are called "Fall and Winter Radishes." Some catalogs use the name "daikon" for all Oriental radishes, although this is really a specific variety. It's not serious because once you get into radishes you won't stop at one, and you will soon learn to recognize different kinds regardless of catalog descriptions. Some catalogs differentiate between Chinese and Japanese varieties. The fact is that in those countries they are grown back and forth, and it makes very little difference which country is credited with any particular kind.

Once you start to zero in on special names, be careful about "icicle" radishes; this name is given to both a white Western variety and a white Oriental variety, and they are not at all alike. Chances are if it is offered for spring sowing it is the Western one; for fall sowing, the Oriental one.

Some suppliers list only three or four varieties; some, like Japonica, which goes all out, list up to eleven (these are sent to you in the original Japanese packets with instructions in Japanese, so save the catalog for the information it contains). Kitazawa lists seven varieties.

Redwood City and Nichols also offer quite a few. It is fun to hunt out new kinds, so I am sure that after you have grown and enjoyed these delicious radishes for a season, you will want to search around for yourself.

CHINESE EGGPLANT   AI KWA
[Solanum melongena]

I sometimes think the man who ate the first eggplant was as brave as the man who ate the first oyster; so many of the plants of this family either are poisonous or have had the reputation for being poisonous that there must have been a number of fatalities in the process of determining which ones actually were safe to eat. In this respect, Europeans and Americans were much less adventurous than people of other countries. The potato, tomato, and eggplant (all cousins) were grown only as ornamentals when they were first introduced to those areas; it was only gradually that cooks were tempted to try them and found them not only safe but good.

The eggplant is a native of tropical Asia and is very popular in China and Japan, where it is grown extensively. For some reason, most people are surprised to find it is part of classic Oriental cookery; perhaps they associate it mostly with the cooking of Italy, which certainly does some wonderful things with it. The Near East, Russia, and India, however, also use eggplant in many, many interesting dishes—so if you like it, the eggplant can take you on a culinary trip around the world.

Culinary and other uses

Sautéed eggplant is popular everywhere; in Japan it is cooked tempura-style; in China it is stir-fried with bean sprouts, peppers, and tomatoes; in Italy it is dipped in flour and sautéed in olive oil.

Roasted eggplant is equally international. The Russians and Near Eastern peoples make a cold relish by roasting it and combining it with olive oil, chopped onion, and chopped tomato, plus salt and pepper. One of the most famous dishes of the Near East, "The Sultan Fainted," is made with eggplant. Stuffed eggplant with roasted eggplant combined with pine nuts, ground lamb, tomatoes, coriander, garlic, and lemon juice filling beautiful purple half-shells is pretty, delicious, easy to make, and inexpensive.

The Japanese excel in the making of eggplant pickles. These are

Chinese eggplants ai kwa

submerged in glass or ceramic containers of *miso*—a Japanese soybean paste available in Oriental specialty shops—for three to four months. They come out delightfully pickled, with a most unusual flavor. A Greek pickle submerges them in vinegar which has been simmered with lemon juice, garlic, and hot water, and refrigerates them in the still-warm liquid for a month or two. A marvelous Italian eggplant pickle is made with garlic and olive oil. The best type of eggplant for pickles is the very small variety which you can grow specially for this purpose; the plants are so prolific that one plant will give you enough of a crop for the average-sized family. If you like, you can pickle them American-style, using any standard pickling recipe, or simply simmering them for five minutes in the pickle liquid left over from a jar of commercial pickles. Cool and refrigerate; eat in about a week.

Eggplant combines well with other vegetables, both in sautés and in casserole dishes. Cut into chunks and marinate in the same liquid as the meat, then charcoal-broil on skewers along with your kabobs. If you wish, you can have skewers of meat and skewers of vegetables, with eggplant, tomatoes, peppers, and small white cooked onions threaded alternately along the skewer.

A wonderful and classic Indian dish is made by baking an eggplant one hour at 350° F. (for an average-sized eggplant). Scoop out the pulp and combine it with Indian spices. You can simplify the recipe by using garam marsala, which is a group of Indian spices already mixed, or you can mix your own combination of ginger, cloves, turmeric, coriander, and at least two green chili peppers, minced. To this, add two chopped tomatoes, a couple of thinly sliced carrots, one potato, one onion, and 3 cups of peas. Fry the whole in safflower oil for about fifteen minutes. It will be mild or hot depending on how many chilis you add; my family likes it really hot. If you want to make it even more filling, add another potato. This can be made the day before. Just stuff it back into eggplant halves and refrigerate. Sprinkle with breadcrumbs combined with minced parsley and reheat when you want it.

Note: Do not pre-salt eggplant. This is a tedious process and a waste of time. It can also be disastrous if you do not wash the salt off thoroughly. Oriental eggplants are not bitter and should be cooked without peeling or salting.

Appearance

As I have already mentioned, eggplant was long grown in Europe and England purely as an ornamental, which tells you how pretty it is. The plant is beautifully and interestingly shaped, compact and moderately low-growing (at least the Oriental varieties). Eggplant flowers are lavender, but the Oriental varieties tend to have flowers of a much deeper hue. It is a lovely plant in flower, even prettier when loaded with fruit. According to variety, eggplants are purple, dark (almost black) purple, brown, green, creamy white, snow-white, gray, and striped. Oriental eggplants are dark purple, creamy, or snow-white. The shapes vary from almost round to narrow and elongated like a zucchini. They are beautifully glossy and very decorative.

When to plant

Eggplants are long-season, warm-weather vegetables. This combination tells you that unless you live in Florida or a similar warm climate you will have to start the plants indoors. This is no great hardship, and I find you can sow the seeds much later than is recommended and still get a good crop. I have even sowed the seeds directly in the ground and had excellent results; the crop was later than indoor-started seedlings, because I sowed the seeds the same time I put out my seedlings, but the harvest season is so long it didn't make any difference in the long run. You can always start two or three seedlings indoors for an earlier crop and let your ground-sown seeds catch up in their own good time. Oriental eggplants are so prolific that you need many fewer plants than if you grew the ordinary varieties.

How to plant

Eggplant seed is slow to germinate. To speed things up, soak the seeds overnight and plant immediately the next morning. If this is inconvenient, keep the soil moist until the seedlings appear. The seeds should be sown ½ inch deep in Cornell Mix.

When the seedlings are about 3 inches high, transplant to small pots. The Cornell Mix in these pots should be enriched with dried manure and liquid fish emulsion.

It shouldn't be necessary to transplant them again until they are ready to be set outdoors. If, however, you see they are outgrowing their container, put them into a larger one. Nature doesn't always follow our calendar, and the wise gardener takes a hint.

Good garden practice recommends starting the seedlings about eight weeks before they are to be set outdoors; since they shouldn't be let out until about two weeks after your last frost date, figure back for your area. Personally, I never start my seedlings that early; I find a month is time enough. This may not work for everyone, so if you try my method, you take your chances. In the garden, the plants should be set 2 feet apart in rows 3 feet apart. Some dwarf varieties can go closer.

Before setting out your transplants, harden them off for two weeks. This can be right after your last frost date, because you will be bringing the plants in at night, and will, I hope, have enough sense not to set them out if the day is unseasonably cold. Whether they are indoors or out, they need plenty of sun.

When preparing the bed for the transplants, cultivate deeply and dig a hole 8 inches deep. Put a cup of 10-10-10 fertilizer and 2 cups of manure in the bottom of the hole. Mix the soil you are going to use to fill the hole with a cup of this same mixture. Set in your seedlings the same height at which they are growing, and water thoroughly once you have pressed down the earth around the plant. Keep moist the first ten days but do not soak them.

Culture

It is only fair that a plant which produces so abundantly should need to be well fed. Eggplant is a heavy feeder and requires deep watering.

During the growing season, fertilize every four weeks to keep the plant from wearing itself out. Manure is a good choice at this time. Mulch about 2 inches deep to provide a cool, moist soil for the feeder roots, which grow very close to the surface.

Harvest

At first it may take you a while to recognize a mature Oriental eggplant, because it will be smaller than the ones you are probably used to. They can be harvested from the time they are the size of a large egg, or a small zucchini, depending on the variety, and it is better to pick them immature than fully ripened. If the seeds are brown when you cut into them, you have waited too long. The skin should be glossy and smooth; a dull skin is another sign of overripeness, although occasionally it is due to adverse weather conditions.

Pick them often and the plants will bear for months—a four-month fruiting period is not unusual. If you are used to Black Beauty and some of the other American fine varieties, you will be stunned the first time you grow Oriental eggplant—instead of a crop of eight or ten fruit you will find yourself picking thirty or forty from a single plant.

Varieties

Here, unlike some other Oriental vegetables, you have a wide choice.

Redwood City, Field, Gurney, Nichols, Japonica, Park, Thompson & Morgan, Le Jardin, Johnny's, Kitazawa, and Hudson all carry Oriental eggplants.

Hudson and Redwood City both carry Kitsuta Chunaga with medium-size fruit—5 to 6 inches long. In addition, Hudson carries Chinese Long, as do Redwood City, Japonica, and Kitazawa. Some of these varieties are as much as 10 inches long and only 2 inches in diameter. There are many other good varieties, most of them much earlier than standard eggplants. Japonica carries Black Prince, which won the Grand Cup awarded by the Japanese Ministry of Agriculture at an All-Japan Eggplant Contest in 1973.

Nichols identifies one of its varieties as Japanese Pickling Eggplant, but this is equally good used in the usual ways.

Three seedsmen (to my knowledge) offer cream or white eggplants: Nichols (which for some reason calls it White Italian), Park (White Beauty), and Thompson & Morgan (Oriental Eggplant).

8 *All About Bean*

Sprouts—NGAR CHOY

Bean sprouts are becoming increasingly popular with Americans. At least, when a fresh-food item, especially a highly perishable one, is regularly carried by the big supermarkets, I think it is safe to assume that a lot of people are buying it; bean sprouts can be found almost always (except in midsummer) in both big and little markets in my area of Connecticut. They are not an easy item for the produce department. Unlike other produce, they are only at their best when freshly made; they cannot be "picked green," ripened by gas or other artificial methods, or held in "cold storage." And if a bean sprout is more than a week or so from the bean, it is fit only for pigs—as many happy pig farmers, who send trucks daily to Manhattan's bean sprout "manufacturers," can attest.

Further evidence of the popularity of this Chinese vegetable is the fact that some of the garden centers and hardware stores now carry "sprouting seeds," along with radishes, tomatoes, and marigolds, on their seed racks.

If you are one of the many consumers who have discovered bean sprouts, I hope you will grow your beans and sprout your own crop.

Bean sprouts are the easiest and fastest fresh vegetable you can grow, and you can do it all in the tiniest kitchen or even without a kitchen.

If you raise your own Chinese beans (full directions for these easy crops are given in Chapter 7), the cost in both time and dollars is negligible, the value in nutrition is enormous, and the addition of this interesting vegetable to your culinary repertoire is a delight.

Bean sprouts have something for everyone. Half a cup of this delicious, crunchy vegetable contains only about 16 calories, yet they are higher in protein than most other vegetables and are loaded with vitamins and minerals; they also contain practically no cholesterol. You can start growing them on Tuesday for dinner on Saturday, and have a fresh vegetable every day of the year.

The most popularly sprouted bean in China is the mung, but all other beans produce interesting sprouts, and each has its own distinctive flavor. By utilizing these different beans, you can serve sprouts more often, without repeating yourself, and enjoy a rich variety of flavors and textures.

Culinary and other uses

Bean sprouts can be eaten raw or cooked, added to your own favorite family recipe or used in authentic Chinese dishes.

A quick confetti salad can be made of bean sprouts lightly tossed with finely chopped carrots and red and green peppers, dressed with rice vinegar and sesame oil. Garnish with a sprinkling of raw or toasted sesame seeds.

Or fill an omelet with bean sprouts that have been stir-fried for one minute with finely diced pineapple (canned in its own juice). After you have spooned in the filling and before folding the other half of omelet over it, top the filling with ice-cold yogurt that has been mixed with a little of the unsweetened pineapple juice (from the can). Serve immediately so that the hot omelet and the chilled yogurt combine in the mouth like a super Baked Alaska. The pineapple won't be too sweet (as long as you use the unsweetened) even for breakfast; the whole is very refreshing. The combination of textures is typically Chinese even if the recipe is strictly my own.

When stir-frying bean sprouts, always add them at the last minute (literally) of cooking. For instance, to make stir-fried beef, toss the beef in a marinade of sherry, soy sauce, a little sugar, and some cornstarch. Then drain and stir-fry for two to three minutes. Add the vegetables and cook for another minute. Stir in the marinade and cook until thickened. Serve immediately.

If you've never made egg rolls, don't be timid about them; nothing could be simpler. I must admit I always buy the egg-roll "skins," but they aren't any harder to make than pancakes, and you can make up a batch to freeze and use when you want to make the egg rolls. The most commonly used egg-roll filling is made with ground pork, or pork strips, raw shrimp, bean sprouts, and celery. The pork should be stir-fried first for about five minutes, then removed and the rest of the ingredients cooked for about two minutes. Add the pork to the pan of vegetables and shrimp, plus sherry and cornstarch mixed with a little water. Cook until thickened, then put aside to cool. Once the filling has cooled to lukewarm, fill the egg rolls, rolling up and tucking the ends in. It is easy to keep the tucked-in flaps stuck to the main part of the roll if you moisten the underside of the flap with cold water before pressing down. Do the same when you reach the end, sealing like an envelope. Some cooks use egg white for this purpose, but so many people are allergic to eggs that I prefer the water method.

The egg rolls can then be fried in a little oil in a skillet, or deep-fried in a deeper pan. They take five or six minutes to turn crispy golden brown (turn them so they brown evenly) and can be set aside under a towel or in a low oven while you make the rest. If you want to make a batch ahead, they freeze beautifully and reheat in ten minutes in a 450° F. oven (preheat the oven, naturally).

In preparing bean sprouts for use, *do not* do it in the Chinese way. For some reason they tediously pick off all the little beans that are left and use only the sprouts. This is not only time-consuming and very frustrating for a busy cook, it also removes a good part of the nutrients and the flavor. Remove only those beans that have not sprouted and any loose husks; do keep the beans on the ends of the sprouts.

When you have bean sprouts handy, you will find many occasions to use them. A clear consommé looks more inviting with a small handful of sprouts dropped in just before it is served; a sandwich of bean sprouts, thinly sliced scallions, and a thick spread of cottage cheese (instead of butter or mayonnaise) will be a welcome change; if you make chow mein, bean sprouts are an essential ingredient.

Although any kind of bean sprout can be used in any recipe that calls for sprouts, you will find that the taste differs according to the bean used; the only way to determine your preferences is to make them all and taste them. There are flavor differences even among the several varieties of the same beans. Soybeans, for instance, make all kinds of sprouts, some somewhat coarse in taste, some very delicate. Since this is equally true of the soybeans themselves, perhaps we should not be surprised that it carries over into the sprouts.

Many catalogs will guide your selection by noting that a particular variety of a given bean is "excellent for sprouting," or "a good bean for green shelling." If you want an all-purpose bean, these guidelines won't mean much, but if you want to sow the crop mostly for one purpose, it can save you experimenting or taking several growing seasons to arrive at the bean that suits you best.

Appearance

One of the interesting things about making your own bean sprouts is the variety of sprouts you discover. With adzuki sprouts, the red beans are very noticeable and create visual interest to any dish in which they are included; the sprouts themselves are comparatively small. Mung beans almost disappear in a forest of white shoots. In all cases, however, the sprouts should be white; green shoots are not desirable and the flavor will not be sweet and delicate. Good sprouts are clean, white, and very crisp.

Equipment needed

There is nothing complicated about bean-sprouting containers; your kitchen is full of them. As long as they will hold the beans, can be drained easily, and won't be needed for a few days, anything will serve. A wide-mouthed jar—peanut butter, some soups (if not redolent of vinegar and spices)—will do fine. Mason jars, with the center lid removed, are excellent. So is a clay flower pot if first scalded thoroughly with boiling water. You can even use a colander or strainer.

You will also need several thicknesses of clean cheesecloth or plastic screening and a rubber band or two.

Preparing the beans

Wash and pick over the beans. Debris and even small insects may sometimes get into beans, but it takes only a minute to check out the small amount you are sprouting. You will need about a ½ cup; beans will make three to five times the volume of sprouts.

Soak overnight in warm water to cover. Do not refrigerate; the beans can be left on the kitchen counter. In the morning, drain the beans in a strainer.

Sprouting

Since the beans will need to be rinsed in clear tepid water two or three times a day, your container should be rigged to make this easy. A mason jar can have a piece of plastic screen put in place of the inner lid; a wide-mouthed jar needs only two or three thicknesses of cheesecloth (or the screening) secured by a rubber band. A flower pot works especially well, with a piece of screening laid across the bottom hole and cheesecloth tied around the top. A colander can be covered with a dish towel.

Put the drained beans into your container. Put the container under the water tap and let the water fill the container. Drain out the water and repeat two or three times. Drain well. Lay the container on its

Two ways to sprout mung beans

side and shake it gently so that the beans spread out along the side. Put aside.

There are only two things to do from here on. The seeds must be kept moist but not wet, and not allowed to get stale or musty. This is easily accomplished by rinsing with fresh water, twice a day in cold weather, three or four times a day in hot or very humid weather. It is very little trouble to slip the container under the tap, fill it, and drain it a couple of times and put it aside again.

The other essential is to keep the sprouts out of the light while they are growing. Sun or bright light will make them turn green and develop too strong a flavor. If you want to experiment, try sprouting a small quantity in the sun and the rest in the dark and judge for yourself. If you use a clear glass jar, cover it with a couple of dish towels; it is even better if you can put the jar on a shelf in a closet but do not stow it away so completely that you forget about it and miss the rinsings. A clay pot is naturally opaque and can be left on the counter as long as it is not in direct sunlight.

As sprouting progresses, the container will gradually fill up with sprouts. After a few crops, you will be able to estimate more exactly what quantity a given container will hold; start with ½ cup the first time. If you overcrowd the container, the beans will not sprout as well and it will be much harder to rinse them properly and prevent mold from forming.

Harvest

Sprouts will take three to six days depending on the variety. On the sixth day, take them out of the jar and rinse in cold water in a large bowl, running your fingers through the sprouts to separate them and rinse them. Remove any bits of hull that float to the surface or any beans that didn't sprout (there are always a few).

The sprouts are now ready to eat.

To store

If you are just storing the sprouts until dinner or tomorrow's lunch, drain and put in a plastic bag in the refrigerator. For longer storage, put back in the jar, fill with cold water, cover, and store in the refrigerator. They will keep fresh for about a week if you change the water daily.

I understand sprouts freeze successfully, but I have never tried it and I can't imagine why anyone would want to.

9 The Chinese
Herb Garden

CHINESE CHIVES • SESAME • CHINESE PARSLEY •

JAPANESE PARSLEY • GIANT GARLIC • WATERCRESS •

GINGER • MULTIPLIER ONIONS • HOT PEPPERS •

DAY LILIES

The use of herbs as food and medicine goes back to the beginnings of man on earth, and Chinese herbs, a product of the accumulated experience and wisdom of an ancient civilization, are not only rich in folklore but also in medicinal, nutritional, and culinary application.

As our civilization has become increasingly industrialized, we have moved from the natural to the synthetic, from the field to the laboratory. In the past few years many people have attempted to reverse this trend by returning to natural foods and remedies, although pharmaceutical houses still seem to be more comfortable with the test tube than the garden. Recently, though, Western scientists and physicians have begun to realize that many of the commonly used herbs of the Far East may have something to contribute to our own still-limited knowledge in this field. They know that some of our most potent medicines—curare, digitalis, quinine, and many, many more—have natural origins, even though these are so buried in brand names that it is usually impossible for the layman to determine whether the composition of a particular pill is organic or chemical.

In China, the reverse is true. Herbs as medicine are as accepted in Oriental medical practice today as they were thousands of years ago, with such strikingly successful results that our universities are now sending groups of American scientists to study firsthand how they are used, and to evaluate their effects. This is only the beginning of an interesting exchange.

Even in the Far East, a knowledge of herbs and their properties was

133

acquired slowly and through much experimentation. Shen Nung, who ruled in China about 2780 B.C., is reputed by legend to be the father of Oriental medicine. He is said to have gone into the countryside and through the mountains with a red whip. When he came upon a plant that was new to him, he would beat it with his whip to release its juices and mash it into a pulp. Then he would taste it to determine its qualities. If it seemed good to him, he would study it further to try to determine what illness it could aid or cure. He must have been a brave man—and a lucky one.

Over two thousand years later an herbal bearing his name was published, but no copies of it are extant today. Later, a version was put together from a variety of sources, but it is not necessarily the same as the original.

According to this herbal, medicines fall into three groups: medicines which restore life, medicines which restore energy, and medicines which cure illness. All known medicines fitted into one or more of these categories and were prescribed accordingly. It was known that some could not be used too long or too often because they contained poisonous as well as beneficial substances. We have this same problem today, even with our laboratory medicines, and the cure is still often worse than the disease.

The Japanese, with their usual good sense in adopting the best from other cultures, soon brought Chinese herbal knowledge to their own islands and also began to gather natural plants that grew in Japan. During this time, it became clear to the Chinese that it would be better not to have to hunt out wild plants but instead to have the most widely used herbs near at hand and quickly available. This was the beginning of the Chinese herb garden.

Not long after, in 701 A.D., under the Japanese emperor Bumbu, the first Japanese herb garden was planted. It was placed under the care of the court physician. The basis of plant selection for this very special garden was the Chinese herbals then in use.

From that time, herb gardens became increasingly important; they were so cherished that special herbs grown in them were among the presents offered in tribute to the reigning emperor.

Eventually herbals became accepted as medical books rather than folklore, and knowledge was accumulated from all over the East, including Korea. In addition, many plants were brought from Europe and Africa which can now be found naturalized near the ancient herb gardens where they were first cultivated.

In 1709 a sixteen-volume Japanese herbal was published; other scholarly works on the subject soon followed.

Herb gardens were sponsored and supported by the governments of both countries, and today the traveler to the East can visit these gardens and browse in them to his heart's content. Private herb gardens were also cultivated; one of the most famous was the Morino Herb Garden in Japan, first planted in 1729 and continued up to the present time. Today it is preserved as a historic site; while it still belongs to the original family, it contains a government-built museum and a rest house for visitors.

Herbs are an important part of traditional Japanese flower arrangements, and are used in considerable quantities in courses given in this subject throughout Japan.

In the West, herb gardens—for both the medicine chest and the kitchen—have long been a tradition; some of our best-known colonial gardens were herb gardens. This chapter will introduce the gardener to some of the little-known Chinese herbs and make it possible for anyone with an interest in this subject to grow them in the United States. Aside from their possible medicinal use, all the herbs in this chapter are good eating and contribute to the delightfully different flavors which characterize Oriental cooking. If you want your Chinese dishes to be authentic, or even if you merely want to ring some interesting new changes on favorite old recipes, learn to grow and use this sampling of Chinese herbs. As a bonus, you will find that many of them are beautiful ornaments and can be combined with flowers for a striking and unusual display.

CHINESE CHIVES   GOW CHOY

[Allium odoratum]

Most windowsill gardeners and those who like an indoor herb garden have grown common chives. The popularity of this onion-flavored herb is surely indicated by the spring offerings of potted chives which appear in every supermarket, where they sell for a dollar or more and are quickly snapped up by cooks eager for fresh snippets for their salads and cookery. Common chives are also frequently grown in the flower garden for their attractive lavender blooms, which make a pretty display over a long period of time.

Chinese chives, though closely related to common chives, are as different as they can be. The blossom is a flat-headed spray of star-shaped white flowers that smell like roses! Two or three pots on a windowsill can perfume your kitchen and be as pretty as any flowering house plant you could grow. The flavor of the leaves is also different from common chives—garlic instead of onion.

Chinese chives cannot be purchased in pots in a supermarket; you must grow them if you want to have them—and nothing could be easier than their culture. They are a very useful and beautiful herb—indoors and out—and you will become very fond of them.

Culinary and other uses

Chinese chives can be used exactly as you use common chives, but allow for the fact that they are more strongly flavored and taste like

Chinese chives (gow choy), **rose-scented**

garlic, not onion. Substitute them in dishes where you usually use common chives; mix with cottage cheese or yogurt, mince for salads, sprinkle as a garnish over hard-cooked stuffed eggs or as a zesty addition to sautéed veal. Toss with bean sprouts for a quick, high-protein salad.

The Chinese often add chives to recipes calling for onions and garlic. They feel the chives enhance the flavor of these other alliums, and there is no doubt they make their own subtle contribution to the overall flavor.

Be sure to add them only during the last few minutes of cooking; Chinese chives have a tendency to get stringy when overcooked, and lose much of their flavor.

The bulbs too can be eaten, like garlic or shallots. Crush and add to boiling vinegar, then set aside for a few days to mellow. Mince and braise with meat or sprinkle over fish before broiling. Heat in melted butter before scrambling eggs. Chinese-chive bulbs are much more delicate than garlic bulbs, and different in flavor from the mildly garlicky shallot; you can experiment with them boldly.

Don't eat up your entire crop; some should be saved for your winter indoor garden, some for next spring's planting.

All chive blossoms are edible and can be eaten fresh or dried. I always keep a couple of dried bunches handy to the kitchen and find many unexpected uses for them. They are much milder than either the leaves or the bulbs, and are very pretty when used as a garnish. If you wish, separate into florets to float on top of a clear soup, and add them after the individual bowls have been filled so that they come to the table fresh and still faintly fragrant. If vichyssoise is one of your accomplishments, give it an exotic touch by adding white chive blossoms along with the traditional chives.

Chinese herbals recommend this allium for the treatment of various ailments. It is especially prescribed as an antidote for ingested poison, and as a way of controlling excessive bleeding. Here again, modern medical knowledge confirms the wisdom of the ancient herbalists; it has been discovered that alliums are effective antiseptics, contain a natural antibiotic, and are rich in sulfur.

When to plant

Indoors, Chinese chives can be planted anytime you please. Outdoors, they need to be planted from seed only once, and are best sown in the spring. Once you have a clump going, you will have a permanent supply of bulbs and will soon be handing pots around to happy neighbors. One seed packet will provide enough, in a few years, for your entire garden club, church fair, charity benefit, or even your local market. Chives are unfussy and prolific, and that is a combination that is hard to beat.

How to plant

Chinese chives germinate just as slowly as common chives, so put the seeds in their pots (I like Fertl Cubes) and patiently keep the soil moist until the tiny shoots are well on their way. The seeds should be sown about ½ inch deep.

Bulbs are even easier to plant. Put about four of them ¾ inch deep in a 3-inch pot and keep moist until they show about 2 inches of growth. I use Cornell Mix for my pots, but Chinese chives are not fussy and will do well in almost any soil—from a rich potting soil to a coarse, gravelly one.

Once the seedlings are about two weeks old, let the soil dry out somewhat between waterings; from then on treat them as you do common chives.

Chinese chives are easily transplanted and settle quickly into a new location. You can even start them in flats, if that is more convenient, without worrying about disturbing the roots when removing them to pots or in-the-ground gardens. This is very convenient if you want to start a large number of seedlings for use in the vegetable garden as companion plants to discourage harmful insects. If you have trouble with chipmunks invading your tulip beds, a generous planting of Chinese chive bulbs will sometimes persuade the chipmunks to move to another location. I can only suppose that they do not like the taste of the chive bulbs and consequently, not wanting to take the chance of biting into one, leave the tulip bulbs alone. This is not a guaranteed solution to loss of tulip bulbs, but it is easier than planting them in individual wire cages (a last resort, in any case). If it does work, the chives can be left in place, since they are so decorative.

Culture

Chinese chives are so tolerant of soil conditions and so compact in growth (they don't get sprawly like common chives) that they make excellent plants for the rock garden, nestling into out-of-the-way corners and sending up their lovely blooms right on schedule every year.

Seedlings transplant easily when four to six weeks old and should be set 8 inches apart in rows about 12 to 14 inches apart. They prefer full sun but will tolerate partial shade.

Fertilize lightly when taking cuttings; otherwise, keep fertilizing on an infrequent schedule.

Harvest

The leaves can be harvested any time after they are about 6 inches high. Cut each shoot to within 2 inches of the ground and take several shoots all the way to that point. Do not clip across the entire plant; the bulbs need some foliage to grow on.

If you want flowers, leave some clumps unclipped until the flower stalks have developed. In practice, you will find that you can clip a little and still get flowers, but until you have become familiar with the growth habit of this particular plant, leave a few clumps alone and let them flower the first time around.

The buds and flowers are a delectable and rare treat; they can be harvested whenever they appear, at any stage.

Do not let the flowers go to seed; there is no advantage to you and it takes energy away from the plant. Cut them all off to eat fresh or to dry, then begin clipping the leaves. Once your chive plantings are well established you will always have enough to grow ornamentally for the beautiful, fragrant blossoms, and for the kitchen as well.

Unlike common chives, Chinese chives don't have to be planted from seed in August for winter use indoors. Separate and pot a clump in early fall and it will grow in your kitchen all winter.

The plants you leave outdoors will die back during the winter and come up again in the spring.

Clumps that have grown too large for their site can be separated either in the spring or in the fall.

Varieties

Sometimes—and this is one of them—the Latin name isn't a completely satisfactory means of identification. Various books and catalogs will list Chinese chives as *Allium schoenoprasum var. tuberosum, A. tuberosum,* or *A. odoratum.* These are all Chinese chives, all grown and used in China. True Chinese chives can always be recognized by their broad, flat leaves, unlike the hollow, rounded stems of common chives. The flowers also differ from common chives in that they are usually white, and are not shaped like rounded balls. Sometimes the flowers will be lavender, but larger than those of common chives.

The most desirable of the Chinese chives, in my opinion, is the fragrant chive, *A. odoratum* (or *A. tuberosum*) which has a white flower with the scent of an old-fashioned rose. The lavender-flowered Chinese chive is garlic-scented but not strongly so.

Japanese names for the various Chinese chives include *nira (A. tuberosum)*, *asatsuki (A. grayi)*, and *gyoj ninniku (A. victorialis)*.

If you hope to avoid the difficulty of locating the variety you want in a seed catalog, you may feel safer buying pots of Chinese chives. But unless you see them in flower, this is no more satisfactory than growing your own, and much more expensive. As an experiment, I bought several pots labeled "Chinese Chives" or "Garlic Chives" from different nurseries. Some turned out to be white-flowered and some purple; it was impossible to tell them apart from the labeling or from the appearance of the leaves. Seeds are easy to grow and the plants take up very little room, so keep track of your seed sources and you will soon find out which seedsman carries what you want.

Tsang & Ma carries *A. tuberosum*. Grace's does not give the Latin name for its variety. Japonica lists *nira* chives.

SESAME   CHIH MA   [*Sesamum orientale*]

In the *Arabian Nights* story of Ali Baba and the Forty Thieves, the fabulous treasure cave could be entered only by uttering two magic words: "Open sesame!" When these words were spoken by Ali Baba in a clear, firm voice, the cave opened and he was able to enter and gather untold riches. When as a child I read this story, I didn't attach any significance to the ritual; "sesame" had a good ring to it and we tended to use it in games and jokes. We were not alone; in the adult world it was used in articles, advertising copy, and other writing as a magic formula for anything literally or figuratively hard to open. It still is, to some extent, although modern education has pretty much eliminated this classic from children's reading lists. (Adventurous readers still occasionally discover the unabridged version, which is rich in language and in material of a decidedly adult nature.)

It was not until I became a gardener that I learned the reference was actually to something real—the sesame seed itself. The author had simply used a common charm that he knew would be familiar to his

Sesame chih ma

readers. The magical properties of this useful herb were so well known that the natives of the East Indies called it "thunderbolt" because of its power to open secret hiding places. In ancient Greece, sesame was a plant sacred to Hecate, goddess of the underworld and of witchcraft, and many spells depended on its use.

Some botanists think that sesame may be the most ancient of all herbs or spices. It apparently was first cultivated in the north of Africa, where the oil extracted from it was known in the Euphrates valley as early as 1600 B.C.; it is also mentioned in Egyptian writings of about that period. It is apparently native to both Asia and Africa, but the exact locations cannot be pinpointed since it has never been found growing wild.

Its use spread throughout the Far East, where butter and olive oil never became popular, and it served both culinary and cosmetic purposes. It came to the American colonies along with African slaves and adapted well to the climate of Texas and other Southern states; wherever cotton grows well, sesame is a good commercial crop.

Today sesame seed is used primarily to produce a very expensive oil; even in China and Japan it is used sparingly in cooking because of its cost. The seeds, both raw and toasted, are used in the cookery of many lands.

Appearance

Like so many Oriental vegetables and herbs, sesame is a beautiful ornamental and would deserve a place in the garden for that reason alone. The plant stands from about 3 feet high and is very erect. Depending on the variety, the flowers range in color from pink and deep pink *(Sesamum alatum)* to lavender-pink or white *(S. orientale)*. They are large and prominent, something like foxglove in shape, and grow along the stem, opening in sequence from bottom to top.

Culinary and other uses

The plant is edible from early leaves to seed. When young, the leaves can be gathered and used, with discretion, in tossed salads or, even better, as a potherb with a few drops of soy sauce and sesame oil added after the leaves have simmered to tenderness. In the South the leaves are used to make a beverage which is considered very soothing and beneficial. To do this, the young leaves are whirled in the blender with a quantity of water and allowed to stand for about five minutes, and then the whole is poured over ice cubes. I keep meaning to try it some summer but so far I never have.

The crop the home gardener may be most interested in is the seeds. These are delicious both raw and toasted; excellent as a snack, a garnish for salads, an addition to stir-fry dishes, or a delicious sprinkle on boiled carrots or beets. If you prefer the toasted to the raw seeds, it isn't necessary to toast seeds on dishes that will be baked since they will be toasted in the cooking process.

When you become familiar with their taste, you will invent ways to use them in everyday recipes. Pressed into pie crust for a peach pie, for instance, they turn a familiar dish into a deliciously exotic dessert.

Each plant produces an enormous quantity of seeds so that you can easily grow enough for a year's use from just a small planting. You will find that sesame seeds, like other herbs, are very expensive to buy, and this cannot help but add to the satisfaction of growing your own.

Sesame seeds are easily made into a paste or butter that is something like peanut butter only much more delicate. It is called tahini in health-food stores and Middle Eastern markets, and lends itself to a wide variety of uses; dressings, candies, pastries, casseroles, and so forth. You can make the paste in your blender with the addition of a little sesame oil (just the way you do with homemade peanut butter) or you can use a Japanese grinder (specially designed for this purpose) which is made of plastic and easy to clean and store.

If you express your own sesame oil, the residue can be mixed with candied lemon or orange peel and honey and shaped into little cakes to be eaten as a confection.

All sesame products are good for you. The seeds and oil are considered particularly desirable today because their fat is polyunsaturated. In addition, they are rich in calcium and Vitamin C, and contain also Vitamins E and F and lecithin.

The oil is very flavorful; a few tablespoons added, in the Chinese manner, at the end of a stir-fry or sauté dish will impart a delightfully nutty flavor to the entire contents. Used in braising delicate vegetables such as finochio, Belgian endive, or even celery, it will create a company dish in just a few minutes of cooking.

When to plant

Sesame is a warm-weather plant and cannot be set out until all danger of frost has passed. If your area has chilly springs, you may want to start it indoors. If so, you might even plant it as early as two months before time to set it out; it doesn't take up much room in the early stages and would give you a good start on the season. In the South it is usually planted about March 15, but even in the South that depends on your local frost date.

How to plant

Sow the seed ½ inch deep, 1 inch apart. If you plant in rows, they should stand about 3 feet apart. The seedlings, which can be eaten, should be thinned to stand 8 inches apart when they are about 6 inches high.

Culture

Sesame requires full sun or a very sunny south windowsill. It will grow in almost any soil, is very drought-resistant, and is a reliable cropper. For superlative results, plant it in a good vegetable-garden soil, lightly limed and manured. It isn't fussy about watering because it has both a deep taproot that will hunt for moisture deeper than most herbs, and a secondary fibrous root system that makes the most of surface moisture. Once you have planted it, sit back and enjoy it until it is time to gather the seeds.

Harvest

Harvesting the seeds is a little tricky because they do not all mature at the same time. This is one of the factors that makes them so expensive to buy; commercial growers like crops that mature all at once so they can send pickers or machines into the field and do the job at one time. For commercial growers a new variety has been developed that doesn't shatter so easily and that matures at about the same time all along the stem. This needn't concern the home gardener, who can harvest the plants as soon as the first seeds become ripe.

The timing depends on catching the first seeds to ripen. Watch the bottom seeds, since they will ripen from the bottom to the top. When the bottom seeds seem to be turning tan and the top seeds seem full-sized though still green, take the whole plant and put it (with as many plants as will fit without crowding) upside down in a paper bag. Hang the bag with a thumbtack in the garage or some other warm, dry place and let the seeds shatter and shell themselves for you into the bottom of the paper bags.

The pods will be quite large and each one will contain about eighty seeds. Since there are usually over a hundred pods to a plant, you can see that you can have a good crop from just a few plants.

How to toast sesame seeds

Most cookbooks tell you to toast sesame seeds in a frying pan over medium heat until the seeds start to jump like popcorn. I don't like this method because you have to keep shaking the pan and stirring the seeds to keep them from burning. Some recipes even suggest frying them lightly in a little sesame oil. This is messy; the seeds tend to stick together, and anyhow they are already 50 percent oil and you don't need to add more oil to them to make good eating.

The method I prefer is to put them in a single layer on a flat pan—a cookie sheet, for instance—and put the pan in a low oven, about 200° or 250° F. Keep a sharp eye on them—they can toast a golden brown in three to five minutes. This is an easy method; no shaking or stirring and you leave them right on the pan to cool. When completely cool, store in a spice jar or other tight container. Be sure not to toast them all; the raw seeds are delicious and useful, and they keep indefinitely.

Varieties

Although I have indicated the Latin name as *Sesamum orientale*, there are many other equally good varieties which you may come upon. *S. indicum* is very common, and Hudson offers *S. alatum* as one of its two kinds. Nichols, Redwood City, and DeGiorgi also offer sesame seeds. In general, look under "Herbs" rather than under "Sesame"; sometimes—as with Nichols—look under "Bene Sesame." The seed pods are generally grayish or tannish to light cream, but black sesame seeds are highly regarded too, so do not hesitate to order these if they are offered. Japanese seed offerings may call sesame seeds *goma*, and the Chinese name may be spelled a number of ways. The black sesame is *hak chih mah* in Chinese and *kuro goma* in Japanese.

CHINESE PARSLEY   YUEN TSAI

[*Coriandrum sativum*]

When you talk of Chinese parsley, it is fashionable among certain gourmet cooks to look very knowing and say, "Oh, you mean cilantro." One name is no more chic or correct than the other, and you would be well within your rights to retort, "Actually, I mean coriander." For Chinese parsley is all of these things. In the Oriental markets, when looking for fresh bunches of this herb, ask for Chinese parsley or yuen tsai. In Spanish markets or when traveling in Mexico or Italy, ask for *cilantro* or *celantro*. When hunting for it at your grocery store, ask for coriander. It is also listed as coriander in most seed catalogs, under "Herbs."

Cookbooks often distinguish between the fresh green leaves and the seeds by using the term "coriander" for the seeds only, no matter what they call the leaves. So much for terminology. If you don't feel like getting involved in all of that, simply stick to the Latin name, which is the same regardless of how and in what country this herb is used.

There is no doubt that Chinese parsley has acquired a certain amount of snob appeal. Not so long ago, seed catalogs, while extolling the virtues of the seed, warned gardeners not to be put off by the "fetid" smell of the foliage; descriptions like "repellent" and "unpleasant" were commonly used, and it was a constant source of wonder among food writers that the seeds could be so delightfully flavored when the foliage was just the opposite.

This was true, however, mostly in English-speaking countries. The rest of the world has enjoyed this unusual herb—fresh, dried, and fruited—from the earliest recorded times. It was used in Egyptian cookery three thousand years ago; natives of Mexico and South America have long eaten it extensively; Italians consider it a major herb, along with oregano and basil. It is absolutely essential if you wish to prepare authentic Chinese dishes. All of these countries regard the scent and flavor of the fresh leaves very differently from America.

So while American seed catalogs may describe the foliage as smelling "like a bedbug," Tsang & Ma says it has "delicious fragrance and flavor, with no hint of bitterness." All Chinese cookbooks say it is aromatic and delicately scented. In fact, the Chinese refer to it as the "fragrant green."

Occasionally, a garden book will compare its taste to that of parsley; in spite of its name, the flavor bears no resemblance to either curly or Italian parsley—it is quite unique. No other parsley is a satisfactory substitute for it.

In case you are worried that your taste may not run to this unfamiliar herb, I should tell you that a Chinese woman who was giving a cooking class I once took brought freshly picked bunches of Chinese parsley as a gift to the class. As she passed the bunches around for us to take, she said, "How do you like the smell?" Everyone thought it was delicious and proved it by enthusiastically eating the dish she prepared that night, liberally seasoned with it.

Like most herbs, Chinese parsley has an ancient history, with a rich vein of mythology. Inevitably, it was used in love potions and as a general aphrodisiac. The Chinese also believed that eating it could confer immortality. Medicinally, it is still valued in some countries as a carminative. It is one of the herbs mentioned in the Bible, in Exodus and in Numbers, where manna is described as "small, round and white like coriander seed."

Culinary and other uses

The leaves should be eaten when young and tender. They can be minced or cut into 2-inch lengths, depending on the dish in which they are to be used. As an ingredient in a salad, they add zest and a touch of the unexpected.

When incorporated in stir-fry dishes, they should be added toward the end of the cooking cycle. The Chinese make a particularly delectable beef stew, simmered with vegetables and seasoned with the Five Spices (a mixture obtainable in Oriental markets) and Chinese parsley. Try it also with an Irish lamb stew, adding it during the last twenty minutes of cooking, or mince and sprinkle over sliced and buttered Jerusalem artichokes. Hard-cooked egg yolks blended with a little sesame oil and mixed with minced Chinese parsley can be stuffed back into the whites for a delicious appetizer.

The flavor of the seeds is somewhat like a spicy citrus—orange with a touch of hot lime is one way to describe it. Since this is the case, it seems only natural that Chinese parsley is so rich in Vitamin C.

The seeds are commonly used whole to flavor breads, puddings, and pastries. Or whirl them to a powder in your blender, and incorporate in a vanilla blanc mange with a thin orange slice or a sprinkling or orange mint as garnish. Add to your next tea bread along with orange and lemon zest and use orange-blossom honey instead of sugar.

In Scandinavian countries, the seeds are often crushed and mixed with flour to make special breads—a custom which may have found its way north from ancient Greece, where the seeds were actually ground up along with the flour for bread dough.

Do not limit your use of the seeds to sweet dishes; they are one of the spices most widely used in Indian curries and their unique flavor is highly regarded in all Indian cookery.

An easy and tasty dish is made by simmering crushed coriander seeds in chicken broth for two or three minutes. Strain the broth and use it as liquid in which to cook rice pilaf. If you are serving this with a chicken curry, chop up two or three oranges and a lemon and cook them along with the rice, stirring when the rice is half done to mix the fruit evenly throughout.

Appearance

Chinese parsley is a pretty plant with lavender flowers. It grows about 2 feet tall and has leaves of two different shapes; the bottom leaves look something like Italian parsley; the top leaves are much more deeply cut and feathery.

When to plant

You can plant Chinese parsley in the spring after all danger of frost has passed, or for a fall harvest. It takes about 60 days to maturity, so a good crop can be had almost anywhere in the United States.

You can also enjoy it year-round by growing it indoors; it does very well in a container on a sunny windowsill.

How to plant

Barely cover the seeds with about ⅛ inch of soil and sow about ½ inch apart. Thin to stand 4 to 6 inches apart when the seedlings have about six to eight true leaves. The thinnings make good eating in a tossed salad.

If you sow seeds you have grown yourself, break open the shell or pod to obtain the individual seeds.

Any good vegetable-garden soil will do unless you are starting them indoors, in which case I recommend Fertl Cubes or peat pots of Cornell Mix.

Culture

Fertilize lightly about every two weeks with a 10-10-5 formula—plus a little lime if your soil tends to be acid. Water two or three times a week if you are growing Chinese parsley in a container; once a week in the garden.

Harvest

You can start to crop the leaves when the plant is about 6 inches high. If this is what you want to do, pull up the whole plant and leave others to grow to maturity—about 60 days—and go to seed. You can grow them quite closely together if you do this because the plants you pull up will make more than enough room for the ones that are left to mature.

To store the fresh leaves, wash them in cold water, drain thoroughly, and wrap in a paper towel. Store in the vegetable compartment of your refrigerator and use as soon as possible. If your vegetable compartment is full, store the damp leaves in a tightly closed plastic bag on a refrigerator shelf.

If all the seeds are allowed to ripen fully on the plant, the pods will shatter, scattering the seeds, and you will lose most of your crop. Instead, as soon as the first seed pods are dry, pull up the whole plant, put it in a paper bag, and hang it in a warm dry place. The bags will catch the ripening seeds in the bottom and will also keep the plant clean.

Note: I have found that unusual weather conditions can hasten maturity considerably. Keep an eye on your plants. They may surprise you by going to seed much earlier than the usual 60 days.

Varieties

Almost any seed catalog that offers herb seeds will list coriander. There are no named varieties offered. Catalogs that specialize in Oriental vegetables may list it as Chinese parsley.

JAPANESE PARSLEY   MITSUBA

[*Cryptotaenia japonica*]

I have often thought it would be fun to plant a corner of an herb garden with all the different parsleys. I would have Italian or broad-leaved parsley, curly parsley, Hamburg parsley, Chinese parsley, and—now—Japanese parsley. And I'll bet there are some parsleys I haven't heard of. If you know of any, please write and tell me.

Japanese parsley is not a real parsley, as you can see from its Latin name, but then neither is Chinese parsley. Since they are all called parsley, however, I would stretch a point for the sake of an interesting garden.

Japanese parsley is almost identical to honewort, which grows wild in this hemisphere—from southern Canada to the south of the United States. Honewort's Latin name is *Cryptotaenia canadensis* and it is sometimes known as wild chervil. The American Indians ate it, and the Swedish plant explorer Peter Kalm wrote that the French in Canada were inordinately fond of it in soup. I have never seen it growing wild, but I am not great on gathering wild edible plants, so perhaps I have missed it.

The Japanese, in their thrifty way, early recognized the value of Japanese parsley and put it under cultivation; today it is widely grown.

Culinary and other uses

Japanese parsley is usually said to be celery-flavored but I personally think it tastes more like Italian parsley—which as you undoubtedly know has a stronger parsley flavor than curly parsley. I would not tend to make a whole salad of just this one herb, but it is good in a mixed green salad with Bibb or salad bowl lettuce, or perhaps Chinese cabbage, which is also mild in flavor.

It is excellent simmered briefly in clear chicken broth, and delectable stir-fried with mushrooms and shrimp. Grow it and taste a leaf yourself; you will soon find many, many uses for this unique herb.

If you like to make quick breads—and who could help but like a bread that takes only fifteen minutes to mix—you might try adding Japanese parsley to your carrot, zucchini, or parsnip bread. A minced tablespoon or two is sufficient to give flavor and aroma to the whole loaf.

Do not hesitate to toss minced spoonfuls on freshly boiled vegetables or on cucumber salads, and add it to canapés of egg, shrimp, fish, or pâté.

The whole plant is edible—seeds, leaves, stem, and small roots—but save some seeds to plant next spring. Use the leaves and stems both raw and cooked. The roots can be blanched for five minutes, then sautéed in sesame oil, or they can be boiled together with diced parsnips.

For a thoroughly English treat with an Oriental flavor, make cucumber sandwiches on thinly sliced white bread and butter, and garnish the cucumbers with minced Japanese parsley. (I like this even better on rye bread but it isn't so "English.")

Japanese cookbooks will always call it mitsuba in their list of recipe ingredients, and Chinese cookbooks written for Americans will sometimes call it by this Japanese appellation. I have, therefore, given you the Japanese rather than the rarely used Chinese name.

In China, Japanese parsley is an important and widely used

medicinal herb; it is also used in Chinese cookery, although not in all regions.

Appearance

Mitsuba is interesting in the garden primarily as a foliage plant. Its flowers are small, white, and umbrella-shaped—as is typical of this family of plants—and somewhat unobtrusive unless you have a wild-flower photographer in the family (as I do). Garden books will tell you quite firmly that the flowers appear at the top of the plant, but don't be surprised when the fruit is ripening at the top if flowers start to appear an inch or two from the soil surface on the lower part of the stems. This is, of course, a second flowering.

The seed pods (or fruit) are always described as long and ribbed—but "long" is relative; they are actually about ¼ inch long at the most.

The leaves look something like those of Italian parsley but just enough different to be recognized as Japanese parsley if you are growing them together.

When to plant

Mitsuba is a reasonably hardy herb and can be planted as early as the ground can be worked. If you are growing it in pots indoors, harden it off before you transplant it to the open garden.

How to plant

Like true parsley, it is best to plant mitsuba as an annual—although it self-sows from year to year.

Japanese parsley is not particularly fussy about soil and is, happily, one of the herbs that will thrive in a moist, shady place; save your sunny areas for plants which won't settle for less.

This is one plant that does not like a rich wood-ash mulch: normally neutral vegetable-garden soil is better—do not put it next to your beets, for instance. Use a 10-10-5 fertilizer.

Unlike the true parsley, mitsuba is not difficult to germinate and will quickly show a bit of green if you keep its planting site moist.

The seeds should be sown ½ inch deep in a standard mix, and kept moist during its entire growing period. Do not let the soil dry out completely at any time.

Culture

If you grow mitsuba in full sun, the leaves may turn yellow and mottled and look unhealthy. If this should happen, remove the discolored leaves and use only the new green ones that the plant will continue to put out from the bottom of the stems. If possible, grow in shade, or partial shade.

For the best crop, plant successively, and take the entire plant when you want it. Leave a few plants to go to seed for next season's crop.

Keep moist, much as you do mint, and side-dress when the plant is about 1½ feet tall with the 10-10-5 fertilizer you used in the beginning; a small amount of manure is beneficial but avoid making the soil too rich. At the halfway mark, water is more important than fertilizer, so if your gardening time is limited, concentrate on the watering.

Harvest

If you have a number of plants, you can gather leaves from them without disturbing the growth of the parent plant; seed production will continue undisturbed. If you prefer, pull the entire plant in about four weeks. If you wait until maturity—60 days—you can harvest the seeds *and* the roots. I generally take some of the plant at each stage, so it is like having three different plants in the garden.

Incidentally, you will find that the seeds you buy may turn out to be different varieties from year to year. Some varieties have a slender white stem, some green. Sometimes the stems are hollow, sometimes not. They all taste much the same, so don't worry.

Varieties

Mitsuba, the Japanese name, is the one used in all the catalogs that carry it—Kitazawa, Japonica, and Nichols. However, in American edible-plant guides, wild chervil or honewort is sometimes mistakenly called mitsuba.

GIANT GARLIC   SUAN   [*Allium sativum*]

Now that the treasures of King Tutankhamen have been exhibited throughout the United States, and we have seen the beautiful gold and jeweled objects which his tomb contained, we should be all the more impressed to learn that among the treasures found in King Tut's tomb is one that's never exhibited or mentioned, one that we can all own for ourselves in our own home—and that treasure is garlic. King Tut's tomb is ancient, but the use of garlic is much more so, going far back beyond recorded history and designated in Chinese writing by a single symbol—proof in itself that a word is very old.

A native of western Asia, garlic was introduced to China in some prehistoric time. During Caesar's time the Roman army ate it in large quantities because they believed it gave strength and courage in battle, and they planted it in every country they conquered. Like so many excellent Roman innovations, garlic was not too favorably received in England, but the rest of Europe took to it and it is now grown and eaten throughout the world.

The Chinese wisely consider garlic a medicine as well as an essential ingredient in their cuisine. Western scientists have confirmed that it stimulates the flow of gastric juices, aiding digestion whenever it is included in a meal. If you have been on antibiotics, garlic—along with yogurt—is thought to help the stomach and intestines renew the helpful bacteria which antibiotics so often destroy. In addition, garlic dilates blood vessels and may eventually be found useful in treating high blood pressure. It is sold in health-food stores throughout the United States in the form of tablets—but the best, most effective, and pleasantest way to take it is minced in a salad, deliciously cooked in a meat casserole, or stir-fried in a wok with other foods.

All garlic has these beneficial properties, but for the home gardener the variety known as giant garlic is of particular interest.

Giant garlic   suan

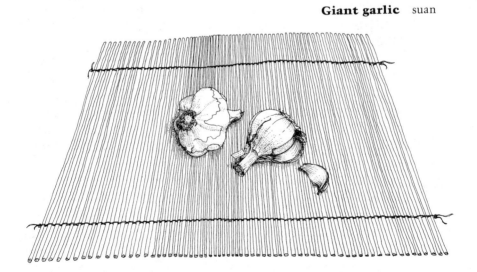

Culinary and other uses

Anyone who has been so timid as not to have attempted garlic in the kitchen will be relieved to hear that there is a garlic that has the flavor without the disadvantages. Giant garlic is much milder than common garlic and does not need to be used nearly so sparingly. Like so many oversized creatures, this mammoth bulb is gentler than its smaller cousin and less liable to create a culinary disaster.

Use giant garlic any way you would use common garlic. In some countries, the cloves are eaten raw—like an onion, with bread, cheese, and wine. It is a healthful, if simple, lunch. I would not go so far as to suggest this repast for Western appetites but this garlic certainly can be used raw in a salad, blended in butter as a spread for making garlic bread, or mixed with cottage or cream cheese, with parsley or grated carrot added for color and additional flavor.

If you still don't want even this mild raw garlic in your salad but would prefer an even subtler garlic flavor, make a garlic vinegar to use in your salad dressings. This is as easy as peeling a garlic clove and dropping it in a small container of vinegar, where, after three or four days, it will have imparted a delicate garlic flavor to the vinegar (the garlic clove can then be removed). I always use the vinegared garlic clove minced in other dishes—but then I am very fond of garlic. If you leave the clove in the vinegar longer, no harm will be done, nor will the flavor get too strong.

For cooking, peel whole garlic cloves, then crush slightly; remove from the dish before serving, so that some unwary guest will not find himself with a whole clove of garlic in his mouth. If cooked slightly in a little oil—as with onions—the flavor will be still milder and very pleasant, even to many people who normally do not like garlic. Leg of lamb rubbed with fresh rosemary, with slivers of giant garlic inserted in slits throughout the surface, is delectable both in the roasting and in the eating.

Some cooks recommend using whole garlic cloves without removing the papery skin; they say this eliminates the aftertaste and odor. I have tried it and invariably find that bits of the skin get loose and into the dish, where they are impossible to locate until chewed on. If garlic is used in proper quantities and browned or otherwise cooked, there is no aftertaste or smell to speak of. Of course, if you make a garlic soup or some similar dish which requires enormous quantities of garlic, I presume you will not choose that night to go to the movies.

The shoots of garlic clumps can be used just like common chives; they are very mild and add a pretty bit of green as a garnish on coddled eggs, creamed vegetables, and clear soups.

To rid the fingers of odor after handling garlic, simply rinse thoroughly under *cold* water. Your hands will come out completely odor-free.

Appearance

Giant garlic looks like ordinary garlic, only more so. A single clove can weigh over a pound and a clump can grow as wide as a dinner plate. If this sounds unwieldy for the small garden, it isn't really. This kind of garlic is much more prolific than common garlic and you will need fewer plants. It is very easy to grow.

Since the bulb is so large, the cloves are also proportionately larger than common garlic cloves, a great help when you are trying to mince or chop a clove. The bother of peeling (greatly simplified by crushing slightly with the flat side of a wide-bladed knife) is nothing with these large cloves.

The stems are narrow but flat and solid (not hollow like some chives) and grow about 24 to 36 inches tall. A flower stem rises up along with the leaves, and the pinkish-lavender flower opens from a papery sheath, but never fully as with other alliums.

When to plant

Garlic can be planted from seed or from cloves indoors at any time. Seed will not produce usable cloves until the second year, but they will give you a nice crop of garlicky shoots for clipping.

Giant garlic can be planted in place outdoors in late fall (about a month before your first frost date) or in early spring. The plant is winter-hardy to about 20° F., but a straw mulch is advisable in severe climates if you plant in the fall. Since it is a perennial, you could leave it in place all year, but it is considered better practice to dig up the mature bulbs, separate into cloves, and replant. You wouldn't get anywhere near as big a harvest from whole bulbs left in the ground, compared to that same bulb separated into cloves and planted individually.

Seeds are usually planted in the spring.

How to plant

Cloves are planted 1 inch deep, about 12 inches apart. If you are not planning to mulch and your winters are cold, plant 2 inches deep.

Seeds are tiny and should be barely covered with about ¼ inch of soil. The plants should stand about 12 inches apart where they are to grow; or they can be sown 4 inches apart and then transplanted to stand the mature distance. All alliums are easy to transplant for all that they look so delicate and frail, but transplanting takes time, so I avoid it when I can.

Since each clove will grow into a bulb containing eight to ten cloves, this is a practical windowsill plant; just one flowerpot will provide the needs of most families. If you want, you can start a second planting of seeds or cloves in a small window box or flat three to four months before harvest of your first crop. This will give you a good start on the seedlings for the next batch. With careful planning, even the smallest kitchen need never run out of fresh, home-grown garlic.

Culture

Garlic likes a sunny location and a sandy loam. Fertilize once a month with a 5-10-10 fertilizer and be careful not to overwater. When the flower forms, snip it off to allow the plant to put all its energy into bulb formation. If you want seeds, leave one or two flowers to form seeds.

The plant will grow most briskly when the temperature is over 65° F. and the days are long. It is very undemanding and can mostly be left to itself.

Harvest

Cloves mature in six to eight months, seeds in about eighteen months. Since it is a perennial, the seeds spend the first season forming a small, immature bulb; it flowers the second season, when a mature bulb will be formed. Sometimes, when you dig up a clump, the bulb will be immature because of vagaries in the weather, soil conditions, and so forth. If this should occur, shrug your shoulders and replant it; it will give you a mature bulb next season. Everything else being equal, the larger the bulb, the better the crop.

You don't have to guess when the bulb is ready to harvest; the tops will turn brown and dry. If they turn brown but not dry, bend them down to earth and they will dry quickly.

Giant garlic will dry and keep just like common garlic. It should be left in the sun for a day or two (but taken in at night). Then any of the papery shell that is loose should be removed, and the roots cut off close to the base of the bulb. Leave the bulb whole; do not divide it into cloves until you need one. At that time, remove as many cloves as you need and leave the rest attached to one another; they will keep much better that way.

Otherwise, store in open baskets or other containers just as you do onions; air circulation is important. Once in a while, turn them over and check through in case any have molded; sometimes only part of a bulb will spoil and the rest can be set aside to use in the near future.

Varieties

Thompson & Morgan carries what they call Jumbo Garlic. They offer seeds only, to harvest in eighteen months.

Nichols has Elephant Garlic, which it claims it has "spent over 25 years selecting for both hardiness and flavor." Nichols gave it the name Elephant Garlic, and recommends it for fall planting. Some very interesting literature on development of the bulb, as well as detailed cultural instructions, is sent with your Nichols order.

WATERCRESS   SAI YONG CHOI

[Nasturtium officinale]

With watercress growing wild throughout most of the ancient world (except in the Americas) it is only natural that man discovered, early in his existence, the edibility of this crisp, pungent herb. It became so popular that it was taken everywhere, and soon was introduced to this continent, where it escaped to grow along brooks and streams throughout North and South America.

In the United States today, however, watercress is mostly used as a garnish, to be put aside uneaten as if it were merely a decoration, whereas actually it is a powerhouse of nutrients.

Elsewhere in the world, watercress is more highly regarded and has been so for thousands of years. The Romans ate large quantities of it, partly because it was thought to prevent hair from falling out. The Greeks regarded it as a cure for insanity, and also for drunkenness (so it was always served at large banquets). Almost all cultures seem to have realized that it had a high Vitamin C content (although they didn't, of course, know there was any such thing as Vitamin C) and used it to prevent diseases caused by a deficiency of that vitamin.

In addition to Vitamin C, watercress contains three times as much Vitamin E as lettuce, and is rich in A, B_1, and B_2. It has almost three times as much calcium as spinach, and is a valuable source of copper, iron, and magnesium. Even if you just use watercress regularly in place of lettuce, you will add appreciably to your intake of vitamins and minerals. All this and it is delicious, too.

While it has long been gathered in the wild, it is no longer so easy to do. For one thing, the plants are much harder to find; for another, even apparently clean streams may be polluted—and not only from running through a cow pasture. Added to this, there is the natural hazard of its affinity for fool's cress (marshwort), which commonly grows along with it and which is unpleasantly poisonous. All in all, you are better off growing your own.

Watercress is rather expensive to buy in the market but nothing could be easier to grow than cuttings—or, if you prefer seeds, they are readily available.

Culinary and other uses

Watercress makes great sandwiches. Cream cheese, cucumber, and watercress on whole-wheat bread is cool, crisp, and flavorful. Or, instead of cream cheese, substitute blue cheese blended with yogurt. For a picnic, pack chicken and watercress sandwiches; the watercress won't go limp on a hot day the way lettuce will.

Make an unusual garnish for a hot or cold soup by whipping lightly salted cream and folding finely chopped watercress in it. Add sprigs of watercress to a mixed green salad or a plate of sliced tomatoes fresh from your garden, the whole lightly dressed with a vinaigrette for a first course on a hot day.

Since the Chinese do not tend to use raw vegetables—unless they have been pickled—watercress is often fried. To make this, quickly stir-fry ginger and garlic in peanut oil, then add watercress, a few tablespoons of chicken stock, a little sherry, and some soy sauce, and continue stir-frying for another minute. Thicken with cornstarch and serve immediately as a hot vegetable. Or use watercress for tempura as the Japanese do.

Cream of watercress soup is a real delight and very quick to prepare. Put the watercress in a blender with chicken stock, ginger, yogurt, and salt and pepper if needed. Blend *very* briefly, then heat to just under the boiling point. Serve hot or cold, with sprigs of fresh watercress as a garnish.

Once you get started on really eating watercress, you will think of many, many ways to use it. Everyone will like it, and only you have to know that it is good for you.

Appearance

As I am sure you know, watercress is a dark-green, small-leaved plant that is usually sold in dripping bunches in the produce market. If it is not moist, chances are it won't be as fresh as it should be. In any case, never buy any that is turning yellow; it's good only for the compost heap.

When to plant

Watercress can be planted anytime. It is customary to recommend sowing the seed in April or May, but this is not at all necessary. Watercress must have wet feet and actually prefers *cool water;* as long as that is provided, it won't pay much attention to air temperatures. In the South, winter seeding is recommended, but here again, the water temperature is the critical factor.

How to plant

You can plant either the seeds or the sprigs. Seeds should be sown on the surface of moist soil and just barely covered with more moist soil. The soil should be rich in humus and lime. In the wild, watercress feeds on leaves and bits of leaf mold that slow-moving water tangles in its foliage; if you can approximate these conditions, your plants will thrive. A flower pot full of well-fertilized, alkaline soil will do fine; it should stand in a container—shallow or deep—of water.

If you prefer, you can germinate the seeds between two layers of moist paper toweling. Once they have sprouted, drop them onto the soil and cover with a little moist sand. I personally don't see any advantage to this method but it seems to suit some gardeners.

What I do is to buy a good, fresh bunch of watercress in the market. I cut the stems into pieces, each piece with a joint at the top. These stems can be rooted in water or soil, whichever happens to be more convenient at the time. They will form roots in a few days and can then be slipped into a pot of moist soil with a bit of the stem out in the air.

Culture

Occasional fertilizing and liming are necessary because keeping the soil moist with fresh, cold water—as you must do—gradually leaches out all the nutrients. I use a Cornell Mix plus lime to start with, and fertilize lightly about once a week with liquid fertilizer. I add more lime about once a month. A good potting soil, however, would be perfectly satisfactory.

It is especially important to put a layer of gravel or moss in the bottom of the pot; if you don't, the soil will quickly wash out through the drainage holes.

Watercress does best in high shade, a term for no sun but plenty of light. I grow it on my porch in the summer, on the kitchen windowsill (facing north) in the winter. It's best to have it in a handy place because it needs fresh water once a day in the winter, twice a day in the summer. If you run into a really hot spell, drop an ice cube into the water rather than letting the tap run. A large-surfaced container, like an azalea pot or window box, will give you a larger crop, since the watercress will spread out into whatever space you give it. Bear in mind, however, that the container must stand in water and that the water must be changed at least once a day. The average window box wouldn't do unless you worked out an outer, waterproof box to stand it in.

Harvest

You can harvest watercress whenever you please as long as you do not let it flower. If it flowers, and especially if it goes to seed, it will be too bitter to be good eating. Seedsmen list it as maturing in 50 days but I never wait anything like that long. Then again, I never plant seed, only stems, so mine can be picked in about ten days.

Once you have it growing, you can easily get more stock by taking cuttings from your own plants and rooting them in water or soil.

Watercress is a good year-round vegetable and no trouble at all; in fact, sometimes I've been too busy to plant stems I had rooting in water and they have flowered and gone to seed before I had a chance to plant or eat them.

Varieties

There are no varieties, but many catalogs list the seeds. Look under "Cress" as well as "Watercress" in the indexes. Hudson, Redwood City, Burpee, Nichols, Stokes, and Harris all list watercress seeds.

GINGER   KEONG   [*Zingiber officinale*]

If you have a spice shelf, chances are that ground ginger is on it. Everywhere in the world, it is one of the most popular and mostly widely used spices. Even the English, who are somewhat conservative in their use of herbs and spices (garlic, for example, has been accepted there only very recently), took to ginger root as soon as it was introduced in that country. In fact, by the fourteenth century, ginger was so well liked in England that its consumption ranked second only to pepper. Queen Elizabeth I and her court dined royally on one of their favorite desserts, gingerbread. Shakespeare, who was always quick to reflect the popular taste, speaks of it as the ultimate love offering when he writes, in *Love's Labour's Lost,* "An I had but one penny in the world, thou shouldst have it to buy ginger-bread."

Many varieties of ginger grow wild from China to the United States, but the finest varieties originated in the East Indies and India. Its use spread rapidly, and by the Middle Ages it was known throughout the civilized world. Since it was usually sold as a living root, ginger was easily planted wherever it was imported, and when it reached the West Indies it found the perfect climate. Today Jamaican ginger is known, even in China, as one of the finest gingers grown anywhere, and it is a principal export of the West Indies.

In addition to the variety of ginger we commonly use, and are most familiar with, there are many other gingers grown in China, Japan, and India. One of them tastes like bergamot, which seems like a waste of good ginger; another is lemon-scented, which might be interesting. However, not all members of the ginger family are edible, so do not buy an ornamental ginger without carefully checking whether it can be eaten.

Ginger root   keong

Culinary and other uses

The variety of ways in which ginger can be used is limited only by the cook's imagination. It is equally good in both main dishes and desserts, hot or cold, in salads or stews. It does wonders for roasts and soups, and in beverages. Ginger lends zest to many bland meat dishes, and eliminates the fishy odors of seafood without spoiling the delicate natural flavors of the fish.

A simple dish of rice pilaf cooked with ginger, scallions, and garlic which have been lightly sautéed in oil becomes a company dish. That old standby gingerbread is still beloved by both children and adults. Try serving it with whipped cream to which you have added a bit of candied ginger.

On a cold wintry afternoon you can offer your grateful guests a nineteenth-century English tavern drink. Sprinkle a little freshly ground ginger on top of a mug of ale (not beer), mull with a hot poker, and serve.

If you like to cook highly spiced food—whether Chinese or Indian—always include ginger among your spices. This is the secret ingredient of those lands; ginger has a soothing effect on the digestive tract and counteracts the turmeric and other hot spices used. Knowing this, you will understand why one of the chief uses of ginger in the Far East is as an aid to digestion. Try it for yourself. You will find that nibbling on a piece of crystallized ginger will relieve discomfort after a too-heavy meal. It is also used to relieve flatulence and as a tonic. In the United States, ginger is commonly employed to make medicines palatable, and to flavor ginger ale, which is frequently recommended for nausea and various stomach disorders.

In addition to its medicinal value, ginger is a good source of Vitamin C; the wise Chinese always took pots of ginger with them on long sea voyages to prevent scurvy—and this was considerably before the British navy learned to achieve the same result with lime juice.

Although it must be used with discretion when raw, a little ginger grated into the dressing for a fruit salad is delightful, and a thin slice added to honeyed hot tea makes a healthful and delicious beverage.

Grated ginger can be used whenever dried ground ginger is called for—in about half the quantity indicated. If you keep a piece of the root in the freezer, grate as much as you need while it is still frozen; it becomes spongy when thawed, and is difficult to grate. Another way of keeping it is to put the root in a small jar, cover with sherry, and refrigerate; it will keep almost indefinitely this way. An editor I know uses vodka instead of sherry—you can take your choice.

A piece of ginger will keep in the refrigerator for about a week, but do not put it in the vegetable compartment. Store it in a plastic wrap by itself. The vegetable compartment is too moist and will tend to mold it.

If you grow your own ginger, you will be able to enjoy "green ginger," which is actually not green but pink. The green refers to the fact that it is not mature, and it is used to describe the immature roots that form from the mature root. If left to grow, they would in time mature, but they are very good eating and particularly good to crystallize or to candy. Look for them three to four months after you have planted the root. In China, these are eaten raw as well as cooked in syrup. When you grow your own ginger, you will always have a supply of the fresh root available, and a beautiful house plant as well.

I should mention, by the way, that today ginger is a common ingredient in men's toilet water, a use which may stem from the old belief that ginger was an aphrodisiac. So potent were its purported qualities that just touching a woman with hands that had been rubbed with ginger was thought to be sufficient to win her heart.

Appearance

Ginger root is a pleasant tan color with a smooth woody look. It grows in a knobby sort of way and can usually be found in the markets perfectly clean and ready to use. This is the part you plant, so try to get a good, firm, fresh root.

The ginger plant itself is reedy-looking and grows about 2–3 feet tall. It is sometimes called "the queen of the greenhouse" because of its brilliant, showy flowers, and many home gardeners grow it as an ornamental, never realizing the buried treasure they have beneath the soil.

When to plant

Ginger usually "rests" during the winter months, so it is planted early in the spring. You can start it as early as you like indoors; outdoors it must wait for really warm weather. In Florida it can be planted in February or early March. In the North, try to start it in January in indoor pots and plant it outdoors in late spring when all danger of frost has passed. The earlier you can start it indoors, the greater the maturity of the root you harvest in the fall. If it is still growing strongly, you can pot it and let it finish growing indoors. If this sounds like too much of a bother, harvest the delicious immature roots instead.

How to plant

The only source I know of for ginger root is your local market. It is commonly sold even in the big supermarkets; if you don't see any, ask the produce manager when it will be coming in. It is normally available all year round, but not all roots will sprout. Buy a large, clean, firm root that is not discolored or spongy. Take it home and cut into 1- to 2-inch pieces; each piece should have at least one "eye" or knob.

Put 2–3 inches deep in a pot of rich potting soil and keep soil moist. After two weeks, if no shoots have appeared, dig up the roots and check them out. If they look the same as when you planted them, wash them off, dry them thoroughly, and put aside to use. If small, pronounced ivory bumps have developed, then replant—these are the beginnings of shoots and show that the root is alive.

When you replant, add a tablespoon of dried manure and work well into the surface of the soil. Continue to keep soil moist all during the growing of ginger, but be sure drainage is good; this plant does not like wet feet.

Sun is desirable for two hours a day but not more—until the shoots are a couple of inches high.

Culture

As the plant develops, numerous reedy shoots will grow and form an interesting clump from which flower stalks will arise in the sixth or seventh month. Ginger is a heavy feeder, and frequent light applications of manure and fish emulsion will benefit it. Liquid compost and a general 10-10-10 fertilizer will also give good results. If you are planting a lot of ginger, space the plants 16 inches apart, the rows 24 inches apart.

Keep the soil moist. If you grow it in the house, put the pot on pebbles and keep the pebbles moist to add humidity to the air around the plant.

Ginger does not like wind. If grown on a terrace, a windbreak should be provided; otherwise put it in a sunny corner that is well protected from wind.

Harvest

The shoots are delicious and can be cut anytime after they are 3 inches high. The roots will continue to sprout if you do not take too many shoots, and this cropping will do the plant no harm. A famous Japanese delicacy is a condiment made by marinating ginger shoots in a vinegar syrup, or in a blend of vinegar, sugar, and sesame oil.

As we mentioned earlier, the roots themselves can be harvested two ways. Baby roots will be pale pink, rather than tan, and can be broken off the main root without disturbing it. These juvenile roots are recognizably gingery but so mild and delicate that you will almost think it is a different plant. This mildness is due to the fact that the flavor and the "heat" of ginger are the result of two different substances; the immature root has not yet developed the gingerin which makes ginger "hot." These baby roots can be enjoyed only by the happy gardener who grows this plant, and is sufficient reason— even if there were not so many others—for including ginger somewhere in the home garden or windowsill. In Japan, the baby roots, marinated briefly in rice vinegar and sugar, are known as red pickled ginger or *beni-shoga*. In China, this is called *soon keong*. You can easily make this delicious pickle in your own kitchen.

Once the stem has withered, the mature root can be dug up whole, or it can be gathered a joint at a time.

In the open garden, the plant will die down over the winter and is best dug up at that time and stored in sand until spring. If you wish to keep the plant in the house, give it a resting period. You can force winter blooms by planting it in a pot about nine months before you want the flowers; it will subsequently go dormant on its usual schedule.

MULTIPLIER ONIONS   CHANG FA

[*Allium fistulosum*]

For most American gardeners scallions are as much a sign of spring as the first robin, but these so-called scallions are, often as not, merely immature onions and not true scallions at all. True scallions never form a bulb; they are grown from seed, not from onion sets; and they will never turn into an onion no matter how long they grow. They are much more economical than immature onions since they increase in number throughout a long season, whereas an onion produces a single immature "scallion" at the expense of a mature onion. So grow your onions to maturity and plant these true scallions for the relish tray.

Multiplier onions are known by many names. In the Far East they are called chang fa in China, *nebuka* in Japan. We call them, variously, Japanese bunching onions, cibol or ciboule, and Welsh onions. They are likely to be found in seed catalogs under any or all of these names.

Multiplier onions are native to Siberia and have no botanical connection with Wales, though they do look a little like leeks and are a common crop in Welsh gardens. They are much more widely used in China, Japan, and Europe than in the United States.

Multiplier onions are an excellent vegetable; easy, prolific, mild or pungent depending on the season, and well worth the small space they take in the garden. They are unusually hardy and can sometimes be cropped even when it means brushing aside the snow to get at them.

Culinary and other uses

Since multiplier onions are scallions, they can be used in any way you are accustomed to use scallions. They are extensively used throughout the Far East, where they are essential in both Chinese and

Multiplier onions   chang fa

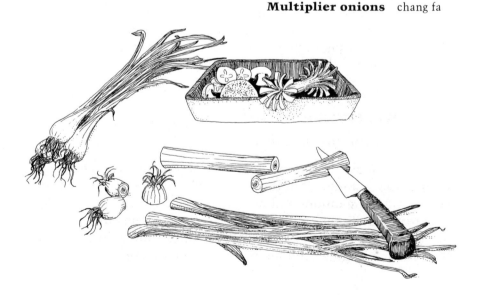

Japanese cuisine—whether specially cut into little brushes as a garnish to a baked fish, sliced thinly for clear soup, or sautéed briefly at the start of a stir-fry dish. We think of them as part of the relish tray, along with radishes, cucumbers, julienne carrots, and celery, and early in the year they are mild enough for everyone to enjoy raw. As the season progresses and the stems thicken, the flavor becomes a little too pungent for most people to eat out of hand. This is when they come into their own in cooked dishes, and if you have never prepared them as a braised vegetable, you will find this delicate and unusual enough to serve as a company dish. It takes only minutes to prepare. Cut the whole onion in half—from green stalk right down through the white part—sauté it in a little sesame oil until it turns golden brown, add enough chicken broth to simmer, cover, and cook for another five minutes. If you want, you can stir in a little soy sauce just before serving, to make it darker and more mysterious-looking, but I like the golden look of the vegetable without the soy. The flavor is as different from the fresh onion as braised leeks are from raw leeks—and it is more delicious than you can possibly imagine anything so simple could be. It is one more proof that tasty dishes don't need to be slaved over.

Appearance

Multiplier onions are scallions, and that is what they look like. In the garden, however, their appearance differs in one important respect from ordinary young onion shoots—the clumps grow with several "scallions" bunched together, almost as if you had planted too many seeds in one spot. It is easy to see why they are called multiplier onions. The shoots divide into more shoots as they grow, and are harvested by pulling shoots away from the main bunch when you want some to eat. Each shoot is a whole scallion.

Another difference, but one which will not be immediately evident when you see them growing, is that multiplier onions never form bulbs. They are perennials, and if allowed, will continue to grow in this form without turning into anything but giant scallions.

I never have enough scallions, so these are a joy; also, you don't have to choose between your onion crop and your early scallions, or feel guilty at the thought that you are sacrificing a large onion.

When to plant

Seeds can be sown either early in the spring for summer use or late in the fall for very early spring use. They are winter-hardy almost everywhere, but to be on the safe side, mulch them in areas where the winters are severe. Of course, if you are growing them on your windowsill, you can sow them anytime you please.

How to plant

The seed is small and should be planted about ½ inch deep. Since the plants are interesting and decorative, don't sow in boring rows like ordinary vegetables, but arrange in clumps throughout the garden as an accent plant. It will act also as a repellent to many garden pests, and will grow very compactly so that it won't be a bother. The stalks are silvery white and about ¾ inch in diameter. Depending on the variety, they will grow from 6 to 24 inches long.

Culture

A high-nitrogen fertilizer is in order for multiplier onions—unlike most onions—because you are harvesting the plant above ground rather than the root. Give multiplier onions a moderately rich soil if you want spectacular plants. I have seen second-year plants individually potted and displayed in greenhouses as exhibition plants; their appearance is so unusual and their size so startling (4 feet high) that they are a conversation piece even with the competition from other greenhouse plants.

They require little care and will self-seed readily. Let the plant do this work for you and transplant the young seedlings once they have reached 4–5 inches in height. This is another vegetable you will have to plant only once for a lifetime supply.

Since the growing season is long—about 120 days—fertilize once a month with a 10-10-5 side dressing in a circle around the clump. Water normally, but do not overdo it.

Good drainage, moreover, is essential to healthy plants.

Harvest

Some varieties will be described as 60 days to maturity, some as 120, and many others as somewhere in between. In practice, the only thing you need to know is that you can count on harvesting any variety you grow in at least 60 days.

To gather, pull an onion gently away from the others, using one hand to pull with and the other hand to hold the clump so that it is not uprooted. The remaining onions will go on growing and multiplying and will not be at all disturbed at the loss. If you don't need the whole onion, you can harvest just a few of the leaves, as if they were chives. I don't ever do this because it is so easy to grow chives for that purpose and I would rather wait and enjoy the scallion, but you can suit yourself. Different varieties will form a different number of whole stalks, but you can always count on several from each clump.

Divide the clumps every three or four years to keep them growing without overcrowding. Always let some go to seed for an additional crop.

Varieties

So many seedsmen carry these onions that you have a wide choice. Read the description in the catalog carefully; not all so-called bunching onions are multiplier onions. Look for descriptions that say "bulbless," "multiplying onions," "grows in clusters."

Among the catalogs that list true multiplier onions are Harris, Hudson, Seedway, Stokes, Nichols, Redwood City, Gurney's, Japonica, Kitazawa, Le Jardin, Hudson, Demonchaux, and DeGiorgi. There are probably others as well, so check your favorite catalog's index.

HOT PEPPERS   LA CHIAO   [*Capsicum frutescens*]

Although I would classify *sweet* peppers as a vegetable rather than as an herb, hot peppers, or chilis, are certainly never eaten as a vegetable—not even in China, where they are an essential ingredient in Hunan and Szechwan cookery. I have, therefore, put hot peppers where the Chinese would plant them, in the herb garden.

Pepper is so much a part of Oriental cuisine that it is necessary to differentiate these hot peppers which you can grow in your own garden from other Oriental peppers which you will encounter in Chinese grocery stores on the spice shelf. *Kinome*, for example, is Japanese pepper leaf and comes from a tree named the prickly ash, which is related to orange trees rather than to the *Capsicum* species. Szechwan peppercorn, hua chiao, is also a different pepper, not even related to our common black peppercorns. They are a very interesting spice. A Westerner's reaction on first eating a dish made with Szechwan peppercorns is usually one of disbelief. The first time I ate them in a Chinese dish, I had been warned what to expect, but my initial impression was that their spicy quality had been overrated; as I opened my mouth to say so I realized it had gone completely numb. This strange numbing effect is typical of Szechwan peppercorns, so that while they are not "hot" in the way of chili peppers, they contribute their own special quality to any dish in which they are used.

Chinese hot peppers are our own native American chilis which the Far East has taken as its own. They are not used in classic Cantonese or Mandarin cooking but are an authentic ingredient in dishes originating in many of the other Chinese cuisines. Native to America, they were discovered by Columbus in his search for a route to the Spice Islands of the East; he brought them back to Europe, where they were warmly received. Those indefatigable sailors and traders the Portuguese took them to India and Asia, where their use and culture spread so widely that for some time botanists thought these lands were their native habitat.

Hot peppers are expensive to buy—dried hot peppers cost over $5 a pound—but they are very easy and inexpensive to grow and take up little space in the home garden. The plants are very decorative and would be perfectly at home in the flower bed.

Culinary and other uses

While hot peppers must be used with discretion, they enhance a wide variety of dishes and are good to have on hand as a staple in the kitchen. They can be eaten both fresh and dried, and strings of dried red or green chilis hung from the kitchen ceiling are a gay—as well as practical—winter decoration.

Although many people are timid about "hot" foods and think they are bad for the digestion, there is increasing evidence to the contrary. Countries such as India which use large quantities of chilis have a lower than average incidence of heart and intestinal diseases. In the United States, research recently undertaken in Texas seems to indicate that chilis serve a useful function in the prevention of heart attacks through their ability to lower the fat levels in the blood; they also have a beneficial effect on circulation. Nutritionists have long known that chilis are very rich in Vitamins A and C, niacin, riboflavin, and thiamin, as well as many minerals. All in all, if you enjoy chilis, eat them with a clear conscience; they not only taste wonderful, they are good for you.

Many Americans are familiar with the name "chili"—mostly through chili con carne, although this popular dish is usually made with the mixture of spices known as chili powder rather than with whole chilis. Chili powder is said to have been the invention of a much-traveled Texan who hit upon that combination of spices in an effort to arrive at a curry powder that would taste like the curries he had enjoyed in India. The chili pepper in chili powder is usually cayenne; curry spice mixtures do include cayenne, but in addition they contain a large proportion of turmeric, the spice that gives curry its characteristic yellow color. The Texan never achieved curry powder but he rested well content with his labors, and created a dish which today is enjoyed throughout this hemisphere.

Although the Chinese do eat some curries, their chief use of chili peppers is to incorporate fresh or dried chilis directly into their cooked dishes.

A typical "hot" stir-fry dish, for instance, is made with thinly sliced beef, thinly sliced scallions, thinly sliced chili pepper (start with *one* the first time you make it), a minced slice of ginger, and snow peas. Stir-fry the beef in peanut oil for five minutes, then add the scallions, ginger, and chili pepper, plus a little soy sauce and a small amount of water. Stir-fry another minute and add the snow peas. Stir-fry one more minute, thicken the sauce with a little cornstarch, and serve with white rice cooked dry.

A spicy eggplant dish that is very good is made with roasted eggplant. Take the hot roasted eggplant out of its skin and combine with cut-up fresh tomatoes, green beans, one or two onions, peas, a couple of minced chilis, and three raw potatoes, cut up. Cook all together in a covered skillet with a little olive oil until the tomatoes are soft but not mushy. Salt to taste and serve hot or cold.

Chili peppers and scallions, thinly sliced and fried lightly in oil, make a delicious sauce for a hearty broiled fish (like mackerel). If the flavor is too strong for you, discard the peppers and scallions after frying and use just the oil to dress the fish. The result will be subtle but delicious and a savory bit of a puzzle to your guests.

If you make pickles, add a chili pepper to the jar when you put it away to "ripen"; remove the chili when serving the pickles.

Chili peppers can become as much of an addiction as garlic, so go easy on your guests if you have become used to eating this fiery herb; chances are they will like your favorite dishes a lot milder than you do.

Hot peppers and garlic whirled in a blender with plain water make a spray that will deter many insects when misted on the foliage of your plants; it will even discourage an occasional woodchuck. Organic gardeners swear by it.

Appearance

Peppers are so beautiful and graceful a plant that they used to be grown as ornamentals. Even today florists offer an "ornamental pepper" which is a popular houseplant. Since hot pepper plants are just as pretty as ornamental peppers, and edible too, why not grow them instead?

Peppers flower freely, with numerous white to greenish-white blossoms which are very decorative against the glossy, dark-green leaves. A pepper plant, like an orange tree (and many other vegetable plants), bears its flowers and fruits simultaneously; a bush full of pretty white flowers and peppers in various colors from green to yellow to red, hanging straight down in colorful profusion, is worthy of your patio or terrace.

When to plant

It is said that peppers should be started indoors in most sections of the country because they are so very sensitive to cold. As usual, I follow my own way, and though I start them in flats, I do so only when I can put them outdoors during the day. I just don't have room to start so many things indoors, and then to nurse them along for a month before the weather warms up.

Since peppers produce fruit very quickly, and since you can pick the fruit at any stage in its growth without waiting for maturity, I would rather save myself the bother of indoor seeding and settle for a slightly later crop than that of the gardener who has planted his seeds earlier. I usually can pick peppers as early as a month and a half after seeding them, and that is quite soon enough for even an impatient gardener.

They are strictly a warm-weather plant and will not tolerate the slightest frost.

How to plant

Seeds should be sown ¼ inch deep about 2 inches apart in a flat of Cornell Mix or some similar mixture. The seeds may be slow to germinate and you can speed up this step by starting them in Fertl Cubes—at least my experience has been that these cubes speed up germination incredibly. In fact, I couldn't believe how much difference the planting medium made, so I tried using Fertl Cubes for Konfrix carrots and curly parsley and they both germinated in barely a week (which is at least twice as fast as usual). The manufacturers make no such claim and I doubt if they even know about it unless they read this book. Of course, you will have to transplant the seedlings as soon as the first pair of true leaves appears; they can go into the flat at that point and you can proceed from there.

As soon as the seedlings are reasonably large and sturdy, and before they outgrow the flat and become leggy, transplant them in the ground or containers. In the ground, they should stand 18 to 24 inches between plants, in rows 24 to 36 inches apart. Two rows set out this way grow together without crowding, to make a very attractive mass, with flowers forming at the top and peppers hanging from every branch. Before putting the plants in place, dig a hole for each one, 6 inches deeper than the plants will be set. Fill with manure plus a cup of 10-10-10 fertilizer. Then fill the hole with regular garden soil.

Culture

Keep well watered. Fertilize when the blossoms first appear and every two weeks thereafter; pepper plants work hard and deserve to be fed generously. They respond very well to manure and a side dressing of 5-10-10. You may find you need to add extra nitrogen occasionally, but if you give too much nitrogen, you will have beautiful foliage but little fruit.

Weeds are no problem because the foliage is so thick it shades the ground under the plants and discourages weed growth.

Harvest

Hot peppers can be picked at almost any stage of their growth unless you want to dry them. For drying, peppers should be allowed to reach maturity. Once they reach maturity, pick them and the plants will continue to bear fruit for months.

Note: Do not rub your eyes before washing your hands when you have handled hot peppers; the capsicum, a volatile oil that makes them "hot," can irritate tender tissue.

Varieties

Most hot peppers turn red, though some, like Hungarian Wax, start out bright yellow rather than green. You can make your own tabasco or hot pepper sauce with the Tabasco pepper; the Jalapeno, one of the hottest, will bring tears to your eyes. All hot varieties are delicious and only experience will enable you to differentiate among them.

You will find at least one variety listed in almost every catalog, except the ones that offer only Oriental seeds. Look through several catalogs to get a wider selection. The smaller varieties are the ones grown in China and are the most decorative to dry.

DAY LILIES   GUM JUM   [*Hemerocallis fulva*]

The day lily owes its name to the fact that its flowers last only for a single day. The plants bloom so profusely, however, that many people don't realize this; during the long flowering season, a clump will always be a mass of blooms and only an observant gardener will notice that these are not the same flowers from one day to the next. Obviously, a plant with this habit of growth will produce an enormous number of buds, and the Chinese, who never waste anything edible, have learned to dry day-lily buds for a special out-of-season treat.

Day lilies are native to Asia, although it is sometimes difficult to remember this when all summer long the Connecticut countryside blooms with these beautiful flowers. Both day lilies and tiger lilies (another escapee) have acclimated themselves so successfully that they form large masses of wild lily plants wherever they are allowed to grow. Since they tolerate almost any soil, and grow in just about every part of America, they are easy to collect from the wild. If you have access to these "wild" lilies, transplant some to your own property or terrace. They will thrive equally well in city or country, wherever you choose to put them. Since they are so decorative, with a long blooming season that cheers up the dry, hot days of summer when other flowers are having hard going, they should be put in the flower garden rather than the vegetable garden. They do not need the regular care and attention that even the hardiest vegetable usually requires, and will thrive more on neglect than on coddling.

Once planted, a bed of day lilies will increase each year. The clumps can be easily divided to be planted elsewhere, and no matter how many you eat, there will soon be more than you can use.

The common day lily *(Hemerocallis fulva)* and the tiger lily *(Lilium tigrinum)* are the lilies most commonly found growing wild in the countryside. In addition, the Chinese use many other lilies, among them *H. minor, Funkia ovata* (Japanese day lily), and *H. aurantidca,* which is fragrant. They are all prepared in much the same way and used interchangeably in Oriental dishes.

Culinary and other uses

In the Orient the most esteemed part of the day lily is the bud, and the Chinese call dried lily buds golden needles—a term you will find

Day lilies   gum jum

among the list of ingredients required for many Chinese dishes. In the market, golden needles are usually offered in the form of a pressed, golden block which is cut to provide the number of ounces you require. If you prepare golden needles from your own garden, the dried buds can be stored, without pressing, in any container that will keep them from reabsorbing moisture. They are 2–3 inches long.

Tiger lilies are the variety usually used for golden needles, but lemon or other *Hemerocallis* species *(H. fulva,* for instance) can be used just as easily. My palate is not so sensitive as to differentiate among these, but perhaps you will be able to—just as a wine connoisseur can tell the different clarets.

Once dried, the buds will keep a long time. To use, soak in warm water for about thirty minutes. Squeeze dry, and cut into lengths the size of the meat and vegetables (all ingredients in Chinese cooking should be cut into similar sizes, and should be able to be eaten with chopsticks without using a knife). Dried lily buds are very nutritious, and you can gather buds all summer long without diminishing growth.

A typical Chinese dish combines mushrooms, shredded pork, scallions, and water chestnuts with dried day-lily buds. The harder bits of stem should be snapped off before the buds are added to the wok. Ingredients should be stir-fried in the order in which they will cook (foods which require longer cooking are put in first), then soy, cornstarch, sugar, and a little sesame oil for flavoring should be added along with a small amount of liquid—chicken broth, or fish broth preferably. Cover, and simmer for two to three minutes. Serve with rice.

For a Japanese dish, cook the buds, without drying, tempura-style. They should be picked when they are plump but before they begin to open.

Since day lilies bloom for a day, you will always have a fresh crop to pick and can serve them as often as you like. There seem to be more recipes for dried than for fresh buds, but once you have become accustomed to cooking them, you may find yourself making up new dishes for both forms.

The bulbs and young leaves of day lilies are also eaten in the Orient, but with so many other things to try, I have never gotten around to them. If they are in your garden, you can try out a recipe if you come upon one that appeals to you.

When to plant

If you order bulbs from the nursery, you will tend to get them either in the spring or fall. If you dig them from along the roadside, you can take them anytime, but they will be easiest to handle in the spring when the shoots are about 3 inches high. They aren't fussy about being moved; you won't have to treat them with any special care.

How to plant

You can naturalize day lilies, put them toward the back of a flower bed, or give them their own bed. As long as they are not in full shade or do not have wet feet, you can put them anywhere and they will reward you with a long season of continuous bloom. The bulbs should be set at the same level as they had been growing (you can tell by the shoots), or if you get them from the nursery, follow the instructions that come with them.

Culture

A little admiration occasionally is a good thing for man, beast, or plant; otherwise day lilies require no care. They dislike a rich soil, and the clumps will not need dividing more than every five years. Even then you don't *have* to divide them, but you will get even more handsome plants if you do.

Harvest

Pick the buds before they open—that's all.

Varieties

There are many Chinese and Japanese varieties. If you choose early, midsummer, and late varieties, you can have lilies in bloom from spring to late summer. The most traditional lily for the kitchen is, however, the day lily or the tiger lily, bought from a catalog or nursery, or collected from the wild. If you want to buy your lilies, look in the flower, not the vegetable, section of the seed catalogs. In addition to the regular seedsmen there are nurseries that specialize in lilies. Almost every catalog, except a strictly fruit or vegetable one, will include a few day lilies.

10 *The Chinese*
Water Garden

CHINESE LOTUS • WATER CHESTNUTS •

VIOLET-STEMMED TARO • ARROWHEAD

If you've always wanted a water garden but thought you didn't have the room, you will be happy to hear that you can have a perfectly beautiful one in an area no larger than a portable washtub—in fact, you can actually have one *in* a portable washtub. Furthermore, all these lovely water plants, exotic as a tropical island, are deliciously edible and are common, everyday vegetables in Oriental cuisine. So scale down your wistful vision of that never-to-be-had villa in Moa-Moa with its acre of water lilies and fan-tailed goldfish complete with a musical fountain that plays on sultry equatorial nights. When I promised you a water garden, what I had in mind is something you can have right here and now—even on a city terrace, a rooftop, or a back yard.

Once you have reconciled yourself to a more modest version, let me hasten to assure you that even your small washtub garden will be beautiful with that loveliest of lilies, the lotus; and while you may not see much open water, you will still have an unusual and almost completely carefree vegetable garden. It will be a delightful conversation piece, can be put in any sunny location you please—even moved around if need be—and will provide you with a good supply of fresh Chinese vegetables unavailable in your local produce market.

The effortless vegetable garden

You will find a water garden the easiest kind of gardening you have ever done. It is particularly good for the weekend—or just Saturday—gardener because it requires practically no upkeep. You don't have to plant seeds or nurse and transplant seedlings. You never have to water (unless your container needs topping up, which rarely happens). No matter how dry your summer, you never need to mulch; fertilizing is occasional and isn't dusty or messy. There are no weeds. If this sounds too good to be true, I must admit that there are very strict limits to the quantity of food you can grow by this method. On the other hand, these vegetables are all very choice—quite rare in the United States—and lend themselves to a great variety of uses in the kitchen; they are quick and easy to prepare. Water vegetables are tasty, both raw and cooked, and will contribute a great deal to your table.

Sources of plants

Water plants are available as plants rather than as seeds. Since they are all grown in water, they are not available from your regular seedsmen but will have to be ordered from water gardens specializing in this kind of plant material. There are a number of these "farms" in California, Florida, Maryland, New Jersey, and other states; I have listed a few in the Appendix and you will undoubtedly come upon others. All those I have been in touch with have been very helpful. They are used to beginners and patient with them, and completely reliable. If you have a choice, order from the source nearest you; traveling is harder on water plants than on other types of plants. If you live near enough so that you can visit your supplier, even better. A visit to a water garden is well worth a day's outing. This is not, however, practical for everyone.

Some water-garden suppliers will be a little baffled at the thought of growing these plants for food. Others are completely familiar with this use of their plants and can pass on the experiences of other water-garden farmers. In any event, do not hesitate to ask them for help or advice. Plan your water garden far enough ahead so that you will have time to ask and get answers to all your questions. The catalogs—with their full-color photographs of dozens of varieties of water lilies—are very tempting.

Size of the water garden

The first step is to decide how large a water garden you want. It can be as small as a 25-gallon container or as large as the in-the-ground pond we imagined at the beginning of the chapter. Or it could be something in between, such as several 25-gallon tubs artistically deployed over a large patio. The room you have and your enthusiasm for this project are the only limits; water gardens are as individual as vegetable plots and you should suit them to your own needs and preference.

An informal water vegetable garden

I would suggest that your first water garden be a small, very limited project. This will give you a chance to see how you like water gardening, whether you have a wet green thumb, and whether you want to grow these particular vegetables. I should warn you, however, that water gardening tends to be addictive; one small tub is likely to grow into a much more elaborate project. Water gardening looks so hard and is actually so easy that the temptation is to undertake a little more each year. Since you are growing edible water plants, there isn't too much danger that you will be inundated with your crops—the danger is that you will be led to overplanting through companion gardening, combining edible with inedible but irresistibly beautiful lilies—a pleasant sort of problem to contemplate but not the subject of this book. As to your edible garden, chances are you will never grow more than you can eat; if you do, all of these vegetables freeze easily and well.

No matter whether you choose a container garden or an in-the-ground pond, you should consult the water-garden sources you are dealing with to check out your plants. They will be able to advise you as to what will work best for your climate and conditions, what kind of containers are available, how much they cost, and what you will need for the garden you have in mind. If you are completely at sea, they will even plan a complete container or pond garden for you. If you prefer to do it all yourself, you will certainly find it much easier than planning the usual vegetable garden.

Container water gardens

Container gardening—whether flowers, vegetables, or fruits—is the modern way to garden. Water gardening is especially well suited to containers. By this we mean not only enclosing the body of water in a container, but also potting each plant or clump of plants in an individual container within the large original container.

Water container gardening is especially simple. The only absolutely essential element required, once the water environment has been stabilized, is full sun. Occasional fertilizing takes care of the feeding (except for the goldfish), and even that is easier than the side dressing required by conventional gardens.

SITING. Water gardening offers the same flexibility in siting as other forms of container gardening; a rooftop, a terrace, a small balcony are all good sites. A sun deck, front doorstep, or breezeway will be immediately enhanced. In-the-ground gardens are often container gardens as well, as we shall see later on in this chapter.

CONTAINERS. Anything that will hold water and is big enough for what you want to grow can be used as a container. Plastic or glavanized-iron containers are usually recommended (although an occasional water-garden expert will frown on metal containers). These can be set inside more decorative containers, such as a half-barrel, for instance, if you feel they are not sufficiently decorative in themselves. Something as simple as a washtub or a child's wading pool works surprisingly well. Water-garden suppliers have all sizes of tubs as well as a number of free-form pools, so you don't have to hunt around if you don't want to. Their prices are reasonable and their advice is free.

I have an old galvanized-iron washtub that I picked up years ago in our local discount store; it has proved to be one of the most useful purchases I have ever made. It started out doing duty as a swimming pool for a couple of wood turtles which wandered across the lawn early one evening when we were having dinner on the porch. My husband, who is very fond of turtles, raced out the door to capture them (turtles move faster than you think when they want to). He built them a fenced-in pen, complete with a sunning rock, greenery, and washtub pool.

After we lost our turtles to some gourmet raccoons, the tub became a container garden, and successively grew beautiful, superproductive crops of peanuts, sweet potatoes, and Chinese flowering cabbages. It is still in good condition, just the thing for a small water garden. A can of spray paint keeps the outside in harmony with its surroundings and the two side handles make it especially easy to move around as landscaping inclinations change.

If I wanted to use the tub as an in-the-ground pond, it would fit comfortably into a small hole dug in the lawn; the edges could be hidden with a little soil and suitable plantings. Or I could make it part of a small Japanese garden, with raked sand or gravel and an ornamental rock or two. The possibilities of water container gardening are obviously limited only by your own imagination.

In-the-ground water gardens

If you have the room and the site, you may prefer a permanent pool for your Chinese water garden. Although there are winter-hardy water plants, these vegetables are not among them, and if you live in an area where the temperatures go below freezing, an in-the-ground water garden of edible plants will be more work than a tub garden. The plants will probably need to be lifted and stored over the winter, or possibly the pond can be winterized with a cover plus deep mulch.

If your in-ground garden is large enough, you can combine the edible water plants with winter-hardy and inedible but beautiful lilies, simply removing the tender ones for winter storage. This task is greatly simplified by planting all material in individual containers. The hardy container plants will stay; the tender ones will lift right out without arduous digging. Your pond will appear undisturbed and in the spring the edible plants can be put back in place with comparatively little bother.

SITING.   Siting a permanent pond must be done more carefully than placing a container that can be moved if you should change your mind. If you are unsure of your own ability to integrate this feature into your present plan, you may wish to consult with a landscape architect. If you feel you can do it yourself, make rough sketches (you don't have to be an artist for these) of different sites to help you get the feel of them.

In siting a permanent pond, it is important to take into account how your present plantings will look when they mature several years from now. A small tree that grows into a large one can turn a sunny site into a shady dell. Think also of the use of the area around the pond; a pond is a pleasant place for contemplation—it is not at its best next to the tennis court.

An in-the-ground water garden doesn't have to be so magnificent that it would be out of place on a small suburban property. It can be as charming as a small woodland pool or as formal as a Japanese garden— all in very little space. Water gardening is what you make it; whatever suits your life-style can be created with very little fuss.

If you are averse to preformed plastic ponds because you think of them as unsightly, with an exposed rim, this is not a problem. The prefabricated ponds are especially designed to be hidden; you can finish off the sides just as you would a completely natural pond. Surround the edges with plantings, build a path, add a rim of gravel. The plastic rim can be completely concealed and is not in any way objectionable. No one dislikes plastic more than I, but even I must admit it has its uses; this is clearly one of them.

Individual containers

Within your main container—whether your garden is in or out of the ground—you now fit individual containers, each one holding one plant or clump of plants. Ideally, these should be plastic; clay pots will soon sour your soil and are generally to be avoided. The plastic pots used for water gardens are shaped somewhat differently from those you use for house plants; they are shaped for greater stability and may be perforated throughout their side surfaces so that water can move freely in and out of the pot. You can best obtain the correct type of container from your water-garden source; the pots are inexpensive and long-lasting.

Square containers take up less room than round containers and can be used for all plants except the lotus, the root of which grows in circles and therefore requires a round container.

The cost involved in planning a water garden using separate containers can be estimated from the following prices listed by one of the water garden suppliers. These prices are, of course, subject to change, and they do not include everything you would need, but they certainly show that a water garden need not be an expensive undertaking.

	DIAMETER	DEPTH	PRICE
Multi-purpose planter:	20″	10″	$ 10–12
Plastic pots:	12″	3″	1.00
	15″	8½″	3.50

If you prefer you can, of course, eliminate individual containers and fill your tub or pond with sufficient soil in which to grow your plants. However, modern water gardening leans toward the use of containers for both tubs and in-the-ground ponds. There are a number of reasons for this preference:

LESS SOIL NEEDED.   Individual containers require much less soil than would be needed if you had to cover the entire bottom to a sufficient depth.

CLEARER WATER.   A muddy bottom tends to make for murky water, especially since the ecology of water plants requires fish, and their movement tends to raise the mud. Fish like to dart in and out of the mud, stirring it up even more.

GREATER FLEXIBILITY.   It is much easier to make changes when all you have to do is lift out a container. Water plants in a muddy bottom require wading into the pond and digging everything out. Even a small tub is much harder to change around if the plants are buried directly in a muddy bottom.

EASIER CLEANING.   Even the most carefully planned water garden may need an occasional cleaning. With container gardening, the individual containers can be set aside; moving buried plants or trying to clean around them would be quite a chore.

EASIER WINTERIZING.   If you live in a climate where the temperature drops below freezing—and this includes most of the United States—you must take out your plants for the winter; it is simple and easy with containers. Removing buried plants might damage the roots and would be much more difficult.

All things considered, I would tend to recommend water gardening in containers. When you become expert in this type of gardening, you may have your own reasons for changing over to direct planting in soil; for a start, stick to containers.

Note: Redwood discolors the water and should not be used either for the main tub or the individual pots. If you like the looks of redwood, use it as an additional container to surround your plastic or metal main container.

Soil

Although I am a firm believer in using Cornell Mix for most container gardening, this is one situation in which it wouldn't work. Water gardens require a good, standard garden potting soil. This means plain potting soil; do not use soil that is mixed with peat moss or manure. If it is clayey, so much the better. Mix half a pot of this soil with the fertilizer specifically recommended for water gardens (available from your supplier) and put this mixture in the bottom half of your pot. Add another quarter-pot of plain soil so that the pot is about three-quarters full of soil. To keep the soil from washing out of the pot, cover the top with ½ inch of gravel, sand, or burlap. This is the basic procedure for potting all water plants. Specific cultural directions, where they differ from this, are given under each vegetable.

SOP

Every kind of gardening has a few terms peculiar to it; water gardening is no exeption. One of the terms you must understand is SOP, which stands for "submerged oxygenating plants." You cannot have a successful water garden without including some SOP to maintain clean water and a healthful environment. SOP consumes most of the carbon dioxide in the water and helps control algae by absorbing the mineral salts in the water. The plants also provide a friendly spot for fish who depend on them for refuge (mature fish, eggs, and fry) and for the oxygen they produce under the water. If you have a muddy bottom, you can plant SOP just by dropping the cuttings into the pond—it's that easy. If you are using containers, the SOP should be planted one-third deep in the center of the container. Recommended rate of planting is two bunches per one 7- or 12-inch-diameter pot, 3 to 5 inches deep. Since you should allow approximately one bunch for every 2 square feet of water surface, you can easily figure out what your particular garden requires. In larger ponds the requirements may be somewhat different and you would want to check this out with your garden adviser.

Fish and snails

In addition to SOP you have to add two other things to your water garden to keep it in proper balance: fish and snails.

Fish act as natural insecticides, eating aphids, mosquito larvae, and other insects which come within their reach. A small tub, with two bunches of SOP, will do well with just two 4–5-inch fish. These can be goldfish or Japanese koi (a decorative small carp). Consult your local fish supplier for breeds and types of fish, but be sure to tell him they are for outdoor use and get instructions for feeding them and the food at the same time. You may find an aquarium store is not equipped to deal with outdoor lily ponds and so forth, in which case your water-garden supplier is; you can order from him.

In severe winters you may want to take a few of the goldfish indoors to seed next year's pond. Goldfish are, however, amazingly hardy; I know of some ordinary aquarium goldfish which were dumped into a shallow pond and have, so far, successfully survived and bred through several unusually cold Connecticut winters.

Water lilies

Unlike the lilies of the field, water lilies do toil and spin—or at least they serve a useful and practical function as well as looking beautiful and being edible. One medium to large water lily should be included for every square yard of surface area in your pond. Since the Chinese lotus requires a fairly large area all its own, small ponds might have to settle for a purely ornamental (and inedible) variety. The lily pads keep oxygen in the water; the oxygen collects on the underside of the pads and is prevented from escaping into the air. Oxygen, in turn, helps maintain the proper water temperature and supports the ecological balance in other ways.

Controlling algae

Up to now we have been talking about things to include in your water garden; algae are something to exclude as much as possible.

Algae are airborne in the form of spores and will begin growing in any body of water that is congenial to them as soon as the weather gets warm. Since they turn the water green, which is considered unattractive, you will want to do whatever is necessary to keep your water sparkling-clear and algae-free. This is not difficult, but timing is important. At the first sign of green water—particularly liable to occur in the early weeks after planting—treat the water with a special preparation which water-garden suppliers sell for this purpose. Repeat whenever necessary to keep the water clear. Incidentally, if you have a natural pond on your property that is unsightly with algae, you can clear that up at the same time.

CHINESE LOTUS   OU   [*Nelumbium nucifera*]

With water lilies, there is considerable confusion in nomenclature; the emphasis tends to be on names and colors, rather than on species. In addition, there are several species which are called either Egyptian lotus or sacred lotus, and this confusion extends throughout the considerable literature on the subject. Most of them are not what I think of as the true Egyptian lotus *(Nymphoea)*, which has an entirely different appearance from the Chinese sacred lotus. The *Nymphoea* lotus has narrow white petals and has been represented in Egyptian art and architecture from earliest times. The *Nelumbium* or Chinese lotus has much wider petals and at one stage of the

Chinese lotus   ou

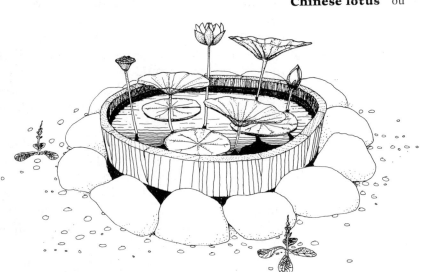

blossoming looks almost like a rose. Both kinds have grown wild in Egypt, so that accounts for some of the confusion.

So far as I have been able to discover, however, all lotuses are edible, so you won't run into any serious difficulty if you order the wrong one. Even our native American lotus *(Nelumbium lutea)* is edible, and was known and used by the American Indians. Specify that you want the *edible Chinese lotus;* you will stand a fair chance of getting what you have in mind, no matter how it is described in the catalog.

From a culinary standpoint, the species which I have named in Latin at the head of this section is considered the most desirable. Refer to the Latin name when ordering; the nurseryman will know what you mean and will tell you if he doesn't carry it. As far as I know all the water gardens I have listed in the Appendix do have this variety.

Since ancient times the lotus has been revered throughout the Near East, India, and the Far East. It is a symbol of purity because it rises from the mud and is undefiled; as such it has been incorporated into the religions of many countries. Some readers will be familiar with the "lotus position," which is the sitting position in which Buddhists meditate, with the legs crossed and each foot, sole turned upward, resting on the opposing thigh. Statues of Buddha frequently show him in this position. It is still used today as a position for meditation, although it is a difficult position to achieve; it has the advantage of being one of the few upright positions in which you can fall asleep without falling over.

In ancient China the lotus was a symbol of female beauty; the bound feet of highborn Chinese women were called golden lilies, after the lotus flower. In spite of this, it would be an excellent flower for the women's liberation movement to adopt since it is the symbol of the only woman to be found among the Eight Immortals of the Chinese—her name is Ho-hsien-ku.

Because the lotus displays all three stages of growth—bud, flower, and seed pod—simultaneously, it is symbolic of the past, the present, and the future. This is sometimes illustrated in Japanese flower arrangements, with the past represented by a leaf that is past its prime or even decayed or worm-eaten, the present by a perfect leaf and flower, the future by a bud. If you attempt this for a flower-show exhibition, be sure the judges are well informed enough to know that the decayed leaf is an intentional part of the arrangement or you are liable to receive a scathing comment on your carelessness, instead of a blue ribbon.

Culinary and other uses

All parts of the lotus are edible and can be eaten raw or cooked. The young leaves (preferably only a few gathered from each shoot) can be added to a salad. They can also be briefly simmered, tossed with sesame oil, and served as a green vegetable. The petals may be floated in clear consommé or cold fruit soup or used as a garnish for salads. To enjoy these out of season, dry them like day-lily buds (don't attempt to dry the lotus bud). The seeds can be dried and eaten out of hand like sunflower seeds or, in traditional Japanese fashion, pickled. Pickled lotus seeds are a classic ingredient in stir-fry dishes.

The root is by far the most widely used part of the vegetable. It is called *lin ngau* in Chinese; its Japanese name is *hasunone*. It is easily recognizable in any dish because of the characteristic pattern the air channels form when the root is sliced; the flowerlike pattern appeals especially to the Japanese, who consider the appearance of their food just as important as its taste. Even when the sliced root is dipped in batter and fried as tempura, the pattern is clearly visible. Combined with shrimp, snow peas, and mushrooms, lotus root makes a quick but elegant company dish.

If you like sweet and sour pork, try adding sliced lotus root the next time you make it; the sauce is particularly compatible with this fascinating vegetable.

Once you have acquainted yourself with the flavor, you will undoubtedly think of many ways to use it, and I predict it will soon be as popular in your kitchen as in an Oriental one.

Note: Do not be afraid that eating the lotus root will make you sleepy. The lotus of Greek mythology and of Tennyson's famous poem is not this water lily but a tree whose fruit is called by the delightful name "jujube." According to Greek mythology, eating the fruit of this tree caused you to while away your days in dreamy languor, forgetful of family, friends, and home. Fortunately (or unfortunately, as the case may be), the lotus lily does not have this effect.

Lotus seed pods are traditionally dried and used for flower arrangements, where they are highly regarded. This handsome plant material is very striking in appearance, and if you have grown tired of peacock feathers, you could do worse than replace them with a few of these unusual decorations. Once dried they keep indefinitely as long as the atmosphere is not too humid. An example of the length of time they remain viable was strikingly illustrated just recently when a Japanese horticulturist, living in Washington, D.C., succeeded in germinating a two-thousand-year-old lotus seed. So when you have tired of your lotus-seed-pod decoration or flower arrangement, don't throw away the seeds—your great-grandchildren might like to plant them.

All in all, if you grow this showy flower and delicious vegetable, the problem will be not how to use it but how to grow enough for all the uses to which you will wish to put it.

Appearance

The lotus lily is an exceptionally beautiful plant, among the loveliest of water lilies. The lily pads are a silvery blue-green and rise well above the water; the flowers grow even higher. Buds take three days to open fully in a fascinating progression of development; they follow the sun during the day and close at night. Seed-pod formation begins after the third day.

Lotus lilies are perennials and, with proper care, will give you years of pleasure—if you can keep from eating them all up.

Culture

The lotus tuber looks something like a reddish-brown banana joined in segments like a string of sausages (a mixed-up description, but apt), and the flesh is light orange.

When you receive it from the water-garden supplier, there will usually be one or more shoots already growing straight up, at right angles to the root. The roots, incidentally, are shipped only from April to June, so get your order in early.

Plant the tuber horizontally, with the sprouts pointing upward, at a slight angle; the end opposite the section with the sprouts should slant slightly downward. Plant it 2 inches deep; the growing tips should stand about ¼ inch above the surface soil in the container. Your container must be round, because lotus roots grow in a circle; if the root were to encounter the corner of a square container, it might die. The minimum-size container to use for a single lotus root is a bushel—or 25 gallons. Fill it with potting soil and fertilizer, as recommended for all water vegetables in this chapter.

A single lotus root can grow as large as 4 feet long and 3 inches in diameter if you let it.

Once the root is planted, fertilize monthly during its growing season (approximately April to September).

Chinese lotus should be grown in full sun. The more sun, the more freely it will flower. Less than full sun will give you some flowers but it will not make the glorious show of which it is capable.

Each water plant has its own requirements as to depth of water in which it grows best. The lotus container should be placed (within the water container) so that there are at least 6 but not more than 10 inches of warm water above the soil line. Do not place in cold water or in a situation where the water will get very cold. Once the plants are established, they will tolerate colder water, but they should not have to start their growth under stress.

The lotus will be set the deepest of your water vegetables, so your main water container need not be any deeper than is necessary to accommodate the lotus. If you are growing it in a pond or in a container that is deeper than this, put some sort of support—a rock, another pot, or something similar—under your lotus pot to raise it to the right height. In a muddy bottom, you may have to build up the soil in that area to achieve the same result. This is another good reason for using containers; it is much easier to set containers at different depths than to create a pond bottom of different depths.

Harvest

The lotus makes a vegetable with a long harvest season because it bears buds, flowers, and seed pods all at the same time, allowing it to be put to many uses simultaneously. Gather whatever part you want, as soon as it is ready. The roots can be harvested at the end of their growing season (usually September), but it is not necessary to use the entire root; take the last segment and the rest of the root can be put aside for next spring's plantings. If you have let your root grow to its full 4 feet, you can take several segments, either to plant or to eat. If you break them apart before storing, you will find shoots growing from each segment by the time you come to plant them in the spring (if, of course, they have been stored properly).

If you want to grow new plants from seeds, it is a very slow process but a most interesting project.

Winter storage

If the roots are liable to freeze if left in the water garden, lift them to store over the winter.

This is a very simple procedure. The lotus lily will go dormant as the cold weather approaches and should then be removed from its container and buried in a container of damp sand—a small carton or wooden box is easily obtained and should be lined with plastic. Keep this container where it will not freeze but will stay cool enough to keep the root dormant and prevent it from starting to grow again; it needs its rest. If the only suitable spot you have is outdoors, protect it with sufficient covering and mulch to keep it from freezing. Usually, even in an apartment, you can find a cool corner—perhaps in the back of a closet—which will have the space required. In many parts of the United States, winter storage can take place right in the water garden; lotus lilies are not winter-hardy but they are not as delicate as they look.

Varieties

A water-garden catalog with its beautiful photographs in full color will tell you more at a glance than any description I could write. Send for a couple to brighten a dreary January afternoon.

In addition to the lovely Chinese lotus offered by most water-garden suppliers, look for the new Japanese dwarf lotus which can be grown in a 10-inch pot. This will not, naturally, produce much of a crop because the root will be small too. It might, however, make it possible for you to grow a lotus where otherwise you would have to do without.

WATER CHESTNUTS   SUI MATAI

[*Eleocharis dulcis*]

Almost anyone who has ever eaten or prepared Chinese food knows about water chestnuts. Every supermarket carries them canned and packed in water, and people who prepare their own Chinese dishes frequently buy a can because the recipe calls for them. Unfortunately, canned water chestnuts, like so many other canned foods, are only a pale version of the real thing; both crispness and flavor suffer in the canning process. With an edible water garden, you can have all the fresh water chestnuts you choose to grow. They are an exceptionally easy crop and multiply rapidly so that you will be constantly replenishing your original plants.

In China water chestnuts have been eaten for many centuries. They are sometimes grown in rice paddies, since they do not interfere with the rice plants; they are also grown in large tanks as a single crop.

Culinary and other uses

Water chestnuts are prized for two characteristics: their nutty flavor and their crispness. They can be eaten both raw and cooked, but if cooked, should be added toward the end of preparation so that they do not lose their crispness.

Slice water chestnuts thin and add them to a tossed salad along with radishes and cucumbers; it makes one of the best salads ever. (The chestnuts should be peeled before slicing.)

A good stir-fry vegetarian dish combines sliced water chestnuts with mushrooms, bamboo shoots, snow peas, bean sprouts, scallions, and taro root. All the ingredients should be either sliced or cut into small pieces so that they can cook quickly; the whole dish won't take more than five minutes, including the gravy made with stock, soy sauce, and cornstarch. If you like a hotter version, add a chili pepper and some grated fresh ginger. For meat eaters, shredded chicken or pork can be cooked first and then the vegetables added.

A clear soup garnished with a few thin slices of water chestnut becomes an authentic beginning to a Chinese meal—although it would do just as well as a starter for a roast beef dinner. If you like creamed vegetables, combine water chestnuts and celery in cream sauce. A popular Chinese dish with a sweet-and-sour sauce (rice vinegar and sugar) includes water chestnuts along with bell peppers, celery, bamboo shoots, and Chinese cabbage. Like most Chinese recipes, cooking time—once the vegetables are prepared—is about six minutes. Water chestnuts are also a good ingredient to include in egg-roll stuffing because they stay crisp even if you make the egg rolls ahead of time and freeze them for later use.

In China, water-chestnut flour is a valued cooking ingredient, but I don't think you will grow enough of your own chestnuts to use them in this way.

Appearance

The value of water chestnuts in a mixed water garden (aside from being good eating) is the contrast of their foliage with other water-plant foliage. Water chestnuts belong to the sedge family and do not have recognizable leaves (at least not leaves that look like leaves). Their leaves resemble coarse chives (the common, not the Oriental variety). Both leaves and stems are erect, like rushes, in tubular clumps of green quills. Water chestnuts are not, of course, true nuts; they are edible roots with a distinctly nutty flavor, especially when freshly gathered.

The chestnuts themselves form in the mud at the base of the stem. When fully mature, they are about the size of a walnut, although the canned ones are usually much smaller. They are covered with a tough brown skin which should be peeled for eating purposes. Once peeled, store them in water in the refrigerator; the white flesh will discolor quickly if left exposed to air. If you need to keep them more than a day, change the water every twenty-four hours.

Culture

Since water chestnuts are members of the sedge family, they are bog plants; their containers should be set shallowly in your water container. The water surface should stand no more than 3 to 5 inches above the soil surface of the container. Individual planters can range in size from 7 inches in diameter and 5 inches deep to 20 inches in diameter and 10 inches deep, depending on how many plants you want to grow and what you want to grow with them. They combine well with most other water plants, including the lotus.

Use the standard soil mixture recommended at the beginning of the chapter.

Harvest

Water chestnuts mature in about six months but can be gathered much sooner if your growing season is not that long or if you will settle for smaller "nuts."

A 25-gallon container will produce about thirty to forty mature chestnuts; smaller containers will produce proportionately fewer.

Winter storage

In climates where roots would freeze under water, they must be stored over the winter. Remove the roots from the water (in their containers) and store in a cool, moist, shady place. The pots should be laid on their sides. Check every so often to be sure the soil has not dried out.

VIOLET-STEMMED TARO   WOO CHAI

[Xanthosoma violacea]

This lovely water plant originated in tropical America. It early spread to Africa and then to Asia, where it escaped to ponds and waterways; it is now an essential ingredient in authentic Oriental cuisine.

You will sometimes find other roots called taro, and this can be especially confusing because they too are used in Oriental cookery. If you grow your own, you will at least know which one you are eating. In the Caribbean and other places, violet-stemmed taro is also known as primrose malanga, Indian kale, and yautia. In looking for recipes in any English-language cookbook, you will have to check all those names in the index; they are used even in some Chinese cookbooks prepared for Americans.

The Chinese name which I have given above, woo chai, is also used for *Colocasia esculenta*.

Culinary and other uses

You can find taro root in the fresh-produce department of markets which cater to Spanish and Chinese consumers. The root is about the size of a large white potato, brownish with a rough, thick skin. It is not particularly attractive—like so many delectable root vegetables—but it is a culinary surprise in the kitchen, where it turns into a delicious vegetable which many gourmets consider far superior to our white potato.

Before I tell you how taro is used in Chinese cuisine, I must tell you of my first conscious experience with it; "conscious" because it was the first time I had knowingly eaten it although I had undoubtedly had it many times before and not known what it was. It was the time my husband brought home a couple of pounds of these strange-looking roots and asked if I would make them as a vegetable with our baked chicken dinner. I said I would if he could tell me how to cook them—and he did. They were scrubbed with a brush and tucked in a corner of the oven to bake along with the chicken. An hour later (it was a small chicken), both were done and we broke open the taro roots, put in a pat of butter, and tasted. They were delicious, really *good*, and that is the opinion of someone who loves white potatoes. I subsequently discovered that I could use any potato recipe, substituting taro, with good results. They are especially tasty in a good rich stew.

To serve them as an Oriental dish, peel, slice, and cook until tender. Meanwhile make a dressing in your blender of toasted sesame seeds, rice vinegar, and a little sugar. Add enough water to make it slightly liquid, heat, and pour over the hot cooked taro.

A very popular taro dish is made with coconut milk, eggs, sugar, taro root, and lime juice. If you would like to try it, follow any standard custard recipe, adding ½ cup mashed taro to three eggs.

Don't forget, also, to try taro pancakes. Make them just like potato pancakes; they are especially good with a spoonful of yogurt over them.

Appearance

The violet-stemmed taro is grown ornamentally in this country, mostly for its unusual foliage. The large arrow-shaped blue-green leaves have violet edges. They grow 5 to 7 inches in length on beautiful violet stems which rise about 2 feet above the water. The mid-ribs and the veins underneath the leaves are also violet. This particular taro rarely flowers, but the foliage is a picture in itself.

Culture

Taro is a bog plant, like the water iris, and should have no more than 3 to 6 inches of water above its soil line. This means that you may have to prop up your taro pot in most water containers to bring it to the proper depth.

The number of taro roots you can put in your plastic pot depends entirely upon the size of the pot. You should put only one root in a 7-inch-diameter pot that is 5 inches deep. A pot that is 19 inches in diameter and 9 inches deep would hold six roots. If more than one root is put in a pot, they should be spaced evenly apart.

Use the standard soil and fertilizer mixture recommended in the beginning of the chapter unless your water-garden supplier gives other instructions.

Harvest

The foliage will die down in the fall. Harvest the roots then; they are as mature as they will get that season. If you wish to eat most of the roots, save the small offsets for next spring's plants.

To store in cold climates, remove the pots (with the offsets in them) from the container and turn them on their sides in a cool, moist, shady place—a cellar is fine. It is important not to let the roots dry out, so check every so often to be sure the soil is moist.

In the spring, when the water warms up, put the pots back in the water container and you are all set for another season.

If you have not eaten all the roots, they may have become too big to continue growing in their original pots, and in that case they should be repotted.

ARROWHEAD   CHEE KOO   [*Sagittaria sagittifolia*]

Arrowhead is a beautiful bog plant native to temperate regions throughout the world. Oriental arrowhead is called chee koo in China, *kuwai* in Japan. It is much more widely used in Japan but also has its place in Chinese cuisine.

Arrowhead   chee koo   **water chestnuts**   sui matai
Chinese lotus   ou
violet-stemmed taro   woo chai

American arrowhead, *Sagittaria latifolia,* is native to North America, and was known and eaten by the Indians long before Europeans came to this hemisphere. It closely resembles the Oriental variety and served the North American Indians as a starchy vegetable, in place of the white potato, which they did not know. Lewis and Clark mention it in their journals as "a principal article of traffic" among the Indians they encountered. It was gathered by the Indian women, who would wade into the water, feel around in the mud with their toes until they encountered the tubers, and free them. As the tubers were released from the pond bottom, they would float up to the surface, where they were easily gathered by the men waiting in canoes.

Culinary and other uses

Only the roots, or corms, of this plant are eaten. They are not edible raw but are easy to cook. They can be roasted like a potato, or boiled. When boiled, they can then be used in many recipes.

The flesh is cream-colored and similar in flavor to a very delicate, slightly nutty sweet potato; unlike a sweet potato, it also makes a good cooked salad. It is one of the ingredients—along with burdock, lotus root, mushrooms, bamboo shoots, and other vegetables—which make up the festive New Year's dish of Japan known as *umani* or Ten-Ingredient Dish. The recipe is complicated and I wouldn't attempt to describe it here, but you can easily find it in a complete Japanese cookbook.

A simple way to prepare arrowhead is to boil it until tender, slice it thin, and serve with butter or sesame oil. If any should be left over, unbuttered, serve cold with a vinaigrette dressing for a luncheon side dish.

This is an easy vegetable to combine with familiar dishes, and the imaginative cook will find it a welcome addition to the culinary repertoire.

The American arrowhead is somewhat nuttier in flavor than the Oriental but not so much so that it will affect the authenticity of your Chinese dishes.

Appearance

Arrowhead is so pretty that it is grown in this country primarily as an ornamental. Once you have eaten it, however, you will want to grow it as a vegetable as well.

The graceful leaves are shaped like our American Indian arrowheads, hence the name. They grow approximately 24 inches long.

The three-petaled white flowers are very lovely, with pronounced golden-yellow centers. They grow on long stems and make very showy spikes which stand out among the dark-green foliage. In the Northeast the American arrowhead blooms in July and is easily spotted along the banks of streams and rivers.

There is no appreciable difference between the American and Japanese, or Oriental, arrowhead, but if you want to be authentic, order from your supplier by the Latin name. If only the American variety is available, however, you will find it most satisfactory. If you live in the country, you can gather the corms of the American variety yourself and transfer them to your own water garden with very little difficulty.

The corms themselves will be gray or yellowish-gray.

Culture

Like so many water plants and root vegetables, arrowhead is a rampant grower. You will have to repot it every year or it will become pot-bound after the first season. Of course, if you use a great many of the corms in the kitchen, you will have to make a point of setting some aside for next year's crop. If you find this difficult, plant more next year.

Since arrowhead is a bog plant, set it no more than 3 to 6 inches below the surface of the water. Plant more sparsely than other bog plants to allow room for the growth of the roots. Plant a maximum of one plant to a 7-inch-diameter, 5-inch-deep pot; 6 plants to a 19-inch-diameter, 9-inch-deep pot.

Harvest

If your main container is large enough so that the water does not freeze solid and the mud does not freeze at all, arrowhead will winter over very successfully. It is best, however, to check this with your supplier, because the plants he sends you may have been grown under milder conditions and not be as hardy as they might be otherwise.

Like so many root vegetables, arrowhead can be harvested all year around. You never need to worry about storing it; just gather it when the menu calls for it.

PART TWO

_____

Container Gardening

with

Chinese

Vegetables

11 *What You Need to Know to Garden in Containers*

Container gardening is a leisure activity that not only costs you practically nothing to start with, but actually ends up paying you to do it. And you don't have to change into tennis clothes, lug skis, or travel to the shore—it's something you can enjoy right in your own home, whether on a city windowsill or a country terrace. In addition, as we will see, container gardening with Chinese vegetables is even more practical, easier, and more fun than growing ordinary vegetables.

Why garden in containers?

Container gardening is very different from in-the-ground gardening. I have known many container gardeners who had always hated the necessary but tedious chores connected with an in-the-ground garden—rototilling, tiptoeing through muddy soil to check on seedlings, tonging slugs off the marigolds, devising traps for rabbits, woodchucks, and even deer. Nor did they look forward to the annual fall cleanup, when the vegetables have slowed down and the weeds have speeded up. Container gardening eliminates all of these chores. It has proved so efficient that many gardeners with more than enough space for an in-the-ground garden have switched to growing their vegetables in raised beds.

In container gardening, the space between rows of plants is never compacted by being walked on, weeds are almost nonexistent, and many pests are eliminated. It is comparatively effortless, and your plants are right within view—a feast for the eyes as well as the palate.

Also, and not to be minimized, there are the conversational advantages. Once you have taken visitors on a tour of your in-the-ground garden, all but the most dedicated fellow gardeners will be happy to return to the screened porch and talk of other things. A container garden, on the other hand, seems to be endlessly fascinating even to the nongardener. Sitting in a living-room window and looking out on a terrace brilliant with peppers, yellow cucumber blossoms, and gleaming white eggplant on lavender-flowered bushes, the conversation turns effortlessly from crime in the streets to "How on earth do you grow those things?" And, amazingly enough, the inquirer seems to really want to know. A sunny window shaded by the snow peas growing to the top of the frame and covered with sweet-pea flowers and beautiful green pods does wonders for everything from a cocktail party to a dinner for two. I'm not suggesting you take up container gardening in order to improve the tone of your social gatherings—but it's a fringe benefit all the same.

Another advantage to container gardening is the joy that only the proselyte knows. Once you have become hooked on it, you will want to share your newfound pleasure with your friends; you will find yourself showering them with priceless—and welcome—gifts. From your garden, and not obtainable in the marketplace of even a large city, you will have seeds, cuttings, roots, and small potted vegetables, and they will be all the more appreciated because they will represent your own labor as surely as a piece of pottery or a watercolor.

Gifts like these are wonderfully free of the invisible price tags which rate the status of the recipient or the giver. Stewart Mott—with his millionaire's penthouse garden—would be just as delighted with a Chinese vegetable plant as the elderly shut-in who misses puttering in her kitchen vegetable patch.

Another advantage to container gardening is that your mistakes are never obvious. In an in-the-ground garden the row of radishes that for some mysterious reason didn't form roots, or the large area which was meant for zucchini but lost its crop to borers, doesn't stand out accusingly bare. If a container plant fails, it can be temporarily retired to a screened corner with your other garden supplies, with no one the wiser. Only your best efforts need be on display. This is good for the gardener's morale as well as his amateur standing. There is nothing more depressing than trying to decide whether leaf miners or you have won in the spinach patch; the container gardener would not hesitate a minute. In container gardening, space is strictly limited; any plant not pulling its weight tends to be quickly replaced by something else.

As it happens, container gardening is much less prone to many of the plagues of the in-the-ground garden, so you will probably never lose your crop to borers or leaf miners. And even if a small infestation of aphids or some such pest does appear, it is much more easily dealt with, since it is not constantly replenished from the weedy meadows around your vegetable garden.

The container gardener can put his feet up on the rim of his barrel of cabbages, contemplate his trellised cucumber vines, and read with detached sympathy the appealing letters to the *Times* from gardeners plagued with chipmunks who have devoured a whole row of newly planted peas, or moles who have tunneled right under a hill of prized melons. That will never happen to him.

With all these advantages, it is no wonder that even the country cousin is turning more and more to container gardening. The raised bed is probably the home garden of the future; patios, terraces, and even small front doorsteps are being pressed into service to produce vegetables for the entire family.

The day may even come when the suburban visitor looks over your container vegetables and says, "If only I could spend the summer in the city." I am exaggerating a little, but not so much as you think, as many a brand-new city gardener knows.

Where and what containers

This is a situation where the cart and the horse must be considered almost simultaneously; it is impossible to decide on the size or kind of container unless you know what it is to hold, but on the other hand, you cannot plan what to put in your container until you know what you want to grow and how much room it will require.

Most of us do not have much free space in our homes. In spite of this, apartment dwellers almost invariably find room for houseplants. If this is your situation, perhaps you would consider throwing out your African violets and growing Chinese vegetables instead. They are equally decorative, less fussy, and deliciously edible.

If you garden at your job and are particularly proud of your philodendron which has now climbed over the door to your office and is rapidly heading for the other wall, visualize instead a Chinese cucumber vine rampant all over your window, and full of fresh crisp fruit (for an office lunch away from the hassle and expense of a fast-food chain). A carton of yogurt with a cucumber just picked off the windowsill might even bring you to the notice of the company president. If you don't have a window, a small desk-sized indoor light garden will grow a fine crop of herbs to perk up the hard-cooked egg or cottage cheese you brought from home, and a bit of ginger shoot plucked from one of the pots can turn the routine office coffee break into a relaxing English-style afternoon tea. If you still prefer black coffee, at least bring a handful of coriander seeds from home—where you have stored a jar of them from last year's crop.

Once you have decided you can find space for your plants, let us see what to put them in.

A container can be anything at all that will hold earth and drain excess water (which usually means punching a few holes in strategic places). Aesthetics aside, a container can be many of the things you usually throw away—milk cartons, plastic bleach bottles, egg cartons (for seedlings), berry baskets, small and large cartons, wooden crates, colanders that have worn out, aluminum pots with holes, aluminum pie plates, cottage-cheese boxes, ricotta-cheese containers (the 2-pound size will grow radishes and other root vegetables), and much, much more.

Containers from the kitchen

If you are one of the many city dwellers who has fun finding treasures in other people's garbage, you have an unlimited source of fascinating objects. Aside from the incredibly useful—and sometimes brand-new—things which are thrown away, many of the items, discarded because they no longer perform their original function, are ideal as containers. And remember, a chipped rim may spoil a piece of pottery for a collector, but is unimportant to the gardener who knows it will be completely covered by foliage.

If you do not care for this casual kind of container, you can have a

Decorative basket and ceramic containers

more conventional garden with classic clay pots; these are available in a good range of sizes. While they are much more expensive than they used to be, they are still comparatively reasonable, and now come in one or two new shapes that are quite handsome. In the large size, however, clay pots tend to be heavy.

Baskets make beautiful containers. To use a basket as the main container, line it with heavy-duty foil or plastic. Baskets can also be used to conceal less attractive containers; hide the rim with sphagnum moss for a finished effect. For a very pretty display, set individual flower pots in a single large basket. If you do this with peppers or lettuce, for instance, the foliage will soon fill the basket and hide the pots. This arrangement is also easy to change or move around.

If you have a collection of odd pieces of pottery, you can use these, provided you work out the drainage problem. Cut-flower containers are designed to hold water; vegetable-garden containers are not.

In addition to all these, there are always plastic containers. Styrofoam is the choice of a number of gardeners at first, but after a season they usually switch to something else. Although sterile and fairly easy to keep clean, foam is very light; a large plant tends to tip over no matter what you do to anchor it. Styrofoam is also surprisingly easy to chip or nick with a gardening tool, or dent when dragging about a hose or even a terrace chair. And somehow styrofoam pots do not age well; they take on a shabby look, indefinable but unmistakable, like a well-pressed dark suit of uncertain vintage which in some mysterious way always reveals its years of wear.

Regular plastic pots, usually green or white, are quite satisfactory. They are much easier to clean than either clay or wood, they do not build up an impenetrable and unsightly crust around the rim, and they can be freshened up in a jiffy with a damp paper towel. I notice that more and more garden-club exhibitions—except where prized and very special containers are used—show their material in simple green plastic pots. They come in a wide variety of shapes and sizes and often outlast clay pots.

Where really large containers are needed, wood half-barrels or tubs are a good choice. They provide support that offsets the bushiest, tallest, most heavily fruited plant, and are attractive no matter how ancient. They fit in equally well with either kitchen cast-offs or elegant Chinese porcelain. A close second, in my opinion, are the old galvanized-iron washtubs, with the advantage of convenient side handles, and a surface that lends itself to either the simplest or the most elaborate artistic treatment. Since I am not in any way an artist, I confine my efforts to whatever I can do with a spraycan for an occasional change of color; the more gifted can paint flowers, fruit,

Chinese motifs, or whatever with ease. The surface is large and takes well to stenciling. For drainage, simply pry the bottom loose of its rim in four places; be sure to cover these openings with enough gravel so that the soil mixture does not clog the opening. If, in spite of all your efforts, it does get clogged, either widen the hole or dig into it with something sturdy until it drains properly again. If you want to take a chance, you can even use the tub without drainage holes; I have raised a number of vegetables this way but it takes practice and a certain amount of luck. You would also have to cover the surface soil with plastic during heavy rain or the pot would be flooded. Considering the low cost of the tub, I would rather put holes in it than worry about overwatering. The only reason for not putting holes in it is that you might want to use it for a water garden at some future date; but plastic tubs are better for that purpose anyhow, so don't worry about it.

Soil

Of all the aspects of container gardening, soil is one of the most critical. It is not, however, nearly so complicated nor so difficult as with an in-the-ground garden.

Since you are providing all the soil starting from scratch, you do not have the unwelcome task of determining what kind of soil you have—which means scientific testing—and then learning how to change it into something better.

Almost no one inherits an in-the-ground garden with suitable soil. It is either too acid or too alkaline (depending on what part of the country you live in), too sandy or too clayey, too compacted or too porous, too full of weed seeds or too poor to grow even a decent crop of weeds. In addition, it is unmovable. You have no control over how much sun or shade it gets, and watering it means watering large areas of soil in which you aren't growing anything except crab grass which blows its seed in on the wind.

Where you are making your in-the-ground garden in a new area, you must take into account competition from the roots of existing trees, the position of your septic field (which can take up a whole backyard), and the garden's attraction for dogs who like to dig in freshly turned earth.

Container-garden soil is always a custom job; as such, it is specially tailored to its purpose. This means, however, that you cannot resort to the simple expedient of bringing in baskets of earth from a nearby park or vacant lot—or from your mother's place in the country. If you do, you will bring many of these in-the-ground problems along with the soil; at its best, it won't be really suitable.

Aside from anything else, garden soil is heavy. Proper watering makes it even heavier. This is a factor to take seriously if you are gardening on a rooftop or in an apartment. Even in a well-built building, the combined weight of your containers might be more than the roof can bear; your entire garden might end up in the apartment directly under the roof. On a smaller scale, you could conceivably have this same problem inside your apartment, on a windowsill or floor.

Another disadvantage to common garden soil is that it is not sterilized. Harmful bacteria, as well as good, abound in even the best garden soil. You would almost surely have to sterilize it if you wanted to avoid problems that could seriously affect your crops. Home sterilizing of soil is not only a bother, it is downright unpleasant. The soil smells simply awful while you are baking it in the oven.

It must be spread out in a shallow layer in a pan in the oven and baked for at least an hour at 250° F. You can imagine how long it would take to do any sizable amount of home sterilizing. As to the smell, some books suggest avoiding this by dampening the soil before baking it. I tried it but it didn't work. First of all, it increased the baking time—and made how long it should take sheer guesswork since it depended on whether the soil was more sand or more clay. Second, it was a toss-up as to whether it smelled worse when it was damp and hot, or when it was drying and hot. Even mincing fresh garlic wasn't enough to offset the odor, which clung to the kitchen with all the tenacity of the aftermath of a fire.

You may wonder whether I am being unduly cautious, and if it wouldn't be worth the chance to use unsterilized soil. It wouldn't. After a couple of flats have succumbed to damping off, you will do anything to avoid it happening again. Damping off is an unpleasant fungus disease which affects seedlings just as they have successfully germinated and are well on their way to becoming plants. One night they will look fine; the next morning they will all be lying pitifully on their sides, obviously in deep trouble. No matter what you do at that point, they will all die. Damping off is invariably fatal. It also means that the fungus is in the soil and anything else you plant in it will inevitably follow the same route. If you have those flats next to others, they will probably be infected too.

Damping off is very easy to avoid. Always use sterilized soil for germinating seeds and for seedlings; damping off will not affect more mature plants, so you can safely transplant them to unsterilized soil once they have passed the seedling stage.

Sterilized soil is easy to buy. I prefer "soilless" mixes, usually peat moss, vermiculite, and sometimes sphagnum moss. Ready-made containers like Fertl Cubes or compacted pots (which expand when watered) are very easy to use and seem to actually speed up germination. They contain fertilizer as well. Once your seedlings have outgrown Fertl Cubes, which happens quite soon, they can be transplanted to peat pots filled with Cornell Mix or its equivalent. Cornell Mix is a sterilized "soilless" formula developed by Cornell University. Several other formulas have been developed since, and you can buy them ready-mixed in garden centers under various names such as Pro-Mix, Jiffy Mix, and Redi-Earth. New ones turn up every season. Although these are convenient and can be bought in very large quantities (which your garden center will usually order for you if not already in stock), it is, naturally, cheaper to mix your own. A lot of garden books make a big production of this but years ago I discovered a foolproof method. With my system, you don't have to dampen the ingredients to keep from choking to death while you mix them, and you mix them right in the container in which they will be stored.

Most of the mixes are composed—more or less—of equal parts of peat moss and vermiculite, plus fertilizer. For instance, a standard mix is 12 cubic feet of peat moss, 12 cubic feet of vermiculite, 5 pounds of a "complete" fertilizer (usually 5-10-5, but this would vary according to what you were growing), 2 pounds of rock phosphate, and 5 pounds of limestone. The good thing about mixing your own is that you can make small adjustments. For instance, you might make one slightly on the acid side, and one a little more alkaline. Label your containers, and you will have exactly what you need handy at all times.

To mix this formula, I simply dump all the ingredients into a plastic garbage can, cover it, and roll it (on its side) back and forth, or over and over, until the contents are thoroughly blended. Since they all look a little different, a glance inside the can will tell you how you are doing. This eliminates tedious, and very dusty, shoveling back and forth into various piles, and then getting the final mix into something that will hold it. It also eliminates having to clean up the

immediate vicinity afterward—the dust generated by this stuff is very
fine and gets into *everything*, including wool socks. It has further
advantages in that you can prepare your mix even on a very windy
day without losing half your fertilizer to the rooftop breezes; and if
the phone should ring right in the middle, you don't have to cover the
various piles of fertilizer before you run to answer.

Keep the can covered when not in use, so that it stays sterilized,
and (for really good garden practice) keep the tools you use for
working with it as clean as possible. If you garden with things that go
into the dish washer (many people use kitchen forks, spoons, and so
forth), you can be sure your utensils are really clean and will not
spread disease from one container to another. If you bring in plants
and seedlings from a commercial nursery, it's a good idea to isolate
them for a week or ten days to make sure they are disease-free. For
some reason, greenhouse stock often comes complete with aphids,
and that is trouble you don't need to spread around.

Note: Always use your soil mix wet and compressed. To get it this
way, soak it in a pail, then, as you fill the container, press down firmly
so that water runs off. Then sow your seeds or set in your plants.

To avoid problems from commercial greenhouses, I usually treat
any potted plant I buy unless it is too big. I dunk it upside down in
warm, soapy water a couple of times, and keep it isolated for about a
week before introducing it to the plant community. This simple
procedure eliminates many pests, and is easy to do in the kitchen
sink. Unfortunately, you can't do that with flats of seedlings, so keep
a sharp eye out for bugs or diseases when you buy them.

If you find liquid fertilizer more convenient—fish emulsion is a
honey, except for the smell—you might like the Connecticut Extension Service mix. It calls for 1 bushel of peat moss, 1 bushel of perlite
or vermiculite, 1 2-inch flowerpotful of limestone, 2 3-inch flowerpot-
fuls of rock phosphate, and a liquid fertilizer weekly according to the
recommendations on the bottle (since this will vary according to
which fertilizer you use). The bottle recommendations, incidentally,
should only be taken as a rough guide. They cannot possibly allow for
all the variables; use your common sense in applying any guidelines
of that sort. A nice feature of liquid fertilizer is that it feeds the
foliage as well as the soil, sometimes giving a boost to a plant that you
may have inadvertently neglected.

Foliage feeding—a comparatively recent discovery—seems to work
faster than fertilizer taken up by the roots. This is especially

noticeable if your plants are yellowing because of an iron deficiency. The effects of a liquid fertilizer with a chelating action (one which helps the plant utilize certain nutrients more efficiently) can sometimes be seen within twenty-four hours.

You may not want to get into a technical study of fertilizers, and it isn't at all necessary, but if you mix your own, you are bound to find yourself almost intuitively knowing what to add to your basic mix for which plant. If, for instance, a plant needs a little more nitrogen and your formula is 5-10-5, you will put a cup of cottonseed meal in along with your mix and think no more about it than a cook adding another pinch of salt.

If this all sounds tedious and like more than you want to know, there is every kind of commercial fertilizer combination you can think of, special ones labeled for special vegetables as well as general ones for a wide spectrum of vegetables. These will give you a very satisfactory crop, and you won't have to do anything except apply them on schedule. If you decide to use them, take into account obvious variables, like fertilizing oftener when excessive rainfall has leached out more fertilizer than usual.

Incidentally, one trick to minimize leaching out—although it works only with small containers you can lift easily—is to take the saucer or whatever you have catching the overflow and dump it back in the pot about an hour after watering. Somehow the plant will hold the additional water then when it wouldn't the first time, and you won't throw out fertilizer-rich water.

After you have been gardening awhile, you will gradually discover new places to put containers. The obvious places, like windowsills, terraces, and rooftops, will be the first to be used up. Raised beds where you had an in-the-ground garden, patios, decks, breezeways, and front steps are also fairly obvious. When you have exhausted those possibilities, look around again.

If you have covered all the ground-level sites (and this includes raised beds), there is still the air. Hanging containers of all sorts are both suitable and attractive for many Chinese vegetables. Cucumbers, for instance, don't care whether they grow up or down—though no one seems to realize it—and neither do snow peas or yard-long beans. Hanging baskets aren't limited to just one level or to eaves. There are many kinds and lengths of brackets which you could use to arrange several rows of baskets up and down a wall or trellis. Plants could grow from one container to another, and intertwine to form a solid wall of foliage. At ground level—underneath the hanging baskets—you could arrange containers of larger plants, like eggplants or peppers.

You don't have to depend on a wall. A very simple arrangement which supports a metal pole horizontally across an open space could be rigged up to hold a number of hanging plants. In addition, any vertical arrangement of containers—on stepladders, bricks, concrete blocks (although these are less desirable since they add so much weight), baker's racks, and so on—will increase your space vertically without crowding plants. You can build shelves across a window so that you triple your windowsill space, or use bookshelves in windy spots to provide a windbreak as well as space for containers. Incidentally, an old bookcase laid on its back makes a dandy container garden.

If you don't have a fence or a balcony, many Chinese vegetables will grow up a single pole firmly planted in the pot. This is pretty and practical; harvesting is easy and you won't miss any of the crop. Herbs can be planted around the base of the pole.

For winter gardening indoors, take advantage of the combination shelves-and-fluorescent-light planters. A large one in front of a living-room window will yield fresh vegetables all winter. Or put a couple of fluorescent lights under the cabinets over your kitchen counter and grow your own herbs fresh, instead of having them all dried and embalmed in little bottles.

No matter how dreary the weather, you'll never get the winter doldrums with a garden in your home; it's a great time to try out new varieties of vegetables. Even if you're having hamburger for the fourth time that week, it's bound to taste better with the help of the watercress from your windowbox, and a chili from the pepper bush.

I hesitate to mention one especially good way to increase your growing area because it is a little expensive, but a window greenhouse is a tremendous help when space is limited. It takes the place of your window and projects out from the side of the building, so you couldn't use it in an apartment without permission. The initial cost is high ($200 to $300), but installation is simple, and it will hold a surprisingly large number of plants. If, in addition, you build your windowsill out into the room by extending it with a board and brackets, you could have a sizable area. This increases your growing season at both ends—spring and fall—and is especially useful for getting an early start without taking over every available surface within your apartment. If you look into this, first study the measurements and see what you want to plant that would fit.

Light

Most vegetables require sun, or its equivalent in light. I find that this is usually discussed very scientifically, in terms of candlepower and so on, but in practice it doesn't seem to be that simple. For one thing unless you worked continually with a slide rule or a light meter, made constant observations, and recorded them on charts like a laboratory assistant with a cage of white rats, you could never take into account all the variables. For instance, a sunny window varies in the amount and quality of sun from month to month as the sun moves across the sky at different heights. There are also the differences due to cloudy or rainy spells, hot, dry, and clear spells, and those in-between days when the cloud cover is high and everything has a glare—the kind of days when your mother used to say at the beach, "Cover up. You can get a bad burn on a day like this." And sure enough, you always did.

With all these factors in mind, the container gardener has a big advantage over the in-the-ground gardener; he can move things around. This means putting your really large containers on a set of large casters. It doesn't mean getting up every day and shifting plants the way some people move furniture. If you run into a couple of weeks of very hot, dry, and possibly windy weather, your plants will begin to look under stress and they should be protected either by moving them to partial shade or by creating partial shade over them. If moving them is impractical, you could use movable lath walls. They are light and easy to secure, and high enough to create partial shade part of the day. Build them with horizontal wooden bases designed to keep them from blowing over. When you don't need them, they will look decorative against a wall. Don't paint them or you may increase the light and heat through reflection; natural laths are best.

If you have just a few plants, keep them on something easily moved, and roll them to a shady spot when the sun gets too strong.

Even plants in a sunny windowsill can get too much sun under certain conditions. In this case, it's easy to have a bamboo shade or a gauzy curtain you can drop down between the plant and the window. This should be used only when the sun is strongest and brightest (which isn't necessarily high noon), then removed so that the plant gets the maximum number of sun *hours*.

Six to eight hours of direct sun will be the most a plant will need for fruit production—cucumbers, eggplants and so on. Foliage vegetables and root vegetables will produce for you with about four hours of sun. Some foliage vegetables will settle for a bright north or east window; some herbs, such as watercress, will be happy with surprisingly low light levels.

If your problem is not enough sun, that must be handled differently. A terrace or rooftop will get more mileage out of the sun if you paint the back wall, or an opposing wall, white. This will work even if the sun doesn't strike the wall directly, but merely surrounding surfaces. If you mulch with aluminum foil, this will not only preserve moisture and repel aphids, it will also increase the amount of light. Obviously, this will not work if the foliage is so thick that it shades the soil, or aluminum, in this case. Try using the foil somewhat in the fashion of the sun reflectors people sometimes use to get a quick tan. Staple it on a frame of a suitable size, and stand it where it will face the sun and reflect it onto the plant. To get maximum use of this device, you could move it every couple of hours as the sun moves. If you don't need that much additional light, just leave it in place, remembering to take it away if the weather turns very hot.

Don't confuse light with heat. Cool-weather crops, such as Chinese radishes, turnips, and cabbages, like sun but not heat. If you grow them on a rooftop or terrace, the surface on which they stand may get very hot, and reflect this heat into the air immediately above it—which is where the plants stand. Partly for this reason, no container should be put directly on a rooftop surface. If you like indoor-outdoor carpeting, you could lay that throughout the area. It would reduce the heat to a tolerable level, and you could always pretend it was grass—or use Astroturf and then it would even *look* like grass. The whole idea bothers me but it is a good one all the same, and many container gardeners have become reconciled to it because it makes so much sense. If you want to be very rustic, spread salt hay over the surface. This is hardly the treatment for an elegant terrace, however. If you are planning to make your garden a regular feature, it might pay you to build a wood deck over whatever surface you have. This could be very attractive as well as useful. Allow space between the floor boards, rather than building a solid floor, or it will collect water. Treat your finished floor as if it were a boat deck and it will last indefinitely. Or use cedar and leave it rough. Don't make the spaces between the boards too wide or the caster wheels will get caught in them.

In the winter, or in windows which do not get full sun, use

fluorescent tubes for supplementary light. Vegetables that set fruit will not usually do so in fluorescent light alone. If you want a plant to set fruit, you must provide the sunlight plus enough supplemental light to make up the difference.

The fluorescent tubes that are used are not the same as those you have in your reading lamp; just take my word for it without going into a lot of technical detail about color spectrums. Buy special fluorescent lights for growing plants; your garden center will advise you.

Any fluorescent light fixture that is worth buying or building yourself should be movable. For a large fixture, the simplest method is to hang it from the ceiling by a chain which can be raised and lowered by its links. A more complicated method is to rig up a pulley. Both work equally well, but you don't have to be any sort of handyman to hang the lights by chains.

The reason for this arrangement is that the lights will have to be raised and lowered to accommodate different-sized plants. If you use the lights for starting seedlings—and you'd be foolish not to—you have to lower them so they rest about 6 inches above the seedlings. If you are just keeping peppers coming on a mature plant, the light would have to be much higher in order to clear the top of the plant.

Seedlings are very sensitive to light levels which are too low for them, and will quickly get undesirably tall and spindly as they reach for a light source. Be sure not to let that happen or the plants will always be weak. Good adequate light is just as important to immature as to mature plants; it is not an ingredient you can skimp on.

To take the headaches out of fluorescent lighting, invest in a timer. Set it to turn the lights off and on automatically, adjusting the schedule as needed. The rest of the time all you have to do is check your plants and see if they seem to be getting enough light. Don't be upset about how long you have to keep the fluorescents on; fluorescents use comparatively little electricity.

Watering

Watering in outdoor containers is not very different from watering an in-the-ground garden. You are usually nearer your water source, and have more control over how much water the plants get. A small dish set out near the plants will give you a rough record of rainfall—an inch of water in the dish will mean an inch of rain (always assuming you started out with an empty dish). Men seem to like to keep track of these things, but in my experience the cat has always taken a drink at the wrong time, or someone bumps into the dish before I have had a chance to do my measuring. I would rather go by the appearance of each individual plant.

Some plants, like some people, are thirstier than others. Plants with a big root system need more frequent watering, as you know if you have played nursemaid to a bonsai tree. A windy or very dry day will evaporate water much more quickly than a still or humid one. With all these factors to take into account, why not just take a look and do what needs doing?

Check the soil under the surface of the container. If it seems dry an inch down, it should be watered. The excess will run off if the soil is the right kind, and you have unclogged drainage holes. Don't let the pot stand in water in the saucer more than an hour; that creates a condition called "wet feet," and most vegetables dislike it. It also reduces the oxygen in the soil, which is definitely not good.

If you have filled your containers properly, there will be some space between the top of the soil and the rim of the container. In watering, fill this space with water; then come back and do it again—three times in all. Just make the rounds, and you won't have any trouble keeping track.

Hanging baskets have to be watered much more often than other containers—I guess because they are so much more exposed. It is customary to line a hanging basket with sphagnum moss and then to fill it with soil. Some vegetable gardeners go crazy trying to grow their hanging vegetables this way. It is true it makes a nice lightweight container, but it's almost impossible to keep it watered. The container will dry out almost as soon as you have your back turned. Plan an overhead support that will take a little more weight, and line the basket with several layers of clear plastic (painter's drop cloths are cheap and big enough so you can cut out any size you need). Then line with *wet* (not damp) moss and fill with Cornell Mix. As long as you do not let the sphagnum moss dry out (and you can tell by the color of it through the plastic) your plant will always have a chance of making it. It is better not to let the mix itself dry out too much either, but the moss gives you a margin. Punch several drainage holes in the plastic after the basket is filled (you can usually slip in a knife or knitting needle). Or make holes in the plastic to conform to your container's drainage holes. The sphagnum moss should keep the soil mix from running out the holes; if it doesn't, you haven't used a thick enough layer of moss.

Watering can be time-consuming in a really large container garden, as in any garden. Whole books have been written about Rube Goldberg contraptions to solve this problem, and I am sorry that I don't have any special ones to recommend. The layout of your apartment or terrace, and its access to water, will in large part determine your own solution, as will the amount of money and time you're willing to invest in setting up an automatic (more or less) watering system. Just remember you may have neighbors under your roof or terrace; they will not welcome you in the role of rainmaker.

The Chinese water garden

Since a water garden must obviously be grown in a container, all of Chapter 10 will be of interest to the container gardener. The chapter covers, among others, chee koo, ou, sai metai, and woo chai.

Ngar choy

Ngar choy can be grown *only* in containers. See Chapter 8, "All About Bean Sprouts."

Not for container gardeners

I would never say unequivocally that a vegetable cannot be grown in a container; determined container gardeners are very ingenious and seem to be able to grow anything they set their hearts on. There are some vegetables, however, that I personally feel are either too much trouble or take up too much space in proportion to the crop they provide. You can grow them if you insist, but I don't feel I can recommend them for container gardening.

Among these vegetables, I would advise against doan gwa (winter melon) because of its size, chung choy (pickling melon) and mao gwa (fuzzy gourd) because of their limited use, dow fu (fava beans), and soybeans. Some container gardeners do grow soybeans, and it certainly can be done successfully; perhaps I am prejudiced against them because I give so many other vegetables a higher priority in my kitchen.

A last note

While container gardening imposes certain special rules and conditions, basic good gardening practice still applies. This chapter particularizes only as regards the special information that applies to container gardening; the reader should also consult the general gardening information in the chapter where each vegetable is described in detail, and available varieties are mentioned by name.

1̇2̇ *Vegetable-by-*

Vegetable Guide to Container

Gardening

Since all of these vegetables are described in detail in other chapters, I will use this section only for the special things you need to know in order to grow them successfully in containers. In every case, recipe suggestions have already been given under the "Culinary and Other Uses" section that accompanies the discussion of each vegetable in the main gardening chapters. You will also find there a description of the appearance of each vegetable, and general cultural directions which you may want to reread. The areas not covered under general gardening—size of container, ability to grow indoors or completely under lights, and similar points—are dealt with here.

The vegetables in this chapter are discussed in alphabetical order of their Chinese names.

Adzuki

Adzuki beans are a useful and interesting vegetable for the container gardener. The beans themselves are exceptionally high in protein—25 percent—as well as in minerals. They are also an excellent bean to sprout. They are rarely grown in the United States and you won't find them in the fresh or dried bean section of your supermarket. Chances are you may never have a chance to taste them unless you grow your own crop. They are very popular in both China and Japan—as a vegetable and for sprouting—and will add an authentic note to your Oriental dishes. As to American cooking, they fit in with our more familiar beans, and can be used green-shelled or dried.

Adzuki are bush beans and very similar to snap beans in their culture. They bear prolifically—an important factor to the container gardener—and the plants are compact and attractive, with numerous flowers in season. Several pots of them could be arranged to form a nice 2-foot-high hedge.

The practical way to grow them is one plant to a container. The container should be 10 to 12 inches deep, at least 6 inches in diameter.

Sow three seeds to a pot, and thin to one when the seedlings have their second set of true leaves. Adzuki beans don't like cold, wet weather, so wait until two or three weeks after the last frost date to plant them. Pick as green beans, or wait about 120 days to pick for dried beans (which you would need for sprouts). If you pick them only for green beans, you can sow several crops during a season, just as with snap beans.

Use the standard soil mix recommended at the beginning of Chapter 11, but add a larger proportion of peat moss to increase the acidity of the mix slightly; adzuki beans grow better in a little acidity. Fertilize when seedlings are about 4 inches high and every two weeks thereafter with 10-10-10. Water regularly.

This is an attractive and practical vegetable that could easily replace the common bean in the container garden.

Ai kwa   Chinese eggplant

An ai kwa plant looks like an eggplant, but the fruit is obviously very different from ordinary eggplants. For one thing it is likely to be white or cream-colored, which is very confusing. The first time I held a white eggplant in my hand, it really took me time to get used to the idea that I could cook it just like any eggplant. Actually, it is easier to cook than any other eggplant, because it doesn't have the least trace of bitterness—not even the most finicky cook would think it required salting before using.

The foliage is exactly like common eggplant but, in my experience, the flowers are a deeper lavender. The plant with its lavender flowers and white fruit is a real showpiece and deserves a special place in your container garden. There are also purple varieties which produce either small, egg-shaped fruit or small, slim versions of the common eggplant shape. The fruit of the white eggplant never gets really glossy; it has the warm, satiny look of a real pearl, and may be shaped either like a grapefruit or a huge pearl, or be slim and about 6 inches long. The purple gets glossy when ready to pick, just like the common eggplant.

This is a perfect vegetable for the container gardener, a showpiece both indoors or out—you can even grow it under lights; it is one of the few plants that will fruit for you under those conditions.

Ai kwa, like all eggplants, is very cold-sensitive and cannot be put outdoors until the *nights* are warm—which means about June in Connecticut. Start the seeds indoors in peat pots because of the long growing season. Once the plant starts to produce eggplant, it will go on and on until stopped by frost.

When the weather has warmed up, the peat-potted plants should be set into 3-gallon containers, one per pot. I prefer to grow one eggplant to a container; it is pretty enough to warrant this treatment. Each bush will bear so many eggplants, that you won't need more than two or three to see you generously through the summer and fall. The plants will grow about 2 feet tall and take 120 days to maturity— but don't wait until then to pick the eggplants or they will be too tough.

Gauging the ripeness of vegetables is a little tricky because they never get as big as the ones in the supermarket; if they start to lose their glow (white) or shine (purple), pick them immediately.

Ai kwa is a heavy feeder. Provide it with plenty of 10-10-5 and manure. Water copiously so that roots never dry out; this means every few days in very hot dry weather.

If you like eggplant, try ai kwa—I think it is worth space in any container garden.

Bin dow **Asparagus pea**

Bin dow, or asparagus pea, is an excellent plant for container gardening. It is very decorative, prolific, and easy to grow. Most varieties, however, are vines and will need strings, a pole, or a small trellis for support. If you prefer, you can grow the bush type.

If space is severely limited, order the "asparagus pea" offered by Thompson & Morgan; it grows only 12 inches high, which will allow plenty of room overhead for hanging baskets. Or you can plant it in the hanging baskets.

Since bin dow is not frost-tender and does best in cool weather, start it outdoors in early spring. It requires full sun. If you want to grow it indoors over the winter, pick a room you keep on the cool side and set the pot or window box in the sunniest window. For best results, plant in a "ditch" so that you can add soil to the container, and cover up the first few inches of the vine as it grows.

Sow the seeds ½ inch deep, about 4 inches apart in a deep window box. Or 3 inches apart in a circle in a round 5-gallon container. Train each vine to a single string if it seems to want to climb. The Thompson & Morgan variety may not need this treatment.

Your standard mix will do fine for this vegetable. In addition, lay down a bead of 10-10-10 fertilizer at the bottom of the "ditch" before you start to fill it in, and again, along the row, when the flowers first form.

Bin dow will flower profusely and be ready to eat within 30 days. Everything is edible—shoots, leaves, blue flowers, pods, and roots.

Since it takes only 50 days to maturity, this is a plant you might easily want to sow over and over again during the winter. Try eating different parts each time, as if it were a completely different vegetable. If you find you like one part more than another, fertilize for that. For the roots, for instance, use a 5-10-10 fertilizer, and add a bead of rock phosphate when side-dressing at flowering time.

Bok choy *Chinese mustard cabbage*

Bok choy looks and grows more like Swiss chard than like our common cabbage. It has thick, wide, curved white stems and tender, dark-green leaves. It is easy to grow and lends itself to container gardening, both indoors and out. Since it is a leafy rather than a fruiting vegetable, it will also do well under lights, so you can enjoy it all winter long.

The stems of bok choy can be cooked like asparagus, the leaves like spinach; it is a popular ingredient in both Chinese and Japanese cookery and is used in some unusual ways.

Since it is a cool-weather vegetable, sow it in early spring, or in midsummer for a fall crop. Indoors, it can be sown at any time. You can crop it like Swiss chard or leaf lettuce, merely taking the outside leaves and allowing the rest of the plant to go on growing; this will work until hot weather affects the growth. I usually find bok choy will grow right through from spring to fall; but in a container garden you may prefer to pick the whole spring crop, use the space for some other vegetable, then replant bok choy for fall or winter use. Succession planting of various vegetables is particularly important to a container gardener, and quick-maturing vegetables like bok choy allow the container gardener to grow a greater variety of good things to eat.

Sow the seed ½ inch deep, 6 inches between seeds. If you don't have much room, one container could, for instance, hold a single bok choy plant as well as radishes, chives, and Tom Thumb lettuce.

Keep well watered and fertilize with a 10-10-5 formula, plus manure, every two or three weeks. Harvest it as soon as you want to, certainly any time from five weeks on. If you wish, you may seed much more closely and have the thinnings to eat for an extra-early crop.

Cee gwa **Chinese okra**

This is not a plant for indoors unless you have a bay window you want to turn into a jungle. On a terrace it would be spectacular, but it does take up a great deal of room; you could grow a number of cucumbers or melons, for instance, instead of one of these vines.

Sow the seeds in a really large container—the 5-gallon size is an absolute minimum—three weeks after the last frost date. Plant 1 inch deep, three or four seeds to a container. Thin to one plant per container as soon as the third set of true leaves appears.

Keep the soil moist for the two or more weeks the seeds take to germinate. Protect the seeds and young seedlings if the nights turn chilly. This is strictly a warm-weather vegetable; if you need a sweater, so will cee gwa.

Use a 10-10-10 fertilizer in your mix and every week thereafter; this plant does not grow on air, and it grows rampantly, so it feeds heavily. Add a little lime at the same time because you are constantly leaching it out with watering, and the soil should be slightly alkaline. Water copiously.

For eating, start picking the fruit when it reaches 4 inches in length. For sponges and other similar uses, allow to mature on the vine, then soak in a pail of hot water for one to three days, at which point you should be able to peel off the skin. Let it dry and use any way that you wish; it is really great in the shower.

Cee gwa grows so fast, you can almost see it. It has abundant pretty yellow flowers, and the fruit is unusual-looking; however, it takes up a large amount of space under container-garden conditions.

Chang fa **Multiplier onions**

No Oriental cook worth her soy sauce would consider going into business without a good supply of fresh chang fa. This isn't easy to have always on hand—not unless you grow it yourself. And chang fa is easy to grow anywhere; anyone can always have a container full.

Chang fa is a true "scallion." If you think scallions are young, immature, common onions, you may be interested to learn that onions are far from ideal to grow for scallions. Aside from the flavor, one reason they are a poor substitute is that one onion will grow only one scallion; at the price of onion sets, that is a far from economical way to grow scallions. A much better method would be to grow chang fa, the multiplier onion.

Multiplier onions start out as one and multiply to a single clump of many. If you harvest some of the "scallions" for the table, the rest of the clump goes on happily multiplying and growing more.

Multiplier onions are often known as Japanese bunching onions, although they are equally popular in China, and widely used in many Chinese dishes. Early in the season, they are mild enough to eat from the relish tray; later in the season they are a little pungent for the average taste and lend themselves better to cooked dishes. In American cooking, they are used just as we use scallions. Chang fa is quick and easy to grow in containers; the leaves can even be clipped like chives.

Sow the seeds in early spring or late fall outdoors; anytime indoors. Chang fa will do well in the winter under lights without supplementary sun. Use a pot with at least a 6-inch *depth* (8 inches would be even better) and at least 8 inches in diameter. You can keep the clump within this diameter by harvesting the outside scallions; a wider pot will accommodate a larger clump.

Since this is a vegetable that likes to reseed itself, you will find young shoots coming up by themselves, if you leave the soil undisturbed. These shoots can easily be transplanted indoors either for winter or next-season use. Once you have planted multiplier onions for a season, you will always have seeds or bulbs for the following season's crop.

The fertilizer should be a little heavier in nitrogen than your standard mix. Water sufficiently to reach the roots, and keep the soil on the moist rather than the dry side.

Chih ma   **Sesame**

Here is another Chinese herb that is so easy to grow and yet so spectacularly ornamental that I can't imagine why more gardeners don't give it room as a house plant.

The flowers look something like foxglove, and range in color from deep pink to white. A single plant can grow up to 3 feet high, but it will flower long before that. If you prefer a shorter plant, pinch it back.

When someone expecting the usual collection of flowering house plants asks what this one is, the usual reaction to your answer is, "It's a *what?*" When that happens you may be forgiven if you feel a twinge of gratification. Of course, I should be excused for feeling that way on the grounds that I can't grow any of the exciting indoor creatures like proteas or even bougainvillea (which looks even lovelier in a single pot than it does on a tropical island). One day maybe I'll have a greenhouse big enough to fill with these beautiful flowers, although—knowing my predilection—I'll be more likely to just grow bigger and better ginger, cucumbers, and melons.

Anyhow, back to chih ma. I don't think I've mentioned that you will have something special to look forward to when you grow your own sesame plants. The leaves as well as the seeds are edible, and you would probably never get to taste them in a lifetime unless you grew them yourself. Use the leaves raw in a green salad. They also make an interesting, cool summer drink (see Chapter 9 for the recipe).

Sow the seeds ½ inch deep in 3-inch pots. Transplant the seedlings to moderately large containers with other herbs and vegetables or to 6-inch pots for individual display. You won't know ahead of time what color flowers any given plant will produce, so it's fun to have several growing.

Sesame will take as much sun as you can give it. In containers, unlike its requirements in the open garden, it needs regular watering because there isn't anywhere else it can go for a drink.

Chung gwa **Sweet melons**

Chung gwa are excellent melons for the container gardener; many varieties weigh only 1 to 3 pounds and grow on correspondingly shorter stems than do our more familiar cantaloupes and honeydews. They are handsome growing up a rooftop, or terrace wall; you can also grow them around chicken-wire cages. The trick is to start the plants *inside* the cage, then train the vines to grow around the outside of it; otherwise, you won't be able to get at the fruit. A chung gwa vine will not climb by itself; the vine will have to be encouraged by intertwining it with cage wire, or by tying it to the wire with soft cord. If you do intertwine it, be sure the flowers are all on the outside; they will form the fruit and you want that where you can reach it.

You can also grow chung gwa indoors, if you are willing to give up a whole sunny window to it for the 80 or 90 days it takes to mature. The flavor of a freshly picked, vine-ripened melon is ambrosia, compared to even the best melon you can buy in the store; it is well worth growing your own.

Like all melons, chung gwa is strictly a warm-weather crop. Sow the seed about four weeks after the last frost date in a 5-gallon container of the standard mix which has been enriched with manure and 2 cups of 5-10-10 fertilizer. Plant four seeds 1 inch deep and thin to two plants when the seedlings are 4 inches high. If you want an earlier crop, start the seeds indoors in peat pots, under lights or in a sunny window.

Keep well watered at all times and fertilize every twenty days. Some fruit may be too heavy for the vine and have to be supported with individual slings; this is especially true of the cantaloupe type, which if they are not supported will tend to slip off their stems when they get ripe. You can plant two different varieties in the same container and interweave the growing vines so that you apparently have two kinds of fruit growing on one vine.

Dow gauk   **Yard-long beans**

I can't think of anything that would be more satisfactory for the container gardener than growing dow gauk. The vines are not aggressive or over-long, the deep lavender flowers are large and beautiful, and the long, slender beans are interesting to look at and delicious to eat. In addition, the vines are quite prolific, so much so that you may have to pick them every day, like snow peas.

Most catalogs will warn you that dow gauk is "an unreliable cropper." I know of this only by hearsay; it has not been so in my own experience. In my garden, the vines bear merrily over a long season and are much more productive than ordinary snap beans. I also find this vegetable completely trouble-free, which is not true of common snap beans; no pests or diseases seem to bother it and it is very tolerant of casual culture.

The one factor that is critical to success with dow gauk is the temperature. Do not plant the seeds in outdoor containers until the weather is warm during the night as well as during the day; night temperatures of at least 65°F. are an absolute must. You will be able to start harvesting within 40 days, so there is no need to rush the planting.

Sow seeds 1 inch deep in a soil depth of 12 inches, 4 inches between seeds. Give each vine a pole to climb, although they will soon intertwine; the only problem in allowing them to do so is that it makes it harder to locate the beans for picking. Fertilize about once a month with 10-10-5.

Harvest when young, up to 18 inches long, before the pods whiten. Mature pods can be shelled and the beans dried.

Foo gwa   **Bitter melon**

I recommend foo gwa for container gardening because it is so unusual. You won't find anything even vaguely like it in your supermarket, and it is guaranteed to add interest to any menu on which it appears. It may take a little while to get used to the flavor, but soon you will like it above old favorites. Besides, it is essential to authentic classic Chinese cuisine.

Start seedlings indoors, if that is convenient, for an earlier crop. Or sow outdoors in a protected spot as soon as all danger of frost is past. If you guess wrong and plant too early, cover the container with plastic and newspapers to protect it from freezing temperatures, especially at night.

Foo gwa is a trellis plant, whether outdoors or on a windowsill. The copious watering it requires is much easier to provide in containers than in conventional in-the-ground gardens. In a container you know that all the water is going to the melon roots, not into surrounding earth. It requires full sun.

The plant is worth a spotlight position since it is quite spectacular both in the flowering and in the fruiting stage.

Sow the seeds 1 inch deep in a really large container—5 gallons would be a minimum size, larger would be better. Fertilize when the plant flowers, and again as the fruit forms. Add cottonseed meal, or other high-nitrogen fertilizer, to your basic mix. The melons are small—about 12 inches long, 2 inches in diameter—and do not require support; the only reason for growing the vines up a support is to keep them from taking up all your garden space.

Since they are often grown purely as ornamentals, you know they will look good in your container garden.

Gai choy   *Chinese mustard*

This mustard is not the same as the hot saffron-colored stuff in which you dip your egg rolls. Gai choy is a green vegetable like spinach and is a good fresh vegetable to always have on hand. It is not so coarse or so pungent as the American mustards of the South; it is just peppery enough to give you a lift when you need it.

The leaves of some varieties are deeply cut and particularly lovely; others are beautifully curled. If you grow several varieties together, you can get a range of color from bright yellow to dark green—much nicer than coleus and edible to boot. Group several flower pots, each with a different variety, for a pretty windowsill or terrace.

When planning your containers, count on the plant growing from 6 to 12 inches. Chinese mustard doesn't take up much room and you can grow a single plant in a 4-inch pot, or two or more in larger pots. They combine well in a container with other vegetables; for instance, beets, radishes and so on. Or you could plant a pot that makes a "mess of greens"—spinach, Swiss chard, and so on, all together. They also combine well with herbs of all kinds.

If you want to grow them indoors under lights all winter, they will do very well.

The only thing that won't work is growing them on a city rooftop in midsummer without shade; they don't like heat.

Since this is a leafy crop, use extra nitrogen in your original fertilizer mix. Sow the seeds ½ inch deep, about 2 inches apart. Pick every other one; those that are left will grow into the additional space. If you want to, and have the room, you can harvest the leaves by cutting them about three-quarters of the way down; the plant will send up new leaves.

Grow the red-stemmed variety for an especially colorful effect.

Gai lohn   Chinese broccoli

Gai lohn is a good choice for container gardeners who want to grow broccoli; it takes up only half the space required by common broccoli and is extremely prolific.

In appearance it is similar to common broccoli but with much smaller "heads." The culture is almost identical; gai lohn is winter-hardy so that it lends itself to both early-spring and midsummer planting.

Sow the seeds ½ inch deep, 1 inch apart, in a 5-gallon container. (For a single plant, use a 12-inch pot.) Thin young plants (which are edible) to stand 6 inches apart.

Your standard container mix is just right. Side-dress with this mix plus a little nitrogen fertilizer when plant is six weeks old.

To keep the plant producing, harvest the center "heads" first, then the side shoots as they mature. The flower buds will have formed by the time the head is ready to pick, and may open once you have picked the stem; cook them as part of the plant—they do not need to be trimmed off.

Continue harvesting as long as the plant produces new heads.

Gow choy   Chinese chives

A perfect plant for the indoor or outdoor container herb garden, gow choy is not only delicious but also brings bloom to what is normally an all-foliage group of plants. Most herbs are clipped steadily, and not allowed to blossom; the fragrant flowers of gow choy are a delightful exception. These beautiful, star-shaped white flowers are richly rose-scented, and can fill a small room with their fragrance. The flowering extends over a long period; even in my outdoor garden—where wind, rain, and summer sun hasten the fading of flowers—gow choy blooms profusely for months. You can clip the leaves, as with common chives, and still get flowers as long as you do not accidentally clip the flower stalk itself, or do not take so much foliage as to discourage the formation of flower buds.

The plant forms a compact, low-growing clump. The flavor of the leaves and flowers is mildly garlic, rather than peppery onion. If you like garlic but never seem to use a light enough hand with it, gow choy is the answer; it never overpowers a salad or a sauce.

Plant individual 4-inch pots to start with. After several months you will have a clump that you may divide. This is a good time to incorporate one of the dividend clumps into a larger container of other herbs or vegetables. Gow choy has an affinity for tomatoes, for instance, and will be helpful in keeping white fly and other pests away from it. Don't eat the bulbs, just the foliage—as with common chives—and always leave enough for the plant to grow on; it won't die down over the winter the way other chives do, if you bring it indoors.

Since gow choy does not smell garlicky, it makes a pretty table centerpiece; three or four pots placed in a Chinese basket, with spikes of snow-white fragrant blossoms and interesting, erect flat leaves, would add an unexpected accent to a Chinese meal or buffet.

It is not always possible to persuade your seedsman that you want the *white-flowered* Chinese chives; you may be sent seeds of another variety that has larger, lavender flowers. These do not have a noticeable garlic scent, although they do not have any rose scent, either. The flowers are similar to, but even more decorative than, the flowers of the common chive. They form lavender balls about the size of a golf ball, are very interestingly shaped, with a fringy look. This, too, would make a nice centerpiece or windowsill ornamental, although my favorite is still the white-flowered variety. If you buy the plants as pots in the nursery, they will often be labeled merely "garlic chives," and you will have to wait until they flower before you can tell which one you have. As an experiment this summer I bought several pots so labeled, and ended up with a mixture of the two kinds; there was no clue on the labels that one was any different from the other.

Plant from seed indoors anytime. Outdoors, early spring is best. The seeds are small and should be sown ½ inch to ¾ inch deep (deeper in cold spring soil). The seedlings have a fragile look, since they are delicate shoots rather than leaves. Their appearance is misleading; they are hardy, transplant easily, and are not fussy about growing conditions, although they respond especially well to full sun. Use the standard mix, although I think gow choy would grow in a city lot. If your sunny spots are preempted, Chinese chives is tolerant of partial shade.

Once you have enough for ordinary culinary purposes, treat yourself to the buds and flowers; these are delicious raw or added to cooked dishes at the very last minute.

Gum jum   **Day lilies**

Day lilies are very useful and decorative in a container garden. They can be grown in large or small clumps, in round or rectangular containers, in sun, partial shade, or full shade. Their spearlike foliage and brilliant orange or yellow flowers provide the perfect background to other, low-growing plants, and they have a long flowering season. They are best, however, grown outdoors.

Bulbs can be ordered from the nursery or gathered in the wild—day lilies can be found growing freely along country roads. In either case, plant them in standard soil enriched with bone meal, then water regularly until they have rooted. Once they have adjusted to their new home, they can be kept on the dry side. Fertilize in midseason with a 10-10-10 formula. They are cold-resistant and can be left in their containers. If you have the time, throw a tarpaulin or heavy plastic over the container to keep the bulbs from freezing during the most severe weather.

The size of the container depends on the number of day lilies you wish to grow. To start with, choose a container twice the size of the clump. Day lilies spread rapidly and you may soon find that they have outgrown their container. Overcrowding will mean fewer flowers, so the clump must be divided whenever it has outgrown its container. Just dig down between the roots with a sharp trowel, and lift out whichever bulbs you wish. They can be replanted in another container or given as a gift to a friend or neighbor.

All of this plant is edible.

Ho lon dow   **Snow peas**

When I tell container gardeners they can grow fresh peas on their apartment windowsills, they tend to look at me in disbelief. The more experienced they are, the more they know for an absolute fact that even if it were physically possible to produce the peas (which it is), the crop would be so small as to be silly. No sensible city gardener is going to give up valuable windowsill space for a handful of peas. If I am able to persuade them that snow peas are different, and to give this amazing vegetable a chance, they are always delighted with the results.

The secret of snow peas is partly that you eat them pod and all. Instead of ending up with a large bowl of discarded pods and a few tablespoonfuls of peas, you have a big bowl of edible sweet pods, all of which taste like the very finest early June peas.

In addition, snow peas are very prolific and produce with an abandon that makes a windowsill area seem like much more. It hardly seems fair that with all these advantages, snow peas are also one of the most decorative vegetables you can grow. Their beautiful violet-lavender blossoms are, naturally, as profuse as the pea crop, and they stand out from the vine so that they are quite showy. The delicate tendrils and tender green of the pretty leaves are also decorative. All in all snow peas make as pretty a window trimming as you could wish.

If you have a terrace wall, a balcony, or even just some straight poles in a container, you can grow a really sizable crop. Imagine inviting friends over for a Chinese meal, and handing one of them a bowl with instructions to "pick some snow peas, please."

Another nice thing about snow peas is that they don't really tie up your windowsill all that much. They are harvested so early in the growing season that you can then turn their space over to melons, peppers, eggplant, and so on.

Since snow peas require 8 to 10 inches soil depth, you may want to set the container on the floor just below the windowsill. You can use a narrow windowbox as long as it is that deep—it's the depth, not the width, that is needed. If you put the container on the floor, remember you must first start it in light. This is one crop that will fruit under lights, but if you grow it exclusively that way, be sure to pick a low-growing variety like Dwarf Grey Sugar which usually stays within a 12-inch range. This would probably be your best bet for a windowsill too, so try it the first year. Under some growing conditions it will keep on well past the 12-inch mark; if so, pinch back the growing tip.

On a terrace or in some other outdoor situation, peas can be sown while you are still shivering from the cold, "as early as the ground can be worked." To a city dweller this means about six weeks before the last frost date in your area. If you have a protected terrace wall and are willing to put some mulch over the containers at night, you can start them in New York City on St. Patrick's Day.

The dwarf varieties won't actually need strings or other support, but if you have the room, you may find they do better and grow taller with something to grow on. Try them both ways and see what works for your situation.

Snow peas (ho lon dow) **in a window box**

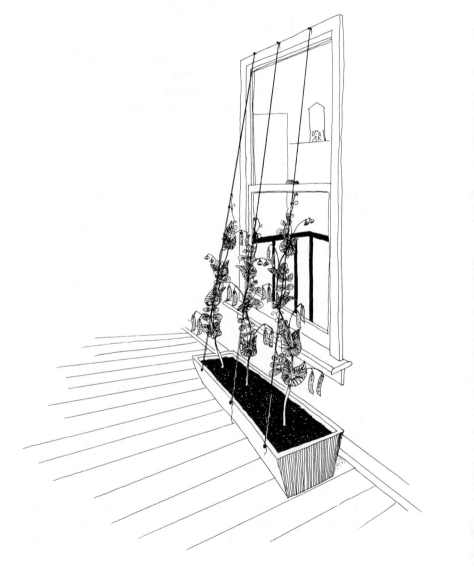

Sow the seeds in a trench about 4 inches below the usual surface of the soil. When the plants are about 6 inches high, fill in the trench with the same mix you used originally. If vines are not covered up with this extra soil, they will dry out along the first several inches, and this will put stress on the plant. You will still get a crop, but it won't be as large as if you took this little extra bit of trouble.

Keep the soil well watered; it should always feel a little damp to your fingertips. Under windy conditions, it is advisable to mulch. In addition to the fertilizer in your mix, add wood ash if you have it. If you don't, use greensand, manure, or cottonseed meal instead. Mix this into your standard "soil" before you fill the container, or spread a layer of it on top of the container when it is half full of soil. Side-dress lightly or water with a liquid fertilizer every couple of weeks.

Having snow peas in nearby containers is much better than having them in an in-the-ground garden—once they fruit they have to be picked at least once a day, and it's easy to forget. It is important not to let the peas get past the stage of barely outlining the pod; they can go from a tiny small pod to one ready for the wok literally overnight. You can keep them in a plastic bag in the refrigerator for about a week, but after that they will not have that marvelous just-picked flavor. Do not string them before refrigerating; that is best done just before cooking.

As we have said, snow peas are one of the few vegetables—other than root vegetables—that will fruit under indoor lights. The only difficulty is keeping them under control. Rigorous pinching back will be necessary even with the dwarf varieties; otherwise the vines will soon be growing over the lights instead of under them.

Hwa choy **Flowering cabbage**

If ever there was a natural for container gardening, it is hwa choy. The plant is compact of growth, easy of culture, beautifully colorful, and deliciously edible. As if all that were not enough, it even comes in two sizes—regular and miniature—to accommodate any container situation. By the way, I don't know why, but many books and seedsmen will say this kind of cabbage is not edible. It is.

I like hwa choy best when grown alone—one to a container. Nevertheless, *miniature* hwa choy is an excellent bedding plant and can be combined successfully with other vegetables or with flowers. A 4-inch pot will hold one miniature hwa choy, an 8-inch pot will hold one regular-sized plant.

Hwa choy can be grown outdoors in the sun or indoors under

lights. The miniature size is particularly attractive indoors when individually potted. The only difficulty with growing it indoors is that its color is brought out by cold weather. Until its foliage is "turned" by cold, it looks like a particularly lovely dark-green cabbage with beautiful purple veins. If you grow it indoors, you may have to put it outdoors until the temperature has done its job. I have often thought that perhaps putting the plants in the refrigerator for the same period would solve this problem but I have never tried it, so I only offer it as a *possible* solution.

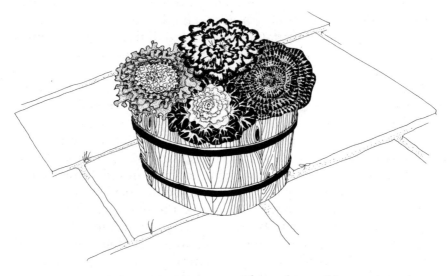

Flowering cabbage　hwa choy

The seeds can be grown in small flats and transplanted, or sown directly in the container where they are to grow. Since hwa choy is planted in midsummer for a fall crop, the former would be better; you won't be tying up a container unnecessarily (and can use it instead for lettuces, radishes, or other quick-maturing vegetables). The cabbage plants can be grown in a flat for several weeks—time enough for two crops of radishes. Another advantage to not sowing it in place is that the young plants can later be set in their containers more deeply than otherwise. Cabbages grow on "stalks" and these must be covered with soil, or else the weight of the cabbage head might break them. If you plant the seeds directly into their permanent containers, leave space in the pot so that you can add the necessary soil; it should come right up to the bottom of the mature cabbage head. Taking this into account, sow the seed ½ inch deep. A 10-10-5 fertilizer should be applied in thirty days.

The cabbages make the best eating when young, before they turn color. The colors are, however, so beautiful that this will be a hard decision; they range from pink to red to green-and-white.

Kee chi **Chinese cucumbers**

Kee chi is the name for the many varieties of Chinese cucumbers, all of which grow on pretty vines with a profusion of bright-yellow flowers, and with cucumbers of various shapes and sizes. Serpent cucumbers curl in a surprisingly lifelike fashion, yard-long cucumbers seem to grow and grow; each variety has its own special charm. They are just as easy to grow as common cucumbers, and just as crisp and fresh, with maybe an even sweeter flavor. (I've never grown a Chinese cucumber that tasted bitter.) Since a single vine will grow well in a 1-gallon container, I would suggest using a 5-gallon container and planting several different varieties. They can comfortably intertwine on a trellis and you will have all different kinds growing together in one large cucumber "patch." Kee chi vines are very amenable, and can be pinched back, trained to grow in any direction you please—including up or down—and will even grow upside down from a hanging basket.

In addition to all its other charms, the Chinese cucumbers are "burpless," and much easier on the digestion than the common cucumber.

For an early crop, sow indoors in peat pots. Otherwise, sow the seeds ¾ inch deep about 3 inches apart. Thin to allow about 10 inches between plants when seedlings are 4 inches high.

Fertilize every three weeks with 5-10-10 enriched with wood ash and manure. You must water copiously; cucumbers are as thirsty as melons, and that's saying a lot. The foliage will wilt in very hot weather, but that won't bother the plant a bit as long as the roots are moist and cool. If the foliage doesn't shade the base of the vine, mulch the surface of the container to help keep the roots happy. Remember, soil dries out much more quickly in a container than in an in-the-ground garden.

Some varieties will grow up to 24 inches long, so unless you know your variety, you won't know from the size when it is getting overripe (except, of course, that it will gradually turn color). Pick your cucumbers while they are still young and you will keep the vine producing more heavily. If you want to let one grow to see how big it will get, pick it the minute it begins to turn yellow or orange (it won't be good eating, but it is important to pick it for the plant's sake).

Keong **Ginger**

Even if fresh ginger root were not almost essential to Chinese, Japanese, Indian, and many other cuisines, as well as an eye-opener when used in old favorites like gingerbread, ginger would be worth growing merely as an ornamental houseplant.

It comes up quickly from store-bought root and, though it is a heavy feeder, requires very little care other than fertilizing and watering. Nothing in the way of pests or diseases seems to bother it.

To start a ginger plant, take a piece of firm, light wood-colored root—a whole knob will ensure that you get at least one bud—and plant it 3 inches deep in a 6-inch pot. When the shoots have reached about 10 inches, repot in a larger container. From then on, repot as needed, until you have reached a 5-gallon container, which will be enough to accommodate the full-sized plant. Fertilize every two weeks with 5-10-10, plus manure.

Do not put ginger in *full* sun until the shoots are 3 inches high; partial or even full shade is better. It can be set outdoors once the air is warm and the nights no longer cold. Take it indoors for the winter when the nights start to drop down to around 50° F.

If you let the plant grow to maturity, it will reward you with beautiful white flowers. No one but you need know that it is also your private ginger plantation. To harvest, dig away enough soil to expose the root. Cut off the baby roots—they are rosy-pink and tender-looking, rather than tan—for a special treat. The baby roots will be distinctly gingery in flavor but not hot, and you will find they add interest to many dishes where you never used ginger before. When harvesting the mature root, always leave the plant enough to grow on. Let the plant "rest" for two months, in dryer soil—without fertilizing—every ten months.

La chiao **Hot peppers**

I don't know why "ornamental peppers" are such a popular house plant when the real thing is just as pretty, and produces enormous quantities of edible fruit. There is almost no more attractive vegetable—for outdoor or indoor gardens—than pepper plants. The leaves are a glossy dark green, the white flowers with their yellow centers are

Hot peppers (la chiao) **in a paint can**

delightful, and the colorful fruit leaves nothing to be desired. Hot peppers are ornamental at all stages of their growth, and the fruit goes on being decorative after it is picked if you dry it in strings to hang from the rafters or kitchen ceiling.

Although it is better to start your peppers in Fertl Cubes or peat pots, you can seed them directly in 10- to 12-inch pots or in larger containers grouped along a terrace wall. Combine them with lettuces and herbs and put them under hanging baskets of tomatoes for a handsome display.

Your pepper plants, like most vegetable plants, will have flowers and fruits at the same time, and stay decorative right through the summer. Indoors they will grow all year round; outdoors they are warm-weather plants and can be set out for the summer, brought in for the winter. If a plant wears itself out fruiting, discard it and start a new one for an endless supply of this useful herb.

Hot peppers are offered very erratically in the market, and just when you have your heart set on that special Chinese, Mexican, or Indian dish, you won't be able to buy them; if you grow your own, you will always have them handy.

Sow seeds ¼ inch deep. If you are doing a row of them in a window box, set the plants about 18 inches apart. You can always prune them back if they seem to be getting out of hand.

One plant indoors will surely be enough, especially since hot peppers require as much full sun as possible, and supplemental lighting won't do much for setting fruit if you skimp on direct sun.

A 5-10-10 fertilizer once a month, or a liquid fertilizer in a weak solution with every watering, should keep your plants healthy and productive. If you don't seem to be getting fruit but the foliage looks healthy, you are either providing too much nitrogen or keeping the plant too cool.

Remember chilis can be picked at all stages of growth. Their color indicates their age; yellow or green is early, orange is getting mature, red is mature. You can grow peppers that are hot or hotter, so try several varieties and then settle down to the ones that suit you best.

Lobok   *Chinese radishes*

Radishes are such a popular vegetable that I imagine most container gardeners already grow them—but even if you do, lobok is special. And as long as you are going to garden in containers, you might as well grow the special—rather than the ordinary—vegetables.

From the moment the first true leaves appear, the daikon radish—to give one example—tells you it is different from other radishes. Instead of the familiar, coarse radish foliage, you will see beautiful, gray-green, oddly cut leaves unlike those of any vegetable you have ever grown. The root itself is pure white, long and graceful, with a mild, sweet flavor. Other Chinese radishes come in all colors and sizes; there are slender white icicles (not to be confused with the common radish most seed catalogs call "icicle radish"); gigantic radishes that weigh up to 65 pounds (you need a 5-gallon container for this one), and delicately rose-pink radishes. There are also purple and black ones.

They are as easy to grow as common radishes. Most of them are sown in midsummer for fall and winter use. There are Chinese radishes for spring and summer too—just read your seed catalogs carefully.

Sow the seeds 1 inch deep, 1 inch apart—except for the larger varieties, which must be spaced proportionately to their growth. Since this is a root vegetable, you can keep an eye on the root formation, and thin out as they get crowded. Even tiny radishes make good eating, and the leaves of young radishes are as delicious as the roots. Use 5-10-10 fertilizer and fertilize lightly but often. Water regularly so that growth is not checked by a dry spell.

If you want to try something new, let a few plants go to seed and use the seeds in your next tossed salad.

Lobok can be grown outdoors, indoors, and under lights, all with equal facility. It is undoubtedly the easiest of all vegetables to grow and often the quickest. Spring varieties are handy for intercropping with slower-growing vegetables; they are picked and gone long before your tomatoes, corn, or eggplants need the space.

Lou teou   **Mung beans**

Mung beans are pole beans, so they naturally take up more room than bush beans, but they are still well suited to container gardening. They have a clinging-vine habit of growth and will wrap themselves around anything handy; you will have to train them to whatever support you provide, and keep them off your other vegetables. If you are so ambitious as to be growing corn, put mung beans in the same container and let them climb up the stalks; they won't hurt the corn and will not come to maturity until after you have eaten the last ear.

Mung beans do best in really hot weather. Since they have a long growing season, set your containers in the warmest, least windy place you have. If you can place the containers against a wall, a drop sheet of plastic lowered over them during the cool nights of the first few weeks of growth will make them even more comfortable. The plastic will keep in the warmth built up in the wall during the sunny hours, and the beans will stay cozy all night; drop the plastic an hour or so before sundown so as not to lose any of the heat from the wall. If you can rig up this kind of protective plastic housing, you can plant the beans as soon as the days warm up; otherwise, you must wait until night temperatures reach 60° to 65° F. Plant the seeds 4 inches apart in a long narrow container; just be sure to allow a soil depth of 12 inches.

Use your standard mix, but fertilize with 10-10-5 when the pods start to form. The vines will produce large numbers of pods which you can gather when young—like snow peas—to eat pod and all. Mung-bean sprouts can be grown only from mature dried beans— allow about 120 days for mature beans to form. This is an inexpensive way of acquiring a good supply of this expensive bean, so if you like bean sprouts, you will definitely want to grow your own mung beans and dry them for sprouts. See Chapter 8.

Mung beans are a very satisfactory crop for the container gardener and can be grown indoors as well as out if you train them in front of a sunny window.

Mitsuba **Japanese parsley**

If you have grown herbs at all, you have probably grown curly parsley. The gourmet gardener might also have included the broad-leaved Italian parsley for its stronger flavor and more definite contribution to the kitchen. Most gardeners, however, have never even heard of Japanese parsley or mitsuba.

Mitsuba is grown primarily for its foliage, which looks very much like Italian parsley, only with a prettier leaf. It also forms a sturdier plant, and is very tolerant of partial shade; it doesn't like a really hot, sunny spot.

If you let it flower, the small white blossoms will quickly turn to seed. To gather the seed, cut the whole stem to within 2 inches of the base, and let it dry on paper toweling. The toweling will hold the seeds as they dry and fall off; they are caraway-shaped. The part that remains in the ground will start to grow again. The seeds can be thoroughly dried; then plant them, for an endless supply of this useful herb. They germinate quickly, and a pot of this plant tied with a saffron-yellow ribbon would make a nice Christmas or hostess gift.

Plant anytime indoors, in very early spring outdoors. Sow seeds ½ inch deep, keep moist, and use a 10-10-5 fertilizer once a month.

I find it almost hopeless to try to describe new flavors, so all I will say is that this is a very agreeable herb, essential to Oriental cooking and a welcome addition to Western dishes.

Mizuna **Chinese potherb mustard**

Grow this exactly like gai choy (Chinese mustard). It has beautiful light-green foliage, distinctive and attractive. It will grow again after cutting or can be cropped a few leaves at a time. The flavor is not at all hot but very delicate. Do not combine it with other greens; it is so mildly flavored it should be used alone or in clear soups, or with other mildly flavored vegetables. If used with young turnips, for instance, add it at the last minute so that it doesn't overcook.

Because it grows quickly and can be harvested at any stage—like lettuce—mizuna is a particularly good vegetable for the container gardener. Another plant can soon take its place; in fact, it can be grown several times during a season, or indoors all winter. It will thrive under lights or in a partly-sunny window. (While it grows well in full winter sun, it doesn't require it.) In the summer, it may—again like lettuce—do better in partial shade, although it will only wilt, not bolt, if it gets too hot.

Ngau pong   **Burdock**

Ngau pong needs a container that is at least 12 inches deep—and practically nothing else. Sow the seeds 6 inches apart and cover with 1 inch of soil.

If you want, you can plant it in the fall and let it come up and surprise you in the spring. Indoors, you wouldn't want to tie up the room, but on a terrace, with little else planted, this would be a good vegetable to have growing through the winter for an early-spring treat. Otherwise, plant it as early in the spring as the spirit moves you.

Germinate the seeds indoors; unlike the plant, the seeds like it warm and cozy. Soak overnight in warm water and plant the next morning ½ inch deep, 5 inches apart. You are primarily interested in the root, so you want a fertilizer high in phosphorus and potassium rather than nitrogen; 5-10-10 is the magic formula, and additional rock phosphate in thirty days makes a welcome addition to the pot.

Since you are growing ngau pong in 12 inches of soil, you won't get a full 24-inch root; this means an earlier harvest, and that is all to the good. If you really are fond of this delicious root, you can crowd it even further by growing it indoors in still-smaller pots. Just to be sure to harvest the roots by the time they have exhausted their container; they will be sweet and delicate. We eat baby carrots and baby beets, so why not baby burdock?

If you leave the plant undisturbed and don't harvest the root, burdock will die down over the winter and come up again each season. There isn't much point to letting it do this as the roots are best the first year. Treat it like an annual and plant it from seed each season.

This is a very versatile and nutritious vegetable. See Chapter 7 for recipe suggestions.

Nung gwa   **Chinese pumpkin**

Nung gwa is the perfect answer for the container gardener who would like to grow pumpkins. Our common orange pumpkins are unsuitable for container culture; both the vines and the fruit grow too large. Nung gwa, on the other hand, grows on short vines and the fruit is small enough to be practical. They are also much more decorative than common pumpkins. Nung gwa will climb a trellis or string, and the fruit can be supported by individual slings if any seem to be getting too heavy for the vine.

The growing season is long, so start nung gwa indoors in individual peat pots. Plant in 5-gallon containers—two plants per container—about four weeks after the last frost date. Plant two different varieties and you will have a fascinating display of interesting pumpkins. There are many varieties to choose from.

Nung gwa is a heavy feeder and should be fertilized weekly once the vines are 12 inches long; 10-10-10 is your best choice. The regular feeding will keep the vine growing, whereas overfertilizing would make the plant brittle. Light, frequent feedings are what is wanted. Copious watering is necessary; the roots should never be allowed to dry out.

When the fruit is ripe, the stems will turn brown and dry.

Nung gwa is a nutritious vegetable and—since it is a pumpkin—an unusual one to find in a container garden; you will be very pleased with it.

Pai lo po   **Chinese turnips**

Chinese turnips are excellent vegetables for the outdoor container garden. Almost any size container will do as long as it has at least 10 inches of soil depth. Turnip greens are pretty, and such good eating that a special variety, Shogoin, the "foliage turnip," is grown exclusively for its greens.

Pai lo po is a cool-weather vegetable and can be planted in early spring for a late-spring crop, or in midsummer for fall use.

Sow seeds ½ inch deep, about ½ inch apart. Since the greens are so good to eat, I plant closely so that I will have an early crop of very young greens. Thin to 6 inches apart for mature turnips.

Pai lo po will benefit from adding rock phosphate to your standard soil mix. Fertilize about every three weeks from the time the plant is about 3 inches tall. Keep well watered but not wet. It is most important to keep vegetables growing briskly; any check in growth will affect the flavor and texture.

Enjoy the young turnips rather than waiting the full 35 to 70 days (depending on variety) to maturity. You will be able to use the space for other vegetables and for a second crop of pai lo po.

Pe tsai *Chinese celery cabbage*

Pe tsai is the "Chinese cabbage" you may have seen in your supermarket produce department; you can easily grow your own. Pe tsai takes up less room than the common cabbage, since it grows tall instead of wide; it is entirely different in appearance. What this means in practical terms is that it will grow in a much smaller container; common cabbage needs 20 inches between plants, pe tsai only 12. Sow the seed in place in midsummer for fall eating, ½ inch deep. For early-summer use, seed should be sown in the early spring, but I would think that the container gardener—with so many other spring vegetables to choose from—might prefer to keep this as a fall crop. An 8-inch pot will hold the tall Tientsin variety; a 10- to 12-inch pot is needed for the chunky Napa type.

Use a 10-10-5 fertilizer and water copiously. A little lime is also a good idea, since your mix may be slightly on the acid side and this vegetable prefers an alkaline soil. You'll have pe tsai on the table about 70 days after planting the seed.

Sai yong choi *Watercress*

Unless you have a clean, unpolluted brook running through your country property, the only way to grow sai yong choi is in a container. It is a natural for the city apartment because it sits happily on almost any windowsill—or on the kitchen counter—and prefers little or no direct sun. Sai yong choi seems to live mostly on water, and spreads rapidly over the entire surface of the container.

You can start it from seed but I never do; I use a fresh bunch from the market. To start your plants, break each stem into pieces, each one containing a joint near the bottom. Remove any leaves that would lie under the soil. Poke all the little pieces of jointed stem into the soil so that the joint is covered by soil.

Add lime to the standard mix when rooting the plant, and monthly thereafter. Use a weak solution of liquid fertilizer once a week.

Change the water once a day by emptying yesterday's water out of the dish and filling it with fresh water run through the top of the pot.

Watercress (sai yong choi) **for the kitchen counter**

Harvesting watercress is as easy as breaking off a sprig; hold onto the bottom with your other hand so as not to uproot the plant. If you grow it from rooted joints rather than from seed, you can start picking it within a week to ten days. Cropping won't hurt the plants a bit; in fact, you *must* pick it occasionally to keep the plants from getting too tall, or from going to seed. This is no hardship; watercress has no calories and is a storehouse of vitamins and minerals.

I think more people would grow watercress at home if they knew how easy it is; I hope now that you know, you will always have a pot growing nearby.

If you prefer, root the stems in water so you can see for yourself that they are really growing. A bunch from the supermarket, kept in a glass of water for several days, will form numerous roots. Since, however, it will root at every joint, you should take a little extra trouble and break up the bunch before putting it in the glass. If your watercress is growing well but you don't need any for the kitchen, break off some of the taller stems, separate them into joints, and put them in new pots—or in the old one, if there is still room. A pot of sai yong choi would be a thoughtful Christmas gift.

Occasionally, when rooting new stems, some of the leaves will turn yellow. Just remove them. If a stem is accidentally pulled out of the soil for any length of time, it will too—just discard it. Other than that, I can't think of anything that ever goes wrong with a container of this attractive plant. You can, of course, grow it all year round.

Shungiku   **Garland chrysanthemum**

Grow shungiku instead of common garden chrysanthemums and you will be able to have your flowers and eat them too. The only difference between the two chrysanthemums is that common chrysanthemums are generally not considered edible—otherwise they resemble shungiku closely. In addition to its edibility, shungiku has a pleasant odor; it is also called "fragrant greens." The combination of fragrance and flower makes it a very attractive container vegetable. If you are willing to dispense with most of the flowers—the greens are, after all, the main crop—you can grow shungiku in a partially shaded spot, leaving your sunny areas for more demanding plants. On a rooftop, protect it from the wind. This is a plant that will do well in a sunny window or under lights.

Plant in pots from 4 inches in diameter on up—larger pots will give you larger plants—in early spring. In a large pot, shungiku could grow to 4 feet, but since you should crop the leaves when the plant is 6 inches high, it will probably never attain its full growth. If a plant seems to be getting out of hand, pinch off the top and the plant will get bushier rather than taller. The greens will be ready to harvest in about 30 days.

Shungiku is pretty combined with lettuces and other low-growing greens in a large, wide container. For instance, if you plant it in the center of a ring of Tom Thumb lettuces, with their miniature rosettes of light-green leaves against the darker green of shungiku, you will have quite a picture.

Add manure and cottonseed or other high-nitrogen fertilizer to your standard mix; fertilize again when seedlings are 3 inches high. It is long-blooming and should be fertilized lightly when the flowers form and every two weeks thereafter. Once the flowers form, the foliage will turn bitter and will not be as good to eat.

Suan *Giant garlic*

Suan garlic is an enormous variety that is as mild as it is big. The oversized cloves peel in a jiffy—especially if you first crush them with the flat side of a wide-bladed knife or Chinese cleaver. You can almost use suan as a vegetable, because the garlic flavor is pleasant but not overpowering; it is especially useful in salads where ordinary raw garlic might offend an unwary diner.

Ideal for container gardening, jumbo garlic produces a large crop of edible shoots and bulbs. It also has an aborted but typical allium flower with the characteristic lavender color. The bulbs tend to split apart when dried so that the individual cloves are released—another time-saver for the busy cook—and can be stored in much the same way you store regular garlic. Braided in strings and hung from the ceiling, though, they will tend to separate and fall all over the place as they dry, so this is one way I wouldn't advise storing them.

Suan is a plant for a larger container than regular garlic. The bulbs sometimes grow as large as a dinner plate, so you obviously cannot grow them to maturity in a 3-inch pot. But if you want to start them out in small containers, they transplant with very little fuss. An azalea pot would grow a nice clump. A large container will enable you to plant a combination of suan with leafy vegetables; the vegetables would be gone, of course, before the suan had matured.

Plant the seeds ¼ inch deep, the bulbs 1 inch deep. You can do this indoors any time of year; outdoors, start the seeds in late fall, the bulbs very early in the spring. Suan is truly winter-hardy—up to 20° F.—so you don't have to take it indoors if you don't want to. An empty half whiskey barrel turned upside down, plus a straw mulch or a plastic covering—over the whole container—will usually keep soil within reason even in Northeastern regions.

Put your garlic containers in full sun, whether on windowsill or terrace, and fertilize frequently with 5-10-10 (you are looking for root, not foliage, development). Watering will be necessary more often in containers; it is important not to allow the soil surrounding the roots ever to dry out completely. On the other hand, never let the containers stand in water or the bulbs may rot.

Figure eight months to maturity for bulbs; next season for seeds. If you want to plant seeds in small containers the first season for clipping (as if they were garlic chives), you will hardly notice the passage of time. By spring, the little bulblets can be planted like cloves, and you will have mature giant garlics by fall.

If harvest time arrives and the tops should be turning brown but aren't, bend them over. They will promptly conform to the normal schedule, and you can harvest them shortly thereafter. As with the rest of the onion family, store them in a cool (not cold) place, very dry, with good air circulation.

Sun Bamboo

There are so many varieties of sun, or edible bamboo, that there is bound to be one for your container garden. It is an especially useful plant for container gardeners because it can be used to provide light shade to soften the harsh effect of full sun in midsummer. (Bamboo varieties that are not called edible can be eaten, but they are bitter.)

While I recommend the so-called edible bamboos, since they are sweeter, you can eliminate the bitterness of other varieties quite easily. Cook the shoots for ten minutes in boiling water, and drain. Repeat the process. They can then be used as you would any bamboo shoots—in stir-fry dishes, egg rolls, and so forth. But regardless of the variety, only the young shoots are edible.

Bamboo requires at least a 5-gallon container; if it is larger, so much the better. You will automatically keep growth under control by gathering the young shoots. If you can't eat that many in season, blanch and freeze for out-of-season use.

Bamboo plants make a most attractive foliage and windbreak plant, interesting at every season. Many varieties are winter-hardy and can be left outdoors year round.

Don't plant more than one clump in a 5-gallon container, and don't fertilize if you use the standard mix to start with. This is an easy plant to care for; it doesn't even expect much in the way of water. (I don't mean, however, that you can keep it as dry as a cactus).

Bamboo is fun to have because it grows so fast that it gives you something to look at when everything else is dormant. If you want privacy for your terrace or rooftop, bamboo will give it to you more quickly than anything I know. It is completely wind-resistant and great for windy city gardens. Be sure that you know how high the variety you are considering will grow. The tallest varieties, which grow up to 120 feet, would hardly be suitable for a container garden.

Yuen tsai Chinese parsley

Yuen tsai isn't really a parsley at all, but I don't think that's any reason not to include it in a parsley window garden—along with curly parsley, Italian parsley, and Japanese parsley. Or, if you like, you could

A Chinese windowsill herb garden

grow them all in one container for an attractive mixture of leaf shapes and shades of green. If you are lucky—and even on a city rooftop it is possible—you may find one morning that one of your true parsley plants is host to a handsome green-and-black-striped caterpillar, which will turn into a swallowtail butterfly if it survives. I don't find that these creatures do much harm to parsley plants, but they can completely strip a large fennel plant in a single day, so remove them hastily if you are growing fennel and should ever find any there.

Yuen tsai is also the herb coriander; you probably have the seeds on your spice shelf. (At least, I hope you have the *seeds*; ground coriander is a waste of spice-shelf space because it loses its flavor when ground and stored.) To make ground coriander, put a few seeds in the blender, and let it whirl away until they have become powdered. Or grind them with your Chinese mortar and pestle.

But let's get back to growing your own fresh coriander—which is what the recipe in your Chinese cookbook means when it calls for a bunch of "Chinese parsley."

Plant the seeds ½ inch deep in a small peat pot or in Fertl Cubes, and keep moist and out of the sun until the second or third pair of true leaves. Then put them into a 3-inch pot, or into a larger container with other vegetables or herbs. A container of lettuces and herbs is particularly nice because you have the makings for an instant salad all in one place.

Although yuen tsai is sold in Chinese markets by the bunch, there is no reason for you to harvest the whole plant at one time. Its distinctive flavor is welcome in all sorts of salads and cooked dishes, but usually a little goes a long way; cut what you need, it won't hurt the plant. You can take a few sprigs at a time, just as you do with other parsleys. If you should let it flower and go to seed, collect and dry the seed, and cut the plant back to about 2 inches high; with luck it will send up new shoots and grow again for you. If it doesn't, you have the seeds and can easily start new seedlings.

Yuen tsai doesn't like very hot weather and should be moved off a sunny windowsill in midsummer. On a terrace, it can be relegated to a partly shady spot. As with all leafy crops, a high-nitrogen fertilizer is called for, but not too much, please. If you grow it to seed, dry some for your spice shelf and label it "coriander."

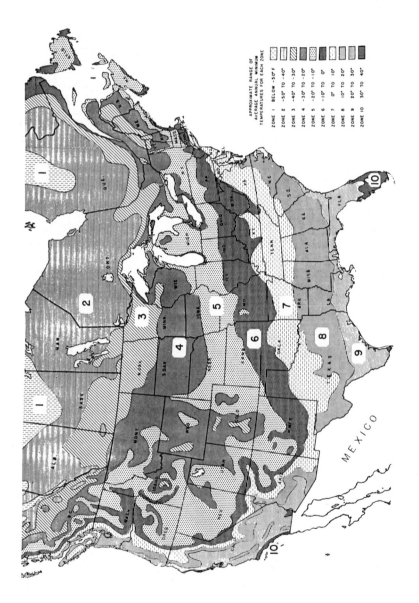

Zones of plant hardiness

APPENDIX

Oriental/English Vegetable Guide

ADZUKI **ADZUKI BEAN**

AI KWA **CHINESE EGGPLANT**

BIN DOW **ASPARAGUS PEA**

BOK CHOY **CHINESE MUSTARD CABBAGE**

CEE GWA **CHINESE OKRA**

CHANG FA **MULTIPLIER ONIONS**

CHEE KOO **ARROWHEAD**

CHIH MA **SESAME**

CHUNG CHOY **PICKLING MELON**

CHUNG GWA **SWEET MELONS**

DOAN GWA **WINTER MELONS**

DOW FU **FAVA BEANS**

DOW GAUK **YARD-LONG BEANS**

FOO GWA **BITTER MELON**

GAI CHOY **CHINESE MUSTARD**

GAI LOHN **CHINESE BROCCOLI**

GOW CHOY **CHINESE CHIVES**

GUM JUM **DAY LILIES**

HINN CHOY **AMARANTH**

HO LON DOW **SNOW PEAS**

HWA CHOY **FLOWERING CABBAGE**

KEE CHI **CHINESE CUCUMBERS**

KEONG **GINGER**

LA CHIAO **HOT PEPPERS**

LOBOK **CHINESE RADISHES**

LOU TEOU **MUNG BEANS**

MAO GWA **FUZZY GOURD**

MITSUBA **JAPANESE PARSLEY**

MIZUNA **CHINESE POTHERB MUSTARD**

NGAR CHOY **BEAN SPROUTS**

NGAU PONG **BURDOCK**

NUNG GWA **CHINESE PUMPKIN**

OU **CHINESE LOTUS**

PE TSAI **CHINESE CELERY CABBAGE**

SAI YONG CHOI **WATERCRESS**

SHUNGIKU **GARLAND CHRYSANTHEMUM**

SOY **SOYBEANS**

SUAN **GIANT GARLIC**

SUI MATAI **WATER CHESTNUTS**

WOO CHAI **VIOLET-STEMMED TARO**

YUEN TSAI **CHINESE PARSLEY**

Sources for Chinese Water Garden Vegetables

Bee Fork Water Gardens
Route 1
Box 115
Bunker, Mo. 63629
Catalog: $2

Hermitage Gardens
Route 5
Canastota, N.Y. 13032
Pools and accessories only

Slocum Water Gardens
1101 Cypress Gardens Road
Winter Haven, Fla. 33880

Three Springs Fisheries
Lilypons, Md. 21717
Catalog: $1

William Tricker, Inc.
74 Allendale Avenue
Saddle River, N.J. 07458

William Tricker, Inc.
7125 Tanglewood Drive
Independence, Ohio 44131

Van Ness Water Gardens
2460 North Euclid Avenue
Upland, Calif. 91786
Catalog: 50¢

Sources for Oriental Vegetable Seeds or Roots

Burgess Seed & Plant Co.
Box 2000
Galesburg, Mich. 49053

W. Atlee Burpee Co.
Warminster, Pa. 18974

Comstock, Ferre & Company
263 Main Street
Wethersfield, Conn. 06109

DeGiorgi Company, Inc.
Council Bluffs, Iowa 51501

J. A. Demonchaux Co., Inc.
225 Jackson
Topeka, Kans. 66603

Ferndale Gardens
702 Nursery Lane
Faribault, Minn. 55021

Henry Field Seed & Nursery Co.
Shenandoah, Iowa 51602

Fruitland Nursery
307 Whitley Drive
Fruitland, Idaho 83619

Grace's Gardens
Autumn Lane
Hackettstown, N.J. 07840

Gurney Seed & Nursery Co.
2nd and Capitol
Yankton, S.D. 57078

Joseph Harris Co., Inc.
Moreton Farm
Rochester, N.Y. 14624

J. L. Hudson, Seedsman
P. O. Box 1058
Redwood City, Calif. 94064

Japonica Nursery
P. O. Box 236
Larchmont, N.Y. 10538

Johnny's Selected Seeds
Albion, Maine 04910

Kelly Bros. Nurseries, Inc.
Dansville, N.Y. 14437

Kitazawa Seed Co.
356 West Taylor Street
San Jose, Calif. 95110

Le Jardin du Gourmet
West Danville, Vt. 05873

Nichols Garden Nursery
1190 North Pacific Highway
Albany, Ore. 97321

George W. Park Seed Co., Inc.
Greenwood, S.C. 29646

The Redwood City Seed Co.
P. O. Box 361
Redwood City, Calif. 94064

Seedway, Inc.
Hall, N.Y. 14463

Stokes Seeds, Inc.
Box 548
Buffalo, N.Y. 14624

Suttons Seeds
Reading, England

Thompson & Morgan, Inc.
P. O. Box 24
401 Kennedy Boulevard
Somerdale, N.J. 08083

Tsang & Ma International
1556 Laurel Street
San Carlos, Calif. 94070

Some Common Sources for Organic Fertilizers

FERTILIZER	MAJOR BENEFITS	SOURCE	SIGNS OF DEFICIENCY
Nitrogen	Promotes growth of plant above ground, especially foliage	Dried rabbit and poultry manure; castor bean plants; dried seaweed; shellfish	Unnaturally pale green or yellow leaves
Phosphorus	Encourages strong stems, feeder and base roots	Rock phosphate; fish emulsion; bone meal; fish and shellfish	Poor fruit set; weak stems; malformed or distorted roots; purple cast to foliage; yellowing of leaf margins
Potassium (Potash)	"Winterizes" plants; increases resistance to excess nitrogen; makes plants resistant to extremes in temperature; benefits base root development	Greensand; granite dust; wood and other ash	Lower leaves turn brown and die; weak stems; weak, stunted base leaves

*Organic fertilizers are also available premixed in various proportions—10-10-10, 5-10-10, and so on.

Glossary of Chinese Vegetables

ENGLISH NAME	CHINESE NAME	LATIN NAME	ALSO KNOWN AS
adzuki bean	adzuki	*Phaseolus angularis*	*azuki* (Japanese)
amaranth	hinn choy	*Amaranthus gangeticus*	Chinese spinach, callaloo, *hiyu* (Japanese), *bhaji* (Indian)
arrowhead	chee koo	*Sagittaria sagittifolia*	*kuwai* (Japanese)
asparagus pea	bin dow	*Psophocarpus tetragonolobus*	goa bean, winged bean
bean sprouts	ngar choy		
bitter melon	foo gwa	*Momordica charantia*	
Chinese broccoli	gai lohn	*Brassica alboglabra*	Chinese kale
burdock	ngau pong	*Arctium lappa*	*gobo* (Japanese)
Chinese celery cabbage	pe tsai	*Brassica pekinensis*	*hakusai* (Japanese)
Chinese chives	gow choy	*Allium odoratum*	*nira* (Japanese)
Chinese cucumbers	kee chi	*Cucumis sativus*	
day lilies	gum jum	*Hemerocallis fulva*	
Chinese eggplant	ai kwa	*Solanum melongena*	aubergine
fava beans	dow fu	*Vicia faba*	broad beans
flowering cabbage	hwa choy	*Brassica oleracea*	flowering kale, ornamental cabbage
fuzzy gourd	mao gwa	*Benincasa hispida*	little winter melon
garland chrysanthemum	shungiku*	*Chrysanthemum coronarium*	*tung hao tsai* (Chinese)
giant garlic	suan	*Allium sativum*	
ginger	keong	*Zingiber officinale*	*shoga* (Japanese)
hot peppers	la chiao	*Capsicum frutescens*	chili peppers

ENGLISH NAME	CHINESE NAME	LATIN NAME	ALSO KNOWN AS
Japanese parsley	mitsuba*	*Cryptotaenia japonica*	
Chinese lotus	ou	*Nelumbium nucifera*	sacred lotus
sweet melons	chung gwa	*Cucumis melo*	
multiplier onions	chang fa	*Allium fistulosum*	Japanese bunching onions, *nebuka* (Japanese), Welsh onions, cibol, ciboule
mung beans	lou teou	*Phaseolus aureus*	
Chinese mustard	gai choy	*Brassica juncea*	India mustard, *takana* (Japanese)
Chinese mustard cabbage	bok choy	*Brassica chinensis*	white mustard cabbage
Chinese okra	cee gwa	*Luffa acutangula; L. cylindrica*	luffa, loofah, dishrag gourd, vegetable sponge
Chinese parsley	yuen tsai	*Coriandrum sativum*	coriander, cilantro
pickling melon	chung choy	*Cucumis conomon*	*uri* (Japanese)
Chinese potherb mustard	mizuna*	*Brassica japonica*	*shui tsai* (Chinese)
Chinese pumpkins	nung gwa	*Cucurbita pepo*	
Chinese radishes	lobok	*Raphanus sativus*	daikon
sesame	chih ma	*Sesamum orientale*	*goma* (Japanese)
snow peas	ho lon dow	*Pisum sativum*	sugar peas, edible-podded peas
soybeans	soy	*Glycine max*	*shoyu* (Japanese)
violet-stemmed taro	woo chai	*Xanthosoma violacea*	primrose malanga, Indian kale, yautia
water chestnuts	sui matai	*Eleocharis dulcis*	
watercress	sai yong choi	*Nasturtium officinale*	
winter melon	doan gwa	*Benincasa hispida*	white gourd, wax gourd, ash melon, *calabaza China* (Spanish)
yard-long beans	dow gauk	*Vigna sesquipedalis*	asparagus bean

*In a few instances I have given the Japanese rather than the Chinese name because that is the way the plant is listed in all the seed catalogs.

Planting Guide

VEGETABLE	SEED DEPTH (INCHES)	DISTANCE BETWEEN PLANTS (INCHES)	DISTANCE BETWEEN ROWS (INCHES)	COOL OR WARM SEASON	DAYS TO MATURITY
adzuki beans	½–1	2–3	18–30	warm	120
amaranth	¼	½	18	cool	30–90
asparagus pea	½	4	18	cool	50
bitter melon	1	6–8	48–60	warm	60–75
Chinese broccoli	½	1	12	cool	60–80
burdock	½–1	6	20	cool	45
Chinese celery cabbage	½–1	1	30–36	cool	70–80
Chinese chives	½	12–14	20	cool	24–90
Chinese cucumbers	½–¾	3	48	warm	60
Chinese eggplant	½	24	36	warm	60–75
fava beans	2½	4–6	18–25	cool	65–90
flowering cabbage	½	8–10	16	cool	55–75
fuzzy gourd	1	2	36	warm	75–85
garland chrysanthemum	¼–½	2	18	cool	25–60
giant garlic (cloves)	1	12	24	cool	180
ginger	3	16	24	warm	90–130
hot peppers	½	2	24–36	warm	65–85
Japanese parsley	½	6	18	cool	60
sweet melons	1	18	60	warm	115–130
multiplier onions	½	10	18	cool	55–120
mung beans	½	6–8	24	warm	90–120
Chinese mustard	¼	2	12–18	cool	35–50
Chinese mustard cabbage	¼	¾–2	12	cool	35–50
Chinese okra	1	3–6	60	warm	115
Chinese parsley	⅙	½	18	warm	60
pickling melon	½	4	60	warm	65
Chinese potherb mustard	¼	2	18	cool	30–60
Chinese pumpkins	1	18–36	60	warm	130
Chinese radishes	1	2	18–30	cool	60–80
sesame	½	1	36	warm	30–45

VEGETABLE	SEED DEPTH (INCHES)	DISTANCE BETWEEN PLANTS (INCHES)	DISTANCE BETWEEN ROWS (INCHES)	COOL OR WARM SEASON	DAYS TO MATUR- ITY
soy beans	1½–2	2–5	24–30	warm	75–115
snow peas	6	2–3	6	cool	50–85
winter melon	1	8–10	48	warm	150
yard-long beans	½–1	4	24	warm	60–90

State Agricultural Experiment Stations

ALABAMA
Cooperative Extension Service
Auburn University
Auburn 36830

ALASKA
Agricultural Experiment Station
University of Alaska
College 99701

ARIZONA
Cooperative Extension Service
University of Arizona
College of Agriculture
Tucson 85721

ARKANSAS
Cooperative Extension Service
University of Arkansas
Fayetteville 72701

CALIFORNIA
Agricultural Extension Service
University of California
College of Agriculture
Berkeley 94720

COLORADO
Cooperative Extension Service
Colorado State University
Fort Collins 80521

CONNECTICUT
Cooperative Extension Service
University of Connecticut
College of Agriculture & Natural
  Resources
Storrs 06268

DELAWARE
Cooperative Extension Service
University of Delaware
College of Agricultural Sciences
Newark 19711

DISTRICT OF COLUMBIA
Cooperative Extension Service
The Federal City College
1424 K Street, N. W.
Washington, D.C. 20005

FLORIDA

Cooperative Extension Service
University of Florida
Institute of Food & Agricultural
  Sciences
Gainesville 32601

GEORGIA

Cooperative Extension Service
University of Georgia
College of Agriculture
Athens 30601

HAWAII

Agricultural Extension Service
University of Hawaii
Honolulu 96822

IDAHO

Cooperative Extension Service
University of Idaho
College of Agriculture
Moscow 83843

ILLINOIS

Cooperative Extension Service
University of Illinois
College of Agriculture
Urbana 61801

INDIANA

Cooperative Extension Service
Purdue University
West Lafayette 47907

IOWA

Cooperative Extension Service
Iowa State University
Ames 50010

KANSAS

Cooperative Extension Service
Kansas State University
College of Agriculture
Manhattan 66502

KENTUCKY

Cooperative Extension Service
University of Kentucky
College of Agriculture
Lexington 40506

LOUISIANA

Agricultural Experiment Station
Louisiana State University
Agricultural College
Baton Rouge 70800

MAINE

Cooperative Extension Service
University of Maine
College of Agriculture
Orono 04473

MARYLAND

Cooperative Extension Service
University of Maryland
College Park 20740

MASSACHUSETTS

Cooperative Extension Service
University of Massachusetts
College of Agriculture
Amherst 01002

MICHIGAN

Cooperative Extension Service
Michigan State University
College of Agriculture
East Lansing 48823

MINNESOTA

Agricultural Extension Service
University of Minnesota
Institute of Agriculture
St. Paul 55101

MISSISSIPPI

Cooperative Extension Service
Mississippi State University
State College 39762

MISSOURI

Cooperative Extension Service
University of Missouri
College of Agriculture
Columbia 65201

MONTANA

Cooperative Extension Service
Montana State University
Bozeman 59715

NEBRASKA

Cooperative Extension Service
University of Nebraska
College of Agriculture & Home
  Economics
Lincoln 68503

NEVADA

Cooperative Extension Service
University of Nevada
College of Agriculture
Reno 89507

NEW HAMPSHIRE

Cooperative Extension Service
University of New Hampshire
College of Life Sciences &
  Agriculture
Durham 03824

NEW JERSEY

Cooperative Extension Service
Rutgers College of
  Agriculture &
  Environmental Sciences
New Brunswick 08903

NEW MEXICO

Cooperative Extension Service
New Mexico State University
Box 3AE, Agriculture Building
Las Cruces 88003

NEW YORK

Cooperative Extension Service
Cornell University
College of Agriculture
Ithaca 14850

NORTH CAROLINA

Cooperative Extension Service
North Carolina State University
P. O. Box 5157
Raleigh 27607

NORTH DAKOTA

Cooperative Extension Service
North Dakota State University of
  Agriculture & Applied Science
University Station
Fargo 58102

OHIO

Cooperative Extension Service
Ohio State University
Agriculture Administration
  Building
2120 Fyffe Road
Columbus 43210

OKLAHOMA

Cooperative Extension Service
Oklahoma State University
201 Whitehurst
Stillwater 74074

OREGON

Cooperative Extension Service
Oregon State University
Corvallis 97331

PENNSYLVANIA

Cooperative Extension Service
Pennsylvania State University
College of Agriculture
323 Agricultural Administration
  Building
University Park 16802

RHODE ISLAND

Cooperative Extension Service
University of Rhode Island
Kingston 02881

SOUTH CAROLINA

Cooperative Extension Service
Clemson University
Clemson 29631

SOUTH DAKOTA

Cooperative Extension Service
South Dakota State University
College of Agriculture
Brookings 57006

TENNESSEE

Agricultural Extension Service
University of Tennessee
Institute of Agriculture
P. O. Box 1071
Knoxville 37901

TEXAS

Agricultural Extension Service
Texas A & M University
College Station 77483

UTAH

Cooperative Extension Service
Utah State University
College of Agriculture
Logan 84321

VERMONT

Cooperative Extension Service
University of Vermont
State Agricultural College
Burlington 05401

VIRGINIA

Cooperative Extension Service
Virginia Polytechnic Institute
Blacksburg 24061

WASHINGTON

Cooperative Extension Service
Washington State University
College of Agriculture
Pullman 99163

WEST VIRGINIA

Cooperative Extension Service
West Virginia University
Morgantown 26506

WISCONSIN

Cooperative Extension Service
University of Wisconsin
College of Agriculture
432 North Lake Street
Madison 53706

WYOMING

Agricultural Extension Service
University of Wyoming
University Station Box 3354
Laramie 82070

INDEX